de Gruyter Studies in Organization 26

Human Resource Management

de Gruyter Studies in Organization

Innovation, Technology, and Organization

A new international and interdisciplinary book series from de Gruyter presenting comprehensive research on the inter-relationship between organization and innovations, both technical and social.
It covers applied topics such as the organization of:
— R & D
— new product and process innovations
— social innovations, such as the development of new forms of work organization and corporate governance structure

and addresses topics of more general interest such as:
— the impact of technical change and other innovations on forms of organization at micro and macro levels
— the development of technologies and other innovations under different organizational conditions at the levels both of the firm and the economy.

The series is designed to stimulate and encourage the exchange of ideas between academic researchers, practitioners, and policy makers, though not all volumes address policy- or practitioner-oriented issues.
The volumes present conceptual schema as well as empirical studies and are of interest to students of business policy and organizational behaviour, to economists and sociologist, and to managers and administrators at firm and national level.

Editor:
Arthur Francis, The Management School, Imperial College, London, U.K.

Advisory Board:
Prof. *Claudio Ciborra*, University of Trento, Italy
Dr. *Mark Dodgson*, Science Policy Research Unit, University of Sussex, GB
Dr. *Peter Grootings*, CEDEFOP, Berlin, Germany
Prof. *Laurie Larwood*, Dean, College of Business Administration, University of Nevada, Reno, Nevada

Human Resource Management: An International Comparison

Editor: Rüdiger Pieper

Walter de Gruyter · Berlin · New York 1990

Editor
Dr. Rüdiger Pieper
Director of Paul-Löbe-Institut Berlin, Germany

HF
5549
. H78424
1990

157057
Sept. 1992

∞ Printed on acid free paper.
 (ageing resistant — pH: 7, neutral)

Library of Congress Cataloging-in-Publication Data

Human resource management : an international comparison /
 editor, Rüdiger Pieper.
 (De Gruyter studies in organization ; 26)
  Papers delivered at a conference held Apr. 28 — May 1,
1989 at Theodor-Heuss-Akademie.
  Includes bibliographical references.
  ISBN 0-89925-720-8 (acid free paper)
  1. Personnel management — Congresses. 2. Personnel
management — Cross-cultural studies — Congresses. I. Pieper, Rüdiger, 1957 — . II. Series.
HF5549.H78424   1990
658.3 — — dc20   90-40428
                                                       CIP

Deutsche Bibliothek Cataloging-in-Publication Data

Human resource management : an international comparison /
ed.: Rüdiger Pieper. — Berlin ; New York : de Gruyter, 1990
 (De Gruyter studies in organization ; 26 : Innovation, tech-
nology, and organization)
 ISBN 3-11-012573-0
NE: Pieper, Rüdiger [Hrsg.]; GT

Typesetting and Printing: Arthur Collignon GmbH, Berlin. —
Binding: Dieter Mikolai, Berlin — Cover design: Johannes Rother, Berlin.

Preface

This book, *Human Resource Management: An International Comparison*, is the result of an international conference (with the same title) held at the Theodor-Heuss-Akademie in Gummersbach, West Germany, from April 28 to May 1st, 1989. About 60 management researchers and practitioners from 21 countries[1] met to discuss the following questions: How is Human Resource Management structured in the individual countries? What strategies are discussed and what is put into practice there? Where are the differences and the similiarities? To what extent are corporate policy strategies influenced by dimensions like culture and government educational policy or by other national contingency factors? The purpose of the conference was, on the one hand, to compare human resource management strategies from different countries and their influence factors; on the other hand, the questions were to be examined as to what specific problems international companies and companies active internationally have in this area and what strategies have been developed. Almost 20 papers were presented; most of them are included in this volume. In addition, several working groups intensively discussed the national influence factors and the practical human resource management strategies of multinational companies.

The conference was jointly organized by the Friedrich-Naumann-Stiftung, a private foundation, closely linked to the West German Liberal party, and the Institut für Management of the Freie Universität Berlin. On the one hand, it was designed as a start of a series of international conferences for scholars and management practitioners who are interested in the international aspects of human resource management, cross-cultural comparisons and especially in East-West comparisons, i. e. comparisons of management thought and practice in the Western capitalist and the Eastern socialist countries. On the other hand, it was a continuation of a successful cooperation between these two institutions, which in 1988 succeeded in bringing management researchers from both East and West Germany together. Thus, for the first time, business school professors from the two Germanies began

---

[1] Austria, Belgium, Brazil, Canada, Czechoslovakia, East Germany, France, Hungary, Iran, Israel, Italy, Japan, Netherlands, People's Republic of China, Soviet Union, Spain, Sweden, United Kingdom, United States of America, West Germany, Yugoslavia.

to compare management thought and education in their countries in a systematic and non-ideologic way[2].

Major credit goes to the Friedrich-Naumann-Stiftung for sponsoring the conference. The foundation even paid for the air fare of researchers coming from countries as far away as Japan and China. I am especially grateful to Mrs. Margot Viebahn and Dr. Fritz Glashauser who made all organizational and travel arrangements and to the other staff of the Theodor-Heuss-Akademie for their hospitality and for the use of the excellent conference facilities at the academy. The academy proved to be an ideal place for intensive and open discussions. It also provided a very personal and informal atmosphere: very different to what one often experiences at many other conferences held in major hotels. Thus, the people of the Theodor-Heuss-Akademie successfully served as catalysts for quite a number of new cross-border friendship relations and helped in starting several joint, infra-national research projects in international and comparative human resource management. Special thanks to Pete Kercher (Lecco, Italy) and Dr. Dorothy Rosenberg for translating a number of papers and to Dr. Bianka Ralle of the Walter de Gruyter publishing company in Berlin for her support in publishing the papers of this conference.

Berlin, Spring 1990   Rüdiger Pieper

---

[2] The papers that were presented at that conference are published in: "Westliches Management — Östliche Leitung. Ein Vergleich von Managementlehre und DDR-Leitungswissenschaft", edited by Rüdiger Pieper, Walter de Gruyter, Berlin — New York 1989.

Contents

Human Resource Management in Italy
Hans H. Hinterhuber and Monika Stumpf

Human Resource Management in France
Jacques Rojot

Human Resource Management in the Federal Republic of Germany
Peter Conrad and Rüdiger Pieper

Part II
Key Problems of Human Resource Management in Socialist Countries

Human Resource Management in Yugoslavia: Problems and
Perspectives
Dancia Purg

Human Resource Management in Czechoslovakia − Management
Development as the Key Issue
Ondrej Landa

Human Resource Management in the German Democratic Republic:
Problems of Availability and the use of Manpower Potential in the
Sphere of the High Qualification Spectrum in a Retrospective View
Hansgünter Meyer

Part III
Human Resource Management in Asian Countries

Human Resource Management in China: Recent Trends
Wang Zhong-Ming

Human Resource Management in Japan
Yoshiaki Takahashi

Part IV
Human Resource Management and Multinational Companies

Strategic Human Resource Management: A Global Perspective
Nancy J. Adler and Fariborz Ghadar

Human Resource Management in Multinational and Internationally
Operating Companies
Eberhard Dülfer

Introduction

Rüdiger Pieper

> Every aspect of a firm's activities is determined by the competence, motivation, and general effectiveness of its human organization. Of all the tasks of management, managing the human component is the central and most important task, because all else depends upon how well it is done.
> (Likert 1967: 1)

1. Human Resource Management as a Strategic Factor

In the past few years, Human Resource Management (HRM) has become significantly more important world-wide, both in management theory and as applied management practice. The number of scientific articles and books being published in the field has increased rapidly, and new journals dealing exclusively with matters of Human Resource Management have been founded. Numerous conferences, frequently on an international level, are being organized to bring together practioners and researchers. Business schools in Europe and North America have introduced HRM courses into their core curriculum, and partly as a consequence, new textbooks are regularly being published. Companies now claim they are spending more money on personnel and personnel development than ever before. In public speeches, CEOs emphasize that the company's employees are the firm's most valuable asset. It seems that HRM has become a fashionable topic...

Although the question of personnel management is new neither to management practice nor management theory, and has always been a subject for research and teaching, the history of HRM as a specific approach to personnel management is relatively new[1].

---

[1] For a historical overview, see: Wolfgang Staehle: Human Resource Management and Corporate Strategy. The history of theoretical and practical approaches to

The first paper by Wolfgang H. Staehle, professor at the Free University of Berlin desbribes in detail the development and historical roots of the personnel function from its beginnings as personnel administration to finally HRM, and current concepts linking HRM to corporate strategy. However, some central themes should be highlighted here together with a clear definition of what the term HRM means.

The basic starting point — at least for the theoretical discourse — was a decline of human relations philosophy in the late fifties and early sixties followed by the propagation of a different view of the work-force by organisational humanists such as Argyris and McGregor (Wren 1987: 418). To distinguish this new perspective from the old human relations model and its keep-people-happy strategies, Raymond Miles introduced the term "human resources" in 1965. His subsequently published analysis distinguishing between the three models of management: traditional, human relations and human resources (Miles 1975) helped to clarify the meaning of this term which, however, served more as an umbrella definition of a number of related approaches rather than a single theory. What these approaches have in common and what makes them different from traditional management and human relations management is that people are viewed as having the potential to grow and to develop. They constitute a dynamic resource pool of various skills and knowledge. Seen this way, the major task of human resource management is helping the company's employees to actualize and develop their potential in accordance with the needs of the organization and the interests of the individuals in question rather than restricting personnel management to purely administrative tasks.

Since the sixties, numerous new approaches to HRM have been formulated ranging from human capital accounting systems or human asset accounting (Likert 1967) to human capital theory (Schultz 1978) and human resource indexing (e. g. Schuster 1986). All of these approaches specificly treat human labor as the major asset of an organization rather than viewing labor primarily as a cost factor. They also argue that even in an age of high technology, no organization can attain its goals without sophisticated human labor. Thus, companies should invest in the development of their employees. In fact, empirical studies support this argument. Both the popular study of Peters and Waterman (1982) and Schuster (1986), in his more systematic survey of the largest American firms, found that the economic success of a company largely depended on its HRM practice.

---

personnel management in various countries is described in the following articles: Beverly and Stephen Springer. United States; Jacques Rojot, France; Peter Conrad and Rüdiger Pieper, Federal Republic of Germany; and Yoshiaki Takahashi, Japan.

In the eighties, research groups at the University of Michigan (Tichy, Fombrun and Devanna 1982; Fombrun, Tichy and Devanna 1984), Harvard Business School (Beer et al. 1985), INSEAD (e. g. Evans 1986, 1987), University of Stuttgart (Ackermann 1986, 1987) and in Switzerland (Rühli and Wehrli 1986; Krulis-Randa 1988) developed new concepts that looked beyond simple emphasis of the importance of the human factor aimed at integrating the personnel function into general strategic management. Most of these authors argue that such an integration of the personnel function into strategic management forms the major difference between traditional personnel management and the concept of HRM. According to this analysis, HRM can be defined as consisting of the following elements:

— *traditional personnel administration* (staffing, rewarding, work design)
— *personnel development*
— a specific *management philosophy* that values labor as the major asset of an organization and that regards human beings as being able and willing to grow and develop
— the *integration* of the personnel function into *strategic management*

Since the mid eithies some researchers (e. g. Laukamm 1986; Lattmann 1987; see also Staehle, in this volume) have began to use the new term *strategic human resource management* to additionally emphasize the importance of a strategic orientation of the personnel function. While for some of them, this new term stands for a new strategic orientation of personnel management, other authors such as Ackermann (1987) and the researchers of the Michigan group (Devanna, Fombrun and Tichy 1984) argue that strategic HRM should be seen as the over-lapping part of both strategic or general management on the one hand and personnel management on the other.

This, however, is hardly the only issue of controversy and possible misunderstanding in the field. The narrower term "Human Resource Management" itself is often defined and understood in contradictory ways. The definition above is by no means generally agreed up. Textbooks that claim to give a current overview of the field, especially those published in the United States, show a confusing diversity in their understanding of the term. Frequently, they simply use HRM to replace older terms for the personnel function without giving it any new meaning. Some authors argue that "human resource management is a modern term for what has traditionally been referred to as personnel administration or personnel management" (Byars and Rue 1987: 6), while others use it as an addition thus titleing their textbooks "Personnel and Human Resource Management" (e. g. Leap and Crino 1989; Schuler 1987). Schuler e. g. (1987: 5) argues that this addition "recognizes the vital role that human resources play in an organization, the challenges in managing human resources effectively, and the growing body of knowledge and professionalism surrounding PHRM". Even when the term HRM is used, it often stands solely for traditional aspects of personnel administration, namely staffing, rewarding and designing work (explicitly e. g. Bateman and Zeithaml 1990: 432).

However, the Conference on Human Resource Management in an International Comparison and, consequently, this volume, leave the controversy over the meaning of HRM aside, and use a more simplistic approach as its starting point: The organizers simply invited researchers from various countries to present the concepts of HRM being discussed and used in their nations, and to link them to determining or at least influencing environmental factors such as the political and economic system, the educational system, the industrial relations system and the national culture. Whether there is a special understanding of HRM (i. e. HRM in the sense of the above mentioned definition) in the countries in question or whether HRM is just used as another expression for traditional personnel administration or management was left as a matter to explore and discuss.

The cognitive interest of such an international comparison of concepts of Human Resource Management is identical to that underlying most comparative management studies which try to transcend simple description, that is the search for excellence. Since HRM is seen as a strategic factor strongly influencing the economic success of a single company, one can argue that it is also a strategic factor for the success of an entire nation. Since most technologies are available world-wide, technology itself no longer forms the single most important determining factor, but the way technologies are applied, i. e. whether people are educated or trained well enough to use them effectively, has become decisive. Neither technologies nor technical knowledge nor money for investment is confined to national borders. People, however, to a large degree are. Whether a plant is built in India or the Federal Republic of Germany makes a considerable difference to its efficiency, even if exactly the same technologies are being used because the work-force in the two countries is different in regard to, for example, its standard of education and its culture. Thus, companies have to take into account the quality and type of HRM that is prevalent (and which can be achieved) in a country when making investment decisions.

Of course, economic terms are not the only variables in defining the success of a nation[2]. In addition to economic achievements, especially the standard of living, cultural achievements, for example, also play an important role[3]. However, success whether materially or culturally defined depends

---

[2] For this discussion see, for example, Farmer 1984.

[3] See the discussion of a definition of quality of life in the seventies and the search for qualitative standards of measurement (OECD 1973; Zapf 1974; Steinhausen 1975).

largely on the human factor, i. e. on the work of the country's people. The way individuals are valued, treated and cared for in a country, their access to education and development, and the involvement and motivational strategies being used form a major contingency factor for the development of a nation and national wealth (Farmer and Richmann 1965; Parnes 1984).

2. National Human Resource Management Concepts

The sampling included in this volume represents three types of nations or regions:

— countries of the industrialized Western world (United States, Federal Republic of Germany, France, Italy)
— socialist countries in Eastern Europe (Czechoslovakia, German Democratic Republic, and Yugoslavia)
— Asian countries (Japan as an industrialized Asian country, China as an example for a developing country in Asia)

With the exception of China, Third World countries have been excluded in this comparison because they face very specific problems that cannot be compared to those of the industrialized nations. Their major problem is not gaining a competive edge in international economic competition through the sophisticated application of HRM concepts, but simple survival.

In addition to descriptions of national HRM approaches, the volume includes two papers which deal with HRM in multinational and internationally operating companies. Nancy Adler, professor at McGill University in Montreal (Canada), and Fariborz Ghadar, professor at The George Washington University in Washington, D.C., concentrate on the practical impacts that the globalization of markets has on HRM. They criticize that most companies have not yet adapted sufficiently to the changing environment. In most internationally operating firms, the human resource management system is still managed as if the companies were exclusively operating on domestic markets. What they need to apply, however, are global concepts of management in general, and HRM in special. Eberhard Dülfer, professor at Phillips University at Marburg (Federal Republic of Germany), describes the practical aspects of global HRM. He focuses on the special tasks that HRM has in internationally operating firms and highlights strategies for solving the specific problems such companies are facing. The conceptualization and implementation of global HRM is, however, no easy undertaking considering the diversity of the various national environments multinational and internationally operation companies have to deal with. A look at the variety of national approaches to HRM explains the dimensions of this problem.

2.1 HRM in the Western Industrialized World: Contradictory Approaches

With the United States, Italy, France, and the Federal Republic of Germany, this section includes the largest economic powers of the Western world. In regard to their gross national product, these countries hold the places 1 (United States), 4 (FRG), 5 (France), and 6 (Italy). In regard to international trade, they are number one (United States), two (FRG), four (France), and six (Italy). If HRM really is a strategic factor determining the economic success of a nation, the HRM concepts applied in these countries should be excellent.

Beverly Springer, professor at the American Graduate School of International Management in Glendale, Arizona, and Stephan Springer, a private consultant, give an overview of the history of HRM in the *United States* and an analysis of current issues and problems. They highlight the major events in the development of personnel administration and both HRM theory and applied approaches in their country. In contrast to the editor who sees HRM as a relatively new approach to personnel management (also see: Staehle, in this volume), the Springers date the starting-point of HRM to the last century thus coming to a title of their paper that might surprise some readers: HRM in the United States celebrates its 100th anniversary. During this hundred years, personnel management in the United States changed from paternalism and Taylorism to human relations approaches and, finally, to integrated concepts (also see: Wren 1987). Each of these changes reflects both new research results — often even new research paradigms — and new societal and economic problems. Contrasting with this long practical and theoretical tradition in the field and the widely held view that the United States is the birthplace of modern management thought and applied concepts and, especially, of HRM, American companies are far from being perfect appliers of HRM concepts. First of all, the current practise of personnel management often lacks an integration into strategic management. However, as the other papers show, this is also true for the European countries and Japan. Secondly, companies have to face numerous basic problems. The number one problem which the Springers point out is the under-qualification of a large portion of the work-force. American labor is often lacking the skills and knowledge that companies are looking for. In the last two decades, the general standard of education has dropped significantly. Even the famous American business schools are now seen more critically (Cheit 1985; Pieper 1989 b; Hayes and Abernathy 1980). Education has become a major political issue and the problem is evaluated by some as an educational crisis. The issue has two aspects: problems in the educational system and the lack of vocational training. In regard to the first, companies argue that the educational level at both private and state-run schools and colleges has declined. College students frequently graduate without an adequate general education, often lacking basic writing and mathematical skills. Popular majors are increasing in subjects that have no direct application to a future professional career. Vocational training, on the other hand, is excluded from the American educational system and left entirely private employers. Companies which do offer some vocational training to their employees, usually concentrate on skills and knowledges that are directly related to their specific jobs and company needs. The result is a complete lack of widely applicable vocational training.

Another field of HRM activities that is especially highlighted by American authors is intercultural or crosscultural training[4]. While such training often "just happens" in Europe and Asia as a result of the coexistence of various cultures speaking different languages, it forms a special problem for management education and development in the United States[5]. The American conviction that "American way of life" is the single best alternative and their consistent efforts to export it worldwide combined with the long-term dominance of the internal American marked which did not force companies to concentrate on export markets, has led to a certain ignorance of foreign cultures and a wide-spread unwillingness to learn foreign languages. The current clear tendency toward a market globalization, tough foreign competition both world-wide and on the domestic market, and a relative decline in the American economy, are forcing companies to think internationally. As a consequence, they are in need of international, polyglott managers who are provided neither by the school system nor the business schools. Since European high school students are required to learn foreign languages and experience foreign countries and cultures through extensive travel during vacation, they have less need of organized intercultural training. At least in regard to Europe, European companies do not regard such kind of training as a major problem of HRM.

---

[4] There is a vast literature now dealing with issues of crosscultural education and training. For a comprehensive overview see e. g. Torbiorn 1982; Harris and Moran 1987.

[5] Also see Nancy Adler and Fariborz Ghadar: Strategic Human Resource Management. A Global Perspective, published in this volume.

In summary, HRM in the United States can be characterized as being confronted with a lack of well-educated labor. On the other hand it is scarcely regulated by state or federal law, hardly influenced by trade unions or shop stewards, and to some degree as a result it is flexible instead of bureaucratic.

The major difference between HRM in the United States and in *Western Europe* is the degree to which it is influenced and determined by state regulations. Companies in Western Europe have a narrower scope of choice in regard to personnel management than in the United States. The largely unregulated American practice of hiring and firing is illegal in Europe. Employees are less mobile both professionally and geographically. The state also plays a more active role in education; in most countries the school and university system is public; attendance is tuition free. In the German speaking countries, vocational training is also provided in a joint state and enterprise cooperation. German students usually either join a vocational training program or go to university before starting a regular job. Formal certification plays a major role both for personnel selection and professional careers in all of the European countries. As in Japan, the type of education that an individual receives highly determines further career options. In state agencies it also determines income level. Such formal systems additionally reduce professional mobility.

Another major difference between HRM in the United States and Western Europe is the degree to which trade unions and shop stewards are entitled to interfere in and influence a company's HRM policy. In general, HRM is the area of company activities where trade unions and shop stewards have the most say. What has not yet been regulated by the state is left to collective bargaining, usually on the state or a regional level, and to direct codetermination on the company level. In the Federal Republic of Germany, for example, most HRM activities may not be implemented without the approval of elected shop stewards. All three West European papers make these differences very clear.

The third point worth mentioning in the historical development of HRM in Western Europe. Although HRM is usually seen as an American invention — at least in regard to the theoretical discourse — the authors point out that the sophisticated application of personnel management and HRM concepts has a long history in Europe. Peter Conrad and Rüdiger Pieper highlight the integrative function of paternalistic personnel management concepts in the early period of the industrial revolution. These concepts also served to keep the trade unions, which at that time based their activities on the Marxist concept of class struggle, out of the factories. Jacques Rojot also mentions the comprehensive welfare policies that French companies practiced at the turn of the century. Amazingly, these paternalistic methods show a strong similarity to current Japanese practices. In both France and

Germany, personnel management issues were dealt with by management researchers from the very beginning of the establishment of business administration as a subject for research and teaching (see also: Schneider 1987; Staehle 1989). With the exception of Italy, the establishment of a special sub-discipline, however, only happened in the sixties. Nevertheless, a closer look at the history of personnel management theory and practice in Europe shows, that HRM cannot be regarded as a purely American invention.

Although they show a number of similarities, the HRM concepts discussed and applied in the Western European countries are distinct from each other in many regards. A major factor influencing such national particularities are differences in the industrial relations systems.

In his paper on *France*, Jacques Rojot, professor at the University du Maine and at INSEAD, clearly names the French particulars. First of all, most issues of HRM are regulated by law and statutes. "Multiple acts accumulated over the years regulate in minute details many issues which, in many other systems would fall in the realm of collective bargaining". In addition, there is a high degree of state interference, both through direct interventions, an extensive public sector in the French economy, and the French welfare system. In part, Rojot links this to a cultural phenomenon: the strong bureaucratic element in French culture. Secondly, France has a special system for selecting its leading administrators and managers. In general, only those who have graduated from one of the "Grandes Ecoles." will rise to top positions in administration and business. This elitist system is similar to the ranking of universities in Japan. It guarantees that the French ruling elite undergoes the same socialisation thus making it a culturally homogeneous group very distinct from the rest of the work force and foreign managers.

The paper on *Italy*, written by Hans H. Hinterhuber, professor at both the University of Innsbruck, Austria, and the Catholic University of Milan, and Monika Stumpf, assistant professor at the University of Innsbruck, points out that Italian management techniques are "strongly affected by social and institutional factors". However, they are not determined by such external factors since applied HRM approaches vary widely. As in all other industrialized countries, they range from personnel administration ("book-keeping administrative approach") to strategic human resource management. Some fields of HRM, especially management development and education, are heavily influenced by American approaches. Instead of developing national models, foreign concepts are adopted to Italian needs. The influential position of foreign concepts is supported by the fact that in Italy, business administration does not include a special discipline for research and teaching which includes personnel management as a distinct entity. On the contrary, as Hinterhuber and Stumpf mention, it is "split up into

different branches of several economic disciplines". Naturally, such splin-
tering makes it more difficult to develop a specific Italian theoretical approach to HRM. According to the authors, however, this now seems to be
changing.

Another characteristic element of HRM in Italy results from the division
between the country's fully developed North with a strong Middle European
orientation and a developing South that reflects some Arabic influence.
Since the north is highly industrialized as well as one of the wealthiest
regions in Europe, while the south is still a traditional developing area,
HRM in such a dualistic regional structure faces different problems, for
example, existing educational standards, dominant work behavior and attitudes, and the labor needs of companies. As a consequence, companies
active in the north require different HRM strategies than those active in
Southern Italy.

In their paper on HRM in the *Federal Republic of Germany*, Peter Conrad
(Free University of Berlin) and Rüdiger Pieper (Paul-Löbe-Institut Berlin)
begin by asking whether there is anything at all new about HRM. They
come to a mixed conclusion, pointing out both the long history of applied
HRM approaches and the short history of HRM theory in their country.
The only aspect that they regard as being innovative is the integration of
personnel management into strategic management. However, in West Germany as well, such integration is practiced only by a small minority of
companies. The German specifics of HRM are:

- the system of codetermination which guarantees elected shop stewards
  a strong influence on HRM decisions,
- the dual-system of training which provides a vocational training to most
  students who do not plan to attend a university program.

While German codetermination leads to a low rate of labor conflict, the
system of vocational training supplies companies with well-trained labor,
especially the so called *Facharbeiter*. Since this system is run in joint cooperation with state agencies, companies enjoy the advantage of not being
solely responsible for financing such training. In addition, the state and
public run insurance agencies also pay for retraining programs for the
unemployed. Of course, the programs are often organized to meet the actual
needs of the companies. Thus, German companies are, in general, able to
shift costs for development programs to state agencies. This, however, is
not the case with regard to managers. While in the United States and some
other European countries, business schools offer training programs for
managers which can be seen as substitutes for in-house-training, German
universities provide courses only for students joining them immediately after
graduating from high school. As a consequence, management development

is seen the exclusive task of the companies' HRM department. In addition, German managers expect their companies to pay all their expenses.

In short, the industrialized nations of the Western world have developed characteristic approaches to HRM which do show some similarities, but are different, often contradictory, in many aspects. It seems that in practice, a single, universal HRM concept does not exist.

Actually, there are two current developments that have to be faced by HRM in all of these countries. First there are strong tendencies toward flexibilisation in work organization, work place and the benefit system. This is primarily a result of the potential flexibility of a number of new production and office technologies. Fordism has been to a large degree replaced by decentralization through work islands, autonomous work groups, home work, and flexible work hours. A second reason is the continuing individualization of most Western societies which leads to divergent labor needs and forces companies to develop, for example, individual benefit systems (like the cafeteria system) but also gives them added flexibility in work organization and work hours.

The second significant development for HRM is the dimishing power of trade unions. During the last decade, most trade unions in Western Europe and the United States saw a shrinking membership (Müller-Jentsch 1988). With changing value systems, and a process of social differentiation in the industrialized countries (Pieper 1988), the traditional milieus which were especially strong in the industrial areas of Western Europe have been replaced by a strong trend towards individualisation. Some sociologists even ask whether, for example, the working class can still be seen as a socially homogeneous group with shared interests and common values, life styles, and political views (e. g. Offe 1984). As a consequence, the representation of such divergent interests has become difficult. Bargaining processes are no longer restricted to labor-management-relations, but are now equally necessary within the unions. Furthermore, the number of blue-colour workers, who used to form the vast majority of trade union members, is shrinking, while the number of non-unionized white-colour workers in the service sector is growing. Trade unions are loosing their traditional membership reservoir and, thus, their influence. While management might see this development as an advantage and an increase in their scope in countries with a decentralized system of trade unions and collective bargaining, it causes significant problems in countries where management is accustomed to centralized collective bargaining. Bargaining partners which no longer represent a vast majority of labor are unable to guarantee that the result of their bargaining will be accepted by all or most employees. They have lost their socially integrative function. Exploring how the various nations and how companies react to these developments will be an interesting topic for further research.

2.2 HRM in Eastern Europe: Revolutionary Changes

The East European section includes papers from Czechoslovakia, East Germany, and Yugoslavia. Czechoslovakia and East Germany have much in common, especially their similar political and economic structures, and a common history of adaptation to the Soviet-Stalinist model, thus being perfect examples of the Warsaw Pact states. *Yugoslavia*, however, presents a special case. Under Tito's leadership, the country managed to remain independent of Soviet political and economic influence. Thus it was — unlike the Soviet allies and satellites — able to develop its own model of socialism. The Yugoslav model, which attempted to combine socialist ownership with market economic elements under a system of workers' self-management, even became popular in the Western European countries in the late sixties at a time when they were experiencing a heated debate over economic and social reforms. In addition, and partly because of its political attractiveness and the general openness of the country, Yugoslavia became the only socialist state in which Western management researchers have been able to do empirical studies. Comparative management studies often include Yugoslavia as the sole socialist country (e. g. Hofstede 1980; MOW International Research Team 1985; Peck 1975). As a result, the general standard of information on Yugoslavia is far better than for the countries of the Warsaw Pact.

In her paper, Danica Purg, the founder and current director of the first Yugoslav business school (Executive Training Center in Kranj, Slovenia) gives a general overview on HRM management in her country, lists the major determining societal factors and describes actual problems in the field. Much like the global situation of Yugoslavia, which has approached crisis in the last few years, these problems are enormous. At this point, nothing remains of Yugoslavia's former model character. Unlike the late sixties, when the system of self-management played a major role in attempts to reform socialist countries like Czechoslovakia, current reform discussions in the Warsaw Pact states reject the Yugoslav experience and are focusing instead on Western-type management and a free market economy. In the aftermath of Tito's death, the nations of Yugoslavia have lost their willingness to compromise. Since then separatism, economic conflicts between the well-developed, Western-oriented north (Slovenia, Croatia) and the south, a Stalinist come-back in Serbia, a widespread inability and inwillingness to reform, and a galloping inflation-rate (more than 600% in 1989) have shaken the country. HRM — in the proper sense — does not exist in most companies, with the very few exceptions of companies that have a high export-orientation to Western markets. In contrast, the introduction and implementation of HRM concepts have to be seen as a major step in reforming the economic system. The creation of management development programs either within companies or at business schools and universities is a central part of this reform process. Another major point that Purg focuses on is the task that personnel administration used to have in Yugoslavia. As in the other socialist countries, personnel administration is heavily influenced by politics. Thus it is not primarily a management function but a political function often dominated by trade unionist and party interests. As a consequence, personnel administration in Eastern Europe became part of the nations' social policy. Specific to Yugoslavia, however, is the direct influence that the employees may exercise on the personnel function through the system of self management. They may exert direct influence by making decisions themselves or indirectly by electing the managers in charge. Because of these two heavily interfering factors an integration of personnel management into the company's general strategic management was almost impossible.

Ondraj Landa from the Czechoslovak Academy of Sciences points to one of the most central problems facing all socialist countries, and which has also been highlighted by Danica Purg: management education, which Landa sees as the key issue of HRM in his country. In *Czechoslovakia* — as in all other socialist states — training programs for all types of employees have always included technical knowledge and skills. Management development programs, however, concentrated heavily on political education and thus failed to adequately develop behavioral and general management skills. In addition and because of the central-planning system, managers were unable to make their own decisions or to take risks, but worked primarily as bureaucrats who were expected to execute political decisions. Consequently, management positions were seen as purely political functions. The selection process of individual managers and their career progress were based on political criteria, especially membership in the socialist party and its sub organizations (youth movement, trade union, cultural organizations). Political conformism was the major prerequisite for a career in management. Consequently, at both business schools and training and education centers run by the socialist partly where managers were required to attend special classes, training concentrated more on politics, namely marxist-leninist ideology and marxist political economy than on practical business administration. Instead of management, managers had to learn *Leitungswissenschaft* which was originally defined as a kind of socialist management theory, but, in fact, was transformed into a political discipline being mainly descriptive and concentrated on planning issues, general political issues and structural elements of management (Pieper 1989 a). In *Leitungswissenschaft*, behavioral aspects are almost totally neglected (Pieper 1989 c: 193cont.). Where practical aspects are addressed and advice given, it is usually not based on empirical research or theoretical concepts, but on political ideology. Only a

very few recent publications include consideration of the behavioral aspects
of management (in the GDR, for example: Hartmann 1988; Czycholl and
Ebner 1989; Friedrich and Voß 1988). However, neither practical nor theoretical aspects of leadership and motivation are taught at East European
business schools (Pieper 1989). Since neither management nor management
development (in the Western sense) have until now existed in Eastern Europe,
Landa's view that management development is the key issue of HRM in
his country, does not come as a surprise. With recent political changes, his
analysis has become even more timely, especially with the introduction of
free market economies in Poland and the GDR. Since a market economy
cannot function without able and experienced managers, management development is no longer simply a key issue of HRM, but has become a key
factor and a key problem for the current economic reforms. The problem
is that the socialist countries have almost no experience in business education
and management development. They did not even establish a discipline like
business administration until the late sixties (Pieper 1989 a). And when they
did do so, business education still concentrated on politics and descriptive
explanations of the central-planning system. Subjects as central as marketing
and finance were totally excluded. The same is true for personnel management: the socialist countries still have no special discipline like HRM or
personnal administration which could be used for teaching nor does a
general theory of management exist. Since there is no established discipline,
there are no professors in the field, almost no research and no courses
offered by business schools. As a result, East European companies do
practice personnel administration but without a theoretical, analytically-
based concept. In regard to HRM theory and research, the Eastern European
nations are still developing countries that urgently need foreign aid.

Hansgünter Meyer, professor at the East German Academy of Sciences,
highlights a very unique problem: the over-qualification of the work-force
in the *German Democratic Republic*. At first glance, this statement might
sound odd and, certainly, a number of readers will argue that the paper as
a whole tends toward apologism. Since it, too, was written before the
November revolution and fall of the once ruling Socialist Unity Party, which
not only dominated politics but economics and science as well, it had to be
written in a fashion acceptable to the ruling elite[6]. Thus it too, is in a way
a historical document,[7] but one that is still worth reading since the problems

---

[6] GDR's authors were required to have all articles approved for Western publication
by various agencies, i. e. they were censored in case they did not fit into the
currently ruling analysis.

[7] Certain aspects, however, haven been rewritten in February 1990. Taking the
speed of change in Germany into account, these change, too, have a historical
aspect.

that are detailed in the paper still exist. Although hundreds of thousands of GDR citizens fled to the West in 1989 and 1990 — most of them with a good education either in an academic discipline or as skilled workers — leaving the GDR economy with a severe shortage of experienced workers — the country is still unable to employ its work-force at its level of education and training. Another result of the bureaucratic central planning system and the attempt of the socialist party to exert total control, is the top heavy bureaucratic apparatus in state agencies and enterprises. Furthermore, academics often hold jobs that could be filled by semi-skilled labor in this bureaucratic apparatus. Today companies are trying to tackle this problem: one of the major economic impacts of the recent political changes is that administrative personnel are being dismissed, sometimes more than half of the members of a department, often in violation of existing law which officially still protects labor from dismissal. In addition, the secret police and the border police absorbed large numbers of well-trained people and academics (both in part-time and full-time jobs) not for productive purposes but to control the domestic population and foreign visitors.

A second major reason for over-qualification in the GDR is the country's wage system, which tends to favor skilled workers. Academics and people in management positions earn only slightly more (sometimes even less) than skilled workers. Thus, from a financial point of view, academics receive a higher income when working in a non-academic position. Being a taxi driver is financially more attractive than working as, for example, a medical doctor, a teacher or a researcher assistant. At the same time, since all educational and training programs are paid for by the state[8] or companies, people do not regard education as a personal investment. On the contrary, they are delegated by their company to join a program, often against their will.

All three East European papers were written in 1989, i. e. before the peaceful revolution in November and December 1989 which almost totally changed the political situation in the Warsaw Pact states. In Czechoslovakia and East Germany, the former Stalinist governments and single party rule have been abolished. Both countries are actually undergoing fundamental changes that can been seen as a shift from Stalinist command economy to a Western type democracy and market economy. East Germany is on its way to being fully integrated into the West Germany political and economic system. When the conference took place in May 1989, Poland was the only country actually changing from socialism to a free-market society, and the speakers from Eastern Europe were still able to talk about a socialist type

---

[8] All students receive a grant that covers their living costs regardless of the income level of their parents. Employees who are delegated to a training program or night school by their company keep their jobs and their actual income. However, their working hours are reduced.

of HRM. Ondrej Landa from the Czechoslovak Academy of Science explicitly argued that "four decades of socialist societal system have created a new tradition of HRM of its own right, a distinctive HRM culture". With the end of these socialist societal systems one might question whether this argument is still valid and whether, in general, the papers from Czechoslovakia and East Germany are now anything more than relics of a time that has passed. As a matter of fact, these papers include views and analysis that would not longer be applied, and exclude opinions that were then unacceptable for political reasons. They also describe a general situation that no longer exists. However, most of the issues treated by these authors must still be seen as real problems which continue to influence the economic and political changes now taking place in these countries. The former socialist states are not starting from the beginning but must build upon existing structures and culture. Since the people of these countries have undergone a specific socialization in the attempt to create a "socialist personality", they have specific work behaviors, life-styles and even logical structures. Changing this will be more difficult than reforming external structures. Thus even in the medium range future, the application of HRM in the former socialist countries will be different from what is now being practiced in most of the Western industrialized nations. The East European papers, although partly historical documents, help to understand these differences, to explain the determining factors, and to recognize the difficulties that these countries face in their attempt to achieve fundamental change.

2.3 HRM in Asia

The Asian sample consists of Japan and China. The HRM approaches described in the two papers are very different, and to some degree contradictory, since Japan as a highly industrialized country faces problems that cannot be compared to those that China as a developing country has to deal with. In general, HRM in Japan has more in common with the concepts being discussed and applied in the Western industrialized countries than with China, while HRM in China shows similarities to Eastern Europe.

Wang Zhong-Ming, professor at the department of psychology at Hangzhou University, describes the actual problems that HRM in *China* is facing in its attempt to change the country's economy from a centralized planning system towards a more market-oriented economy. He argues that "Human resource management is becoming a key aspect of the current economic and management reform in China". These reforms affect almost every aspect of HRM and management in general. Both the ownership of companies is being changed, usually from state to collective or private ownership (also see: Zhai 1990), and the internal management structure. Most important is the shift from promoting political functionaries to management positions to now selecting or electing managers according to their ability. While the East European countries acknowledge similar problems without testing possible solutions on the large scale or developing a new system of management selection, the Chinese have invented a whole new system. According to Wang, "most cadres in Chinese enterprises are now either elected or selected through some open and democratic procedures". This new system resembles the Yugoslav method of employees selecting the managers of a company. However, the Chinese have also started to use elaborated methods of assessing management and leadership abilities, e. g. assessment centers that are still unknown in Eastern Europe.

Other aspects of Chinese HRM are still very similar to common East European practices. Since all of them used to claim to be socialist, they all had (and partly still have) a wage and benefit system with strong tendencies towards egalitarianism. While this system led to (formal) over-qualification in the GDR, it resulted in a lack of incentives for further training in China. Although more individualistic benefit systems were invented in most socialist countries in the seventies, they still do not motivate labor sufficiently. Another similarity to Eastern Europe is that the political situation in China has changed since the paper was written. At least some of the reforms that Wang describes have been cancelled. Although China has not given up changing its economy to a market system, it has definitely slowed the speed of reform. In addition, movements toward a Western type democracy have been totally neglected. What effect these current developments, which also include a growing scepticism towards academic education, might have on HRM in China is unclear und must be left to further research.

Astonishingly, Wang does not mention culture as a significant factor for HRM in his country. This is in sharp contrast to most Westerners who do research on China. Almost all of them identify elements specific to Chinese culture that have a strong impact on management and, especially, personnel management (e. g. Laaksonen 1988; Meindl, Hunt and Lee 1989). There are several possible explanations for this: Either Wang is relatively blind to cultural specifics of his own country (ethnocentrism), or he consciously concentrates on current macro-economic changes that − in his view − have a greater impact on HRM practise in China than culture. The second explanation conforms with the contingency approach to comparative management which regards culture as one among many determining factors of management in various countries (Miller 1984; Negandhi 1975).

Yoshiaki Takahaski, professor at Chuo University in Tokyo, begins his paper on HRM in *Japan* with some methodological remarks. He names three factors that, in his opinion, are relevant to the comparison of HRM approaches in different countries, i. e. the cultural structure, the economic process, and the internal and external organization of the enterprise. Takahashi argues that an interdisciplinary approach must be taken in order to discuss an international comparison of HRM. He then clearly names the widely-known characteristics of Japanese HRM: life-time employment, seniority wage system, and enterprise unionism, and links them to cultural factors such as the groupist orientation of Japanese people. These characteristic elements, however, are changing due to general social, economic and technological changes in the country. Takahashi identifies the increasing number of employees in the service sector, the internationalization of most companies, the aging of Japanese society, and the growing infusion of microelectronics into work-life as the major factors for current changes that likewise pose new problems for HRM. Actual strategies for handling these problems are the establishment of new education and training systems and a modification of the traditional custom of life-long employment. Currently, companies tend to restrict the number of regular, life-long employees and to use part-time workers instead. Furthermore, they relocate employees within and between departments, or even lend or transfer them to daughter and related companies. Another problem is, however, not mentioned by Takahashi, i. e. changes in the Japanese value system. A growing Westernization or Americanization of the country might lead to a reducation of Japanese groupism and a tendency towards individualistic values. If, in the future, the current process of social differentiation and individualization continues, Japanese companies will no longer be able to practice their groupist approaches to HRM. Some of the attraction of Japanese management would then be lost.

3. No Universal Model of HRM

In comparing HRM in the various countries included in this sampling, one may reach several conclusions:

First of all, HRM seems to be more a theoretical construct than an applied reality. What companies generally practise is personnel management instead of HRM. They usually restrict their personnel policy to what Gaugler (1988) calls the basic human resource functions. According to Gaugler, companies all around the world — disregarding cultural or general environmental differences — have to fulfill a number of duties in the field of personnel management since "no company can do without personnel" (1988: 24). These basic functions are to procure staff, to compensate the employees, and company leadership. The latter also covers motivation, developing the employees' abilities and working climate and conditions. However, HRM as it has been defined at the beginning covers more. It also includes a management philosophy and the integration of personnel management into strategic management. These two elements are often missing in applied approaches. Although most authors mention that a strong and even growing emphasis is being put on developing and training personnel in their countries, the link to strategic management seems to be more the exception than the rule. In countries with a centrally planned economy this does not come as a surprise since, strategies there are formulated on a central political level instead by management. In countries with a market economy, the situation in very mixed: applied approaches range from traditional personnel administration to strategic HRM. What is applied by a company largely depends on the company's own management decisions rather than national characteristics. Thus, among the industrialized nations of the Western world, the enterprise level is more appropriate for comparisons.

Secondly, regardless of whether HRM in the proper sense or personnel management is being applied, both practical and theoretical concepts in the various nations vary widely. What has already been stated for the Western industrialized nations, that there is no single universal model of HRM, becomes even more obvious in looking at other nations. This is not surprising given the significant differences between these countries. Elements in HRM approaches can be seen as characteristic for each nation as a result of their specific cultural, economic, and legal environments. A major factor is the degree of *state interference*. In the socialist countries (Eastern Europe, China), HRM is largely determined by law and politics, thus leaving a minimal scope of choice to the individual organization. In West Europe, state interference is also high. The European welfare and educational systems, although different in many aspects, act as strong determinants. In Japan and the United States, state interference is minimal. In Japan, however, this lack of a legal structure is partly substituted by cultural factors, especially Japanese groupism. The issue of groupism leads to the second major factor affecting HRM in different nations: the *degree of collectivism versus individualism*[9]. While the Asian and the socialist countries in Eastern Europe can be characterized by a high degree of collectivism[10], HRM in the United States is quite the opposite, i.e. relatively individualistic. The West European nations lie somewhere in between showing current tendencies towards increased individualistic concepts.

---

[9] Collectivism versus individualism also forms one of the four dimensions that Hofstede (1980) uses to describe a specific culture.

[10] However, it has to be mentioned that in these countries, the cause for collectivism is different: whereas in Japan and China, cultural elements lead to collectivism, the East European collectivism is a result of Marxist ideology, i.e. politics.

Thirdly, all the papers demonstrate that culture is by far no means the only variable which has an impact on HRM. Some papers do not mention culture at all. It appears that there is nothing like a cultural imperative in HRM as, e. g. Steers (1989) argues. Instead, most papers list a number of significant factors which highly determine applied HRM approaches and influence theoretical concepts. This leads to some of the general methodological problems of comparative management research which also become obvious in the international comparison of HRM: the search for a systematization of determining environmental factors.

4. Some Remarks on Methodological Problems of Comparative Management Research

Such search for determining environmental factors and their systematization has been a matter of controversy ever since comparative management research was established in the sixties.

A number of factors that are important to analysing HRM are enumerated in most of the papers. The authors mention:

- the political system and current political changes
- the economic system
- the industrial relations system
- the legal environment
- the educational system
- demographic factors
- technology and technological changes
- culture.

Although this list helps to understand and identify national differences in HRM approaches, it only has a heuristic character and is by no means systematic. Often the authors have merely enumerated what they see as being important for HRM in their country without applying any basic theoretical concept. This reflects the overall problem of comparative management research: a lack of theory (Miller 1984; Negandhi 1975; Staehle 1989).

The lack of a theoretical foundation is, at least in part, the result of different approaches to comparative management, which until now could not be combined into a single theoretical concept. In the late sixties, when comparative management was still a juvenile field, Schöllhammer (1969) identified a "comparative management theory jungle". In his analysis of the current status, Miller (1984) distinguishes three broad orientations of comparative management studies with divergent theoretical and methodological approaches: an economic development and environmental orientation, a behavioral orientation, and a contingency orientation. The cognitive interest of the first orientation is the search for environmental factors influencing a country's economic growth. Farmer and Richman (1965) founded this orientation in their classical study on comparative management and economic progress. The behavioral approach is directed toward explaining behavioral patterns in different environmental settings. It concentrates on culture as the single most important factor, which is seen as largely determinant for individual and organizational behavior in different nations. This approach, which could better be called cross-cultural comparative research, lacks a common understanding of how culture is to be defined and how — if at all — it can be measured. In regard to measurement there are two schools of thought: quantitative and qualitative (for an in-depth discussion see: von Keller 1982). While quantitative approaches assume that culture can be measured with the traditional methods of empirical social science[11], qualitative approaches use interpretive methods of ethnomethodology. The latter approach is identical to the interpretive school of organizational culture research while the contingency orientation in comparative management resembles the functionalistic approach in the organizational culture debate (Allaire and Firsirotu 1984; Burell and Morgan 1982). By focusing on the relationship between organizations and their national environment, the contingency orientation regards culture as being just one of several invironmental factors. Negandhi (1975), for example, distinguishes economic, political, social, cultural, and legal factors. Phatak (1989) names four contingency factors: a nation's political system and the legal, the cultural, and the economic environment. Without mentioning it explicitly, most of the papers on national HRM approaches in this volume use similar concepts based on a contingency orientation of comparative management. This approach is, however, controversial. Researchers who focus on cultural comparisons argue that differences in the environment are the result of cultural differences. Since nations have different cultures, they consequently have different legal, political, and industrial relations systems. Terpestra and David's (1985) argument provides an excellent example of this point of view. They distinguish between culture on the one hand and cultural systems which organize human behavior on the other. Aspects of such cultural systems are, among others, the technological, the economic, the political, and the legal system. The essence of this view is that nations are equated

---

[11] The study of Geert Hofstede (1980) is an excellent example of this school.

with cultures. Thus, the term culture receives the status of an unspecific umbrella expression under which almost everything can be collected.

Even if the current "comparative management theory jungle" is relatively easy to overlook, the diversity of different conceptual and methodological approaches is not especially helpful in filling the theoretical gap which still exists. In my view, a general social theory able to identify the constitutive elements of any society and, thus, to systematically link culture with other variables that make up a society is needed to replace heuristic enumerations endemic to the contingency orientation or controversal concepts of culture characteristic of the behavioral orientation. A general social theory could serve as a conceptual and methodological framework for comparative management research.

The search for an appropriate social theory to be used as the theoretical foundation for comparative management research, demands new perspectives and requires a new level of cooperation between disciplines. In addition to anthropology, organization theory, management research, and empirical-analytical sociology, social theoretical approaches must be included. Reference to research directed toward the formulation of a general theory of society might be especially productive.

A theoretical concept which I, personally, find especially enriching, and which, to a large degree, has already heavily influenced the sociological, philosophical and methodological discourse in Western Europe and, to a lesser degree, also in the United States (e. g. Bernstein 1985; McCarthy 1981), is "the theory of communicative action" of the German sociologist Jürgen Habermas (1981). The work of Habermas has also recently gained some impact on management thought in West Germany (Pieper 1988; Ulrich 1986). Although this volume is not the most appropriate place for proposing a new theoretical foundation for comparative management research, I shall nevertheless attempt to give a short introduction to this aspect of Habermas' work which seems offer a promising concept to fill the existing theoretical gap and that might also be useful in overcoming the dichotomy between qualitative and quantitative methods, and functionalistic and interpretive approaches.

The "theory of communicative action" (1981), which in many regards stands in the tradition of the Critical Theory or Frankfurt School[12], is an attempt to combine the two main streams of current sociological thought, systems theory and action theory, into an evolutionary theory of society (Habermas 1981). Habermas makes such combination by distinguishing between two spheres of society: system and life-world. System, which is that

---

[12] The most important and well-known proponents of the Frankfurt School are Adorno, Horkheimer, and Marcuse.

part of society driven by certain mechanisms through mediums such as power and money, is constructed with the help of general systems theory (namely the work of Parsons and Luhmann), while the concept of life-world is rooted in action theory and arises from hermeneutics and phenomenology. Its basics were formulated by Schütz (1932), and Berger and Luckmann (1969). System and life-world are not just two spheres of society but also stand for two different perspectives. Whereas life-world is constructed from an inside perspective, i. e. the viewpoint of a participant, an outside observer will portray society as a system of actions which are primarily functional. Life-world is the taken for granted universe of daily social life, a code for social behavior, and the collective interpretation of various generations. It also forms the cultural background of a society which can only partly be questioned and only will be questioned in cases of conflicts. Its mechanism is communication, i. e. language. Its basis is the consensus of the people.

Methodologically, such combination of systems theory and action theory offers the chance to analyse a given society from two different viewpoints with two different sets of methodology. The functional parts of society can be analysed analytically from an observer's perspective, as comparative management researchers in the tradition of the contingency approach already do, i. e. analysing society as a system of functional sub-systems. Life-world, however, has to be seen from the inside perspective of a participant. It can thus only be interpreted by outsiders, but by no means explored through quantitative methodologies. In this regard, comparative management researchers can learn a lot from discussions which are going on in organization theory (interpretive approaches to organizational culture) and, especially, interpretive anthropology (e. g. Geertz 1973; Marcus and Fischer 1986). Instead of exclusively defining a national culture in terms of a limited number of variables, as for example Hofstede (1980) does, we have to understand how members of a culture perceive their life-world. Lifeworld, however, is not identical to what is usually understood under the term culture since lifeworld is not a global concept, but the level of individual perception. By using the concept of lifeworld, we are thus able to distinguish between, for example, various local or socially determined subcultures to get a more differentiated picture of a nation.

The two perspectives of an inside participant and an outside observer must be combined to enable us to a more complex understanding of the functioning of society. "We cannot understand the character of the life-world unless we understand the social systems that shape ist, and we cannot understand social systems unless we see how they arise out of activities of social agents" (Bernstein 1985: 22). It can be added that we cannot compare nations without an understanding and a comparison of both life-world and their social systems.

Of course, the practical impact of Habermas' theoretical concept has still to be further explored. Its potential, however, is enormous if we are willing to omit to stare fixedly at either qualitative or quantitative approaches but start to combine them in order to get a more complex picture of nations and more realistic and differentiated comparisons.

References

Ackermann, K. F. (1986): A Contingency model of HRM-Strategy, Empirical research findings reconsidered, in: *Management-Forum*, Vol. 6: 65—117.
Ackermann, K. F. (1987): Konzeptionen des strategischen Personalmanagements für die Unternehmenspraxis, in: Glaubrecht, H. and D. Wagner (eds.), *Humanität und Rationalität in Personalpolitik und Personalführung*, Freiburg/B.: 39—68.
Adler, N. J. (1984): Understanding the Ways of Understanding: Cross-cultural Management Methodology Reviewed, in: Farmer (ed.), *op. cit.*: 31—67.
Allaire, Y. and M. E. Firsirotu (1984): *Theories of Organizational Culture*, Organization Studies: 193—226.
Bateman, T. S. and C. P. Zeithaml (1990): *Management. Function and Strategy*, Homewood, Ill.-Boston.
Beer, M., B. Spector, P. R. Lawrence, D. Q. Mills and R. E. Walton (1985): *Human Resource Management*, New York—London.
Berger, P. L. and T. Luckmann (1969): *Die gesellschaftliche Konstruktion der Wirklichkeit*, Frankfurt/M.
Bernstein, R. J. (ed.) (1985): *Habermas and Modernity*, Cambridge, MA.
Burrell, G. and G. Morgan (1982): *Sociological paradigms and organizational analysis*, London.
Byars, L. L. and L. W. Rue (1987): *Human Resource Management*, Homewood, Ill. (2nd. ed.).
Cheit, E. F. (1985): Business Schools and their Critics, *California Management Review*, No. 3: 43—62.
Czycholl, R. and H. G. Ebner (eds.) (1989): *Aspekte der Personal- und Organisationsentwicklung in der DDR*, Oldenburg.
Evans, P. (1986): The Strategic Outcomes of Human Resource Management, *Human Resource Management*, Vol. 25, No. 1: 149—167.
Evans, P. (1987): The Context of Strategic Human Resource Management Policy in Complex Firms, in: Lattmann, C. (ed.), *Personalmanagement und Strategische Unternehmensführung*, Heidelberg: 105—113.
Farmer, R. N. (1984): Efficiency of Firms and Countries, in: Farmer (ed.), 1—29.
Farmer, R. N. (ed.) (1984): *Advances in International Comparative Management*, Vol. 1, Greenwich, Con.—London.
Farmer, R. N. and B. M. Richman (1965): *Comparative Management and Economic Progress*, Homewood, Il.
Ferris, G. R. and K. M. Rowland (eds.) (1989): *Research in Personnel and Human Resource Management*, Supplement 1: International Human Resource Management, Greenwich, Con.—London.
Fombrun, C. J., N. M. Tichy and M. A. Devanna (eds.) (1984): *Strategic Human Resource Management*, New York.

Friedrich, W. and P. Voß (eds.) (1988): *Sozialpsychologie für die Praxis*, Berlin (GDR).

Gaugler, E. (1988): *HR Management: An International Comparison, Personnel*, August 1988: 24–30.

Geertz, C. (1973): *The Interpretation of Cultures*, New York.

Habermas, J. (1981): *Theorie des kommunikativen Handelns*, 2 vols, Frankfurt/M.

Harris, P. R. and R. T. Moran (1987): *Managing Cultural Differences*, Houston (2nd. ed.).

Hartmann, W. D. (1988): *Handbuch der Managementtechniken*, Berlin (GDR).

Hayes, R. H. and W. J. Abernathy (1980): Managing Our Way to Economic Decline, *Harvard Business Review*, No. 4: 66–77.

Hofstede, G. (1980): *Culture's consequences: International differences in work related values*, Beverly Hills, Cal.

Keller, E. von (1982): *Management in fremden Kulturen*, Bern–Stuttgart.

Krulis-Randa, J. S. (1988): Personalführung und -entwicklung im veränderten gesellschaftlichen Umfeld, *Schweizerische Zeitschrift für Volkswirtschaft und Statistik*, 124. Jg.: 349–363.

Laaksonen, O. (1988): *Management in China*, Berlin–New York.

Lattmann, C. (ed.) (1987): *Personalmanagement und strategische Unternehmensführung*, Heidelberg.

Laukamm, T. (1986): Strategisches Management von Human Resourcen, in: Riekhof, H. C. (ed.), *Strategien der Personalentwicklung*, Wiesbaden: 77–113.

Leap, T. L. and M. D. Crino (1989): *Personnel/Human Resource Management*, New York–London.

Likert, R. (1967): *The Human Organization*, New York.

Marcus, G. E. and M. M. J. Fischer (1986): *Anthropology as Cultural Critique*, Chicago.

McCarthy, T. (1981): *The Critical Theory of Jürgen Habermas*, Cambridge, MA–London.

Meindl, J. R., R. G. Hunt and W. Lee (1989): Individualism-collectivism and work values: Date from the United States, China, Taiwan, Korea, and Hongkong, in: Ferris and Rowland (eds.), *op. cit.*: 59–77.

Miles, R. E. (1975): *Theories of Management*, New York.

Miller, E. L. (1984): Comparative Management Conceptualization: An Assessment, in: Farmer (ed.), *op. cit.*: 69–82.

MOW International Research Team (1985): *The meaning of work: An international perspective*, London–New York.

Müller-Jentsch, W. (ed.) (1988): *Zukunft der Gewerkschaften. Ein internationaler Vergleich*, Frankfurt/M.

Negandhi, A. (1975): Comparative Management and Organization Theory: A Marriage Needed, *Academy of Management Journal*, No. 2: 334–344.

OECD (1973): *List of Social Indicator Development Programme*, Paris.

Offe, C. (ed.) (1984): *Arbeitsgesellschaft — Strukturprobleme und Zukunftsperspektiven*, Frankfurt/M.

Parnes, H. S. (1984): *People Power: Elements of Human Resource Policy*, Beverly Hills, Cal.–London.

Peck, R. (1975): Distinctive national patterns of career motivation, *International Journal of Psychology*, Vol. 10, No. 2: 152–134.

Peters, T. J. and R. H. Waterman (1982): *In search of excellence*, New York.

Phatak, A. V. (1989): *International Dimensions of Management*, (2nd. ed.), Boston.

Pieper, R. (ed.) (1989): *Westliches Management — Östliche Leitung*. Ein Vergleich von Managementlehre und DDR-Leitungswissenschaft, Berlin — New York.

Pieper, R. (1988): *Diskursive Organisationsentwicklung*. Ansätze einer sozialen Kontrolle von Wandel, Berlin — New York.

Pieper, R. (1989 a): Geschichte von Betriebswirtschaftslehre und Leitungswissenschaft in der DDR, *DBW — Die Betriebswirtschaft*, Vol. 49, No. 5: 577 — 595.

Pieper, R. (1989 b): *Business Schools in den USA. Mythen und Fakten*, Berlin — New York.

Pieper, R. (1989 c): Leitungswissenschaft und Managementlehre — Ansätze eines Vergleichs aus Sicht der Managementlehre, in: Pieper, R. (ed.) (1989): 193 — 245.

Ronen, S. (1986): *Comparative and Multinational Management*, New York.

Rühli, E. and H. P. Wehrli (1986): Strategisches Management und Personalmanagement, in: Lattmann, C. (ed.), *Personal-Management und Strategische Unternehmensführung*, Heidelberg: 35 — 46.

Schneider, D. (1987): *Allgemeine Betriebswirtschaftslehre*, München — Wien (3rd. ed.).

Schöllhammer, H. (1969): The Comparative Management Theory Jungle, *Academy of Management Journal*, No. 1: 81 — 97.

Schütz, A. (1932): *Der sinnhafte Aufbau der sozialen Welt*, Wien.

Schuler, R. S. (1987): *Personnel and Human Resource Management*, St. Paul.

Schultz, T. W. (1978): *Economic Analysis of Investment in Education*, Washington, D.C.

Schuster, F. E. (1986): *The Schuster report: The proven connection between people and profit*, New York.

Staehle, W. H. (1989): *Management*, 4th ed., München.

Steers, R. M. (1989): The Cultural Imperative in HRM Research, in: Ferris and Rowland (eds.), *op. cit.*: 23 — 32.

Steinhausen, J. (1975): *Soziale Indikatoren als Elemente eines gesellschaftlichen Planungs- und Steuerungssystems*, Meisenheim/Glan.

Terpestra, V. and K. David (1985): *The Cultural Environment of International Business*, Cincinnati.

Tichy, N. M., C. F. Fombrun and M. A. Devanna (1982): Strategic Human Resource Management, *Sloan Management Review*, No. 2: 47 — 61.

Torbiorn, I. (1982): *Living Abroad: Personal Adjustment and Personal Policy in Overseas Setting*, New York.

Ulrich, P. (1986): *Transformation der ökonomischen Vernunft*. Fortschrittsperspektiven der modernen Industriegesellschaft, Bern — Stuttgart.

Wren, D. (1987): *The Evolution of Management Thought*, New York.

Zapf, W. (ed.) (1974): *Soziale Indikatoren und Sozialberichterstattung. Konzepte und Forschungsansätze*, Frankfurt/M. 3 volumes.

Zhai, L. (1990): Vom Volkseigentum zur Aktiengesellschaft? Perspektiven der chinesischen Unternehmensreform, *Die Betriebswirtschaft*, No. 1: 103 — 109.

Human Resource Management and Corporate Strategy

Wolfgang H. Staehle

1. From Personnel Administration to Human Resource Management (HRM)

Ever since the personnel function emerged as an independent functional area in companies (especially large ones) at the end of the nineteenth century, it has undergone many changes. Its treatment in the academic sphere has shifted, too. Classically, the task of the personnel function has been to adapt personnel to preexisting structures — the work organization — conceived independently of personnel dimensions. The individual departments of the firm communicate their employee needs, and the job of the personnel department is to meet those requirements in the desired quantity and quality at the proper time and at the proper place. The needed personnel is recruited, screened, and after being hired is managed and attended too. Personnel no longer needed is dismissed, retired, compensated. This instrumental view of labor as an object long dominated the thinking of managers.

That one speaks today of colleagues and human resources should not obscure the fact that the dependency relations involved have not changed; only the appreciation for the value of personnel has increased and has led to its acknowledgment as a strategic factor in the soccess of the company. The success of a company today, so it is said, depends especially on proper selection, development, and compensation as well as on proper deployment and training of its human resources.

Reviewing recent literature on the personnel function, personnel management, and labor relations, one finds a drastic change in perspective. Until the early 1980s personnel management was treated as one operational task among others like procurement, production, and marketing. Meanwhile, there has been a reorientation to an integrative, proactive, and strategic way of looking at personnel in the firm. Personnel management is not reduced merely to the competent use of managerial techniques like manpower planning, labor deployment, personnel development or dismissals by highly specialized employees in the personnel department. Rather, it is a genuine managerial responsibility. All actions or decisions pertaining to personnel are planned and integrated as *human resources activities* and harmonized with corporate strategy. At least that is the claim.

Classically, top management and subordinate line managers have delegated personnel matters to the personnel department, which was constantly assigned new responsibilities (like training, career planning, and personnel and organizational development) as new problems came up. In this manner, personnel departments have grown in a relatively uncoordinated, piecemeal fashion, lacking an integrative, proactive, and, above all, strategic orientation.

The subordination of personnel management to corporate policy and the adaptive role of personnel administration (filling positions instead of shaping them, and coping with the negative impacts of given structures) has repeatedly been criticized. The term personnel management relates to the call to place personnel policy on par with coporate policy and to give personnel policy higher priority than job design and work structuring. In terms of setting goals for personnel development and planning operative personnel responsibilities, personnel management is thereby no longer a matter for the personnel department, at least not exclusively.

There is, hence, an observable trend away from centralizing personnel matters and toward reintegrating personnel functions that used to be separated (such as compensation, performance appraisal, and evaluation procedures) returning them to line responsibilities. In the early 1970s centralization in the Federal Republic of Germany was promoted primarily by new laws on labor relations and corporate governance. As a result of the Codetermination Act of 1976, for example, the executive boards of large firms in West Germany have a labor director, who has responsibility for staff and welfare matters.

These developments represent at least formal recognition that personnel policy is just as much a part of corporate policy as other dimensions are. Changes in the names of positions suggest that the functional shift from employee recruitment to human resources management (HRM) is taking place in other western countries as well. The *Employment Manager* has become the *Personnel Manager*, who has, in turn, given way to the *Vice President for Human Resources*.

In the literature many reasons are cited for the change in viewpoints on the value of personnel (Staehle 1988):

- Increased competition (especially the Japanese challenge)
- New technologies and production concepts (with new sets of professional qualifications)
- Problems with productivity and quality

— Demographic changes (age structure, female employment)
— Value change, new life styles, altered expectations of the world of work)

In this context, personnel development deserves special attention as a key focus of HRM. The accelerating advance of technological developments is leading to an expansion, increase, or shift of job requirements. Because of the differences in the extent to which new technologies are used, however, such changes vary greatly from one plant to the next. Company-sponsored training and development is becoming an absolute necessity since appropriate qualifications cannot be acquired ad hoc from the external labor market.

Management's attitude toward personnel is changing discernibly, not least because of the chronic scarcity of highly skilled workers and the central importance that a highly motivated regular work force has for the success of a firm. Except for a randomly deployable marginal work force, at which *company-sponsored* training and development is usually not aimed, employees today are regarded as a pool of resources to be selectively built up, carefully maintained, and further developed to meet the requirements of the jobs performed.

HRM is necessary for other reasons as well, such as the importance of productivity through people as the fundamental source of efficiency (see Peters and Waterman 1982), or the soft S's (staff, style, skills), as McKinsey has called them. As plausible as all these arguments for HRM may be, however, they are ahistorical in nature and offer no insights into the background of the issues. Another plausible interpretation is that the ramifications of the 1973 oil crisis dramatically showed management in western industrialized nations what it means to be dependent on foreign resources. The oil crisis undoubtedly brought management to come to better grips with the significance of material, financial, and, increasingly, human resources. The roots of HRM go back much further, however.

2. Historical Roots of HRM

The period from the mid-1950s to the early 1960s saw the first works by normative management researchers, who propagated a humanistic image of the employee (Argyris 1957, Maslow 1954, McGregor 1960). In 1965 Miles introduced the distinction between human relations and human resources, and in *Theories of Management* (1975) he described three management models: traditional, human relations, and human resources. In the traditional model, the manager closely and constantly monitors the subordinate, who is regarded as work-shy and demotivated. In the human relations model, the manager is supposed to give the employee, who seeks acceptance and recognition, a feeling of utility and importance. In the human resources model, the manager draws on all the talents and qualities of the employee and promotes the skills of self-determination and self-management.

On the basis of his own empirical studies, Likert (1967) surmised that changes in management style from autocratic exploitation to participation would lead to a better utilization of human resources. Attempting to quantify these changes, Likert collaborated with colleagues from the field of accounting and developed the first human resource accounting system (1967). A voluminous body of literature on this subject has since accumulated. All it still lacks is convincing solutions for the serious problems encountered in evaluation. The literature distinguishes between input-oriented models (*the cost approach*, which has to do with the costs of human resources) and output-oriented models (the value approach, which focuses on performance or the value of human resources). Both methods disregard the fact that the value of an employee cannot easily be expressed in dollars and cents. Moreover, personnel is not the property of the enterprise, as are the assets in the balance sheet, and investments therefore entail greater risks. Despite these shortcomings, the debate about human resource accounting has had a positive impact in that management thinks at least as much about the value of a qualified work force as about other resources. Likert (1967) reported that the managers he interviewed estimated the costs of replacing the entire work force of a company to be three times greater than its total annual wages and salaries.

On the basis of American human resource accounting, new approaches to ascertaining and evaluating human assets have been discussed in Europe as well. In the Federal Republic of Germany in particular, awareness of the value of personnel was constantly heightened in the 1970s by high wage costs and fringe benefits, increased costs of employee turnover, occupational health and safety, industrial injuries, and higher job requirements. This trend was also furthered by the government's Action Program for Research on Improving the Quality of Work Life, the amended Works Constitution Act of 1972, and the Co-determination Act of 1976. In 1973, large firms began to respond to the increased public discussion of corporate social responsibility by considering, and in some cases practicing, an expanded concept of corporate social accounting.

From a political and economic perspective, the foundations for a theory of human capital were laid by Becker (1964) and Schultz (1978) in response to the shock caused by sputnik and the end of the 1950s. In this theory, each employee is an asset that can be evaluated like other assets. Accordingly, expenditures on basic and further training represent investments in human capital.

Classically, *labor is recorded as a cost factor* in the profit and loss account. One goal is to minimize it through personnel-related managerial action. In the theory of human capital, *labor is recorded as an asset* in the balance sheets. The objective is to preserve or enhance its value.

If human resources are seen as an economy's most important source of wealth, then each economic and social policy has to be designed to develop, conserve, and optimize the use of human resources. For Parnes (1984: 16 ff.) governmental human-resource management comprises the following policy areas:

— *HR development* (e. g., academic and vocational training)
— *HR allocation* (e. g., the placement of job-seekers with employers)
— *CR conservation* (e. g., unemployment benefits, job-creation measures)
— *HR utilization* (e. g., productive deployment, minimization of absenteeism, illness, and accidents)

The theory of human capital makes it possible to explain, among other things, why unemployment among highly qualified employees is significantly lower than among their less skilled colleagues. To the employer, highly skilled personnel represent a greater investment in human resources, an investment one does not wish to lose too quickly. It is also possible to explain why highly skilled employees can expect a significantly steeper increase in income in the course of intensive vocational training than less skilled ones. The greater capital investments in vocational training are amortized more quickly.

Schuster (1986) still considers the evaluation problems encountered in human resource accounting to be unsolved and suggests that data from *surveys on the organizational climate* rather than financial data be used to evaluate an organization's human assets. Elaborating on Likert's climate survey, Schuster developed a Human Resources Index (HRI), for which there are norms established for a cross-section of other organizations so as to permit comparison to the sector average. The HRI registers management's utilization of the organization's human resources as perceived by the personnel on a scale ranging from demoralized, underutilized, marginal, and effective to fully committed and utilized.

Schuster (1986) deplores that innovations in HRM in the United States have been nowhere near able to keep pace with those in the technological area. In his opinion, the approaches of HRM have changed little since the 1930s. He attributes the lack of interest shown by most companies in part to the dearth of convincing empirical evidence for the economic advantage gained through such practices. In his view, even the highly regarded study by Peters and Waterman (1982) provides only an anecdotal, unscientific plea to pay greater attention to employees. The Schuster Report, by contrast, covers the one thousand largest U.S. industrial firms as well as the country's largest nonindustrial firms, constituting a vast empirical study on the distribution of six HRM practices (assessment centers, flexible reward systems, productivity bonus plans, goal-oriented performance appraisal, alternative work schedules, and organizational development) that Peters and Waterman consider typical for "attention to employee needs." The central *hypothesis*, which he found to be confirmed in his study, was that the more such HRM practises are used by the companies in the survey, the more the management philosophy is oriented to the employee and the more successful the company is (measured by the rate of return on equity and rate of total return to investors).

To summarize, at least two roots of the current HRM debate can be identified:

(1) a *behavioral* one (employees are seen as a reservoir of many diverse potential skills, and it is the manager's responsibility to find out how best to bring out, promote, and develop these abilities) and
(2) an *economic* one (the personnel is no longer regarded only as a cost factor but primarily as an investment to be protected and increased both microeconomically and macro-economically).

In addition, I see three specifically new aspects in the current HR debate:

(3) the systematic synthesis (integration) of recruitment and employee development measures that had been handled separately until now,
(4) their inclusion in decisions affecting strategies and structures, and
(5) the fact that HR are now viewed from a general management perspective rather than from the perspective of a functional area (like personnel administration) and that management now shares responsibility for HR.

3. Current HRM Concepts

3.1 The Michigan Concept

In the early 1980s a research group working with Tichy at the University of Michigan developed the concept of strategic HRM, meaning the interlinkage of mission and strategies, organization structure, and HRM. However, it puts temporal and substantive priority on mission and strategy, with structure and HR being adapted to strategy. The intention is to seek the *best fit* between all three policy fields, including the environmental areas (economic, political, and cultural forces). In the Michigan approach, HRM consists of four components:

- *Selection*
- *Appraisal*
- *Rewards*
- *Development*

The recruitment plan, performance rating systems, incentive systems, and the personnel development programs are derived from the corporate strategy. In a dichotomy between strategy formulation and implementation, Tichy et al. (1982) clearly regard HRM as a contribution to the implementation of strategy rather than to its design. I have criticized this view elsewhere as the adaptive function of personnel administration.

The four components of HRM become relevant at all three decision-making levels (strategic, managerial, and operational), with strategic aspects of HRM being given priority in the Michigan approach:

- Strategic selection (e. g., strategic planning of personnel needs and control of personnel movements)
- Strategic appraisal (e. g., orientation of rating criteria to strategic priorities)
- Strategic rewards (e. g., motivation and remuneration of employees for meeting long-term strategic objectives)
- Strategic development (e. g., conception of future-oriented training programs and strategically appropriate career planning)

On the whole, the Michigan approach is deeply rooted in the classical line of thinking — implementation and adaptation — and underestimates or overlooks the influence that past personnel policy measures have on the future formulation of strategy.

3.2 The Harvard Concept

Whereas the Michigan approach deals primarily with strategic implementation, the Harvard approach carries on the tradition of the Harvard Business School by emphasizing the general management perspective of HRM (Beer et al., 1985). In 1981 a new required course on HRM was added to the MBA program. It is based on four key HRM *policy areas*:

- *Employee influence* (participation philosophy)
- *Human resources flow* (personnel recruitment, deployment, and dismissal)
- *Reward system* (incentive, compensation, and participation systems)
- *Work systems* (the organization of work)

These policy areas are affected by the interests of the *stakeholders* (share-holders, management, employee groups, unions, and community govern-ment) and *situational factors* (such as work force characteristics, business strategy, management philosophy, labor market, unions, task technology, laws, and societal values). HRM decisions have both *immediate organiza-tional outcomes* (commitment, competence, congruence, cost effectiveness) and *certain long-term consequences* (individual well-being, organizational effectiveness, and societal well-being). Feedback loops indicate the circular-ity of HRM policy choices. Through HRM, for example, persistent neglect of employee interests can lead to corrective legal injunctions, or a deterio-ration in a firm's financial health can cause the owners to demand a change in the HR policy (wages, salaries, and training). A key responsibility of HRM is the integrative harmonization of the four policy areas both among themselves and with corporate strategy. On this point, the Harvard authors see three possible approaches: bureaucracy, market, or clan.

4. The Link between HRM and Corporate Strategy

4.1 The Concept of Corporate Strategy

The concept of "strategy" was introduced by professors of the business policy course at the Harvard Business School (HBS) in the 1950s (Christen-sen et al. 1987, Uyterhoeven et al. 1977) and has been an important part of management training ever since. The concept of "business policy" was made the basis of a course in senior management training at the HBS in 1911. It defines corporate strategy as the setting of a company's long-term goals, the major policies and plans, and the adoption of courses of action for achieving these goals. Within corporate strategy, business strategies are pursued. They are less comprehensive and establish the individual product-market combinations for each sphere of activity (Andrews 1987: 13). Stem-ming originally from the military world, the concept of strategy — choosing resources to achieve preselected objectives — is thereby expanded consid-erably. Strategy in this broad sense also encompasses goal-planning and policy formulation. The *formulation* of corporate strategy (relating external opportunities to internal resources and values) is followed by its *implemen-tation* (designing structures and processes for pursuing the strategy).

The strategy concept described above has been varied and modified many times over the years, but its basic structure has remained the same. The concept has a number of shortcomings, however. By breaking strategy down into phases ranging from the formulation of objectives through the implementation of strategy, prescriptive strategy concepts adhere to the decision-making model of rational choice. Empirical studies, however, tend to indicate that behavior is incremental and only partially rational. Quinn (1980), for example, showed that in reality clear objectives rarely, if ever, exist and that strategic decisions tend to come about incrementally by chance, outside formal planning systems and departments. Are managers wrong if they act accordingly, or are they wrong if they follow the textbook recommendations based on a prescriptive, synoptic approach? There are good arguments for both positions. One thing seems certain today, though. In the modern interpretation of the company as a self-organizing, viable system, the planner can only create favorable conditions for strategic decisions by managers but can never "make" strategy.

Moreover, the Harvard concept is clearly *external*, market oriented. This characteristic makes it difficult, if not impossible, to identify *internal resources* as strategic potential for success (e. g., human resource management). In that sense, Hofer and Schendel (1978: 25) express a more open view when they define strategy as the "fundamental pattern of present and planned resource deployments and environmental interactions that indicates how the organization will achieve its objectives." The primarily external attention to the environment is complicated even more by the fact that one can no longer speak of stable environments. Market satiation and political and social changes make corporate planning difficult. Unpredictable events and sudden threats as well as opportunities (such as the oil crisis, microprocessors, and ecological problems) are constant sources of surprise for companies.

One might ask whether anything can be sensibly (strategically) planned at all under such conditions or whether one would do better to turn instead entirely to *organizational* measures (flexible, organic teams) or *personnel* measures (training, recruitment of flexible, creative employees) in an attempt to ensure a permanent willingness to learn and change in the enterprise. In discerning a shift of focus from strategic planning to strategic management, Ansoff, Declerck, and Hayes (1976) were the first to point out this problem clearly. The new concept of strategic management rests on the basic idea of planned evolution, according to which changes take place in a sequence of tractable, small steps. Strategic management is not a new variant of corporate planning but rather a concept that integrates the company's external strategic planning and internal competence as interdependent spheres of equal status.

This change of paradigms also signals a departure from the one-sided view presented by Chandler (1962) — structure follows strategy — and imbues the opposite relationship with meaning as well — strategy follows structure. After a period of excessive attention to the external environment, theoretical analysis has evolved to focus again on the internal competence of the company and the dialectic interplay of external orientation and internal competence. Ansoff (1984) has developed a *corporate-capability* concept intended to help analyze and improve the efficiency of the internal structure and resources in order to support externally oriented strategic actions.

Hence, strategic management is distinguished from strategic planning by at least three additional aspects, the inclusion of which links strategic planning to organizational and personnel development:

- The simultaneous attention paid to all economic and social linkages with the environment (besides product/market linkages)
- The equal attention paid to both capability planning and strategy planning
- The management of change and of resistance to it.

4.2 Strategic HRM

By virtue of the link between HRM and corporate strategy, two problem areas that have always been handled separately in both theory and practice now come together: market-oriented, strategic corporate planning and resource-oriented personnel planning. The heavy emphasis on the environment in strategic planning and the focus on product/market combinations as the sole potential for success (strategic marketing) long prevented internal resources like human potential from being identified as strategic potential for success. Not until strategic planning was abandoned in favor of strategic management was it possible to gain the perspective that now guides strategic personnel management.

Staffelbach (1986: 100) distinguishes between three stages of development:

Stage 1: Conventional corporate strategy oriented to the product/market concept; personnel management is derived from it

Stage 2: Corporate strategy that takes personnel into consideration; product/market strategies are adapted to the human resources in the company

Stage 3: Personnel management as an integral part of corporate strategy; personnel management contributes to the shaping of product/market strategies.

In the first stage of development, which is still typical of practice in Germany today, personnel strategy results from corporate strategy. Like Chandler's thesis, according to which structure follows strategy, the notion that personnel should be adapted to the strategy is held by most personnel planners. The strategically appropriate deployment of human resources is thereby a means for meeting corporate objectives. Personnel strategy is shaped on the basis of strategies pursued in the functional activities or, if it exists, at the level of strategic business units, for personnel demands can vary considerably from one functional activity to another. Personnel strategies are typical strategies of functional areas and can be broken down, for example, into recruitment, personnel development, and evaluation strategies.

With the personnel planning concept of personnel being adapted to strategy, it is assumed that the human potential needed for the successful implementation of strategy can be procured, at least in the short term. In practice, this assumption has proven to be unrealistic, for it is precisely the resource of *personnel* that requires long-term attention. It is also one of the causes for the failure of ambitious strategies. In that sense it is obvious that one should examine the opposite approach — that of developing strategy on the basis of existing human resources.

Accordingly, an interactive development of strategy and personnel is sought in the second and third stages. Initial strategic considerations are confronted directly with existing personnel resources or examined in terms of their implications for the employees. This is true particularly for strategic investment analyses intended to synchronize investment planning and personnel planning. Every investment is analyzed as early as possible for its impacts on work systems, jobs, and the skills they require so that appropriate personnel planning measures (qualitative, quantitative, and structural) can be taken.

Ultimately, the recommendation of the third stage is: Avoid developing plans for which the skills and resources are yet to be found. Rather, develop the skills and provide the resources so that they can then serve as the orientation for the plans to exploit the chances and opportunities that the market offers!

References

Andrews, K. R. (1987): *The Concept of Corporate Strategy*, Homewood, Ill. 3rd. ed.
Ansoff, H. I. (1984): *Implanting Strategic Management*, Englewood Cliffs, N.J.
Ansoff, H. I., R. P. Declerck and R. L. Hayes (eds.) (1976): *From Strategic Planning to Strategic Management*, London.
Argyris, C. (1957): *Personality and Organization*, New York.
Becker, G. S. (1964): *Human Capital*, New York.
Beer, M., B. Spector, P. R. Lawrence, D. Q. Mills and R. E. Walton (1985): *Human Resource Management*, New York — London.
Chandler, A. D. (1962): *Strategy and Structure*, Cambridge, Mass.

Christensen, C. A., K. R. Andrews, J. L. Bower, R. G. Hamermesh and M. E. Porter
(1987): *Business Policy: Text and Cases*, Homewood, Ill. (6th ed., 1st. ed. in 1965).
Hofer, C. W. and D. Schendel (1978): *Strategy Formulation: Analytical Concepts*, St.
Paul.
Likert, R. (1967): *The Human Organization*, New York.
Maslow, A. H. (1954): *Motivation and Personality*, New York.
McGregor, D. (1960): *The Human Side of Enterprise*, New York.
Miles, R. E. (1965): Human Relations or Human Resources? in: *Harvard Business
Review*, No. 4: 148 – 163.
Miles, R. E. (1975): *Theories of Management*, New York.
Parnes, H. S. (1984): *People Power: Elements of Human Resource Policy*, Beverly
Hills – London – New Dehli.
Peters, T. J. and R. H. Waterman (1982): *In Search of Excellence*, New York.
Quinn, J. B. (1980): *Strategies for Change. Logical Incrementalism*, Homewood, Ill.
Schultz, T. W. (1978): *Economic Analysis of Investment in Education*, Washington,
D.C.
Schuster, F. E. (1986): *The Schuster Report: The Proven Connection between People
and Profit*, New York.
Staehle, W. H. (1988): Human Resource Management, *Zeitschrift für Betriebswirt-
schaft*, No. 5/6: 26 – 37.
Staffelbach, B. (1986): *Strategisches Personalmanagement*, Bern – Stuttgart.
Tichy, N. M., C. J. Fombrun and M. A. Devanna (1982): Strategic Human Resource
Management, *Sloan Management Review*, No. 2: 47 – 61.
Uyterhoeven, H. E. R., R. W. Ackerman and J. W. Rosenblum (1977): *Strategy and
Organization: Text and Cases in General Management*, Homewood, Ill. (2nd. ed.).

Part I
Human Resource Management in the Western World

Human Resource Management in the U.S.- Celebration of its Centenary

Beverly Springer and Stephen Springer

1. Historical Background

The 1990's marks the centenary of human resource management (HRM) in the United States. It is the purpose of this article to discuss some of the hallmarks of American HRM in the 1990's both in terms of the environment which sets the parameters for the practice of HRM and in terms of the tools which are available for the practitioners. Before discussing HRM today, however, it is useful to recall some of the important milestones in its one hundred year history and to note how closely linked that history is to the culture and values of the American society.

The history of HRM in the United States may be said to start when the NCR Corporation established a separate personnel office in the 1890's. This event occurred, in part, because the corporation had reached such a size that specialization was the rational thing to do. American values and American life in that period also played a role. The values of individualism and free enterprise capitalism were strong. The workforce was mobile and contained many immigrants. All of these factors led to an impersonal, task oriented relationship between employers and employed. It was an instrumental relationship little colored by the values of paternalism and obligation that are more common in societies with a feudal heritage. Apprentice systems and labor unions had not spread into the new style corporations so that employers had few constraints on their hiring and firing decisions. The hiring of new employees could be done objectively on the basis of criteria relevant for the job to be accomplished. Employees were a factor of production whose costs were to be handled as rationally as the costs of the other factors of productions. The task of those pioneer personnel managers at NCR was to establish a method by which they could best discern, among a large and diverse applicant pool, the individuals who would make efficient and cost effective employees.

Scientific management, which Frederick Winslow Taylor introduced in 1912, was clearly attuned to the needs and values of the American industrial revolution. Taylorism met the demand of employers to utilize efficiently a larger labor pool containing many immigrants. Employees could be easily trained and as easily replaced for the routine, repetitive tasks prescribed by Taylor. The theory was immensely successful during the period when industry was straining to meet the production demands of World War I. By the 1920's Taylorism began to lose its preeminence as a theory but the remnants of the practise of it still exist in some American organizations. Job analysis, which is very much a part of modern HRM, is also one of its legacies. Perhaps, the most important legacy of Taylorism is that it made science the hallmark of HRM in that early stage of its development. In the decades that have followed with all the schools of HRM that have come and gone, the one consistent factor has been that hallmark. The belief that the selection and motivation of a workforce is an endeavor that is amenable to objective, rational and testable criteria permeates the field of HRM today and directly traces back to its roots in the needs and values of the American society of a century ago.

The second key hallmark of American HRM is the linking of the theory and practice of personnel management with the field of psychology. The relevance of psychological tools was demonstrated by the famous Hawthorne experiment of Elton Mayo of the Harvard School of Business Administration which took place between 1927 and 1932. In the 1950's the term "human resource management" began to be used to designate the expansion of traditional personnel management to include modern psychology.

The development of HRM is influenced predominately by two schools of psychology. Behaviorism is an uniquely American branch of psychology which traces to the work of John B. Watson, who was a contemporary of Taylor. He believed that the study of man could be objective and scientific. In the 1930's behaviorists were leaders in the Institute of Human Relations which was formed at Yale University (B. F. Skinner is the most famous, current proponent of American radical behaviorism.). The work of behaviorists has led to the development of tests and evaluation methods that are so much a part of modern HRM. Humanistic psychology is the other school that has influenced American HRM. It began in the 1930's, when a young behaviorist — Abraham Maslow — broke with behaviorism and started a "third force" in American psychology. (Rolle May and Carl Rogers were also associated with this new school.)

The work of Maslow was extremely influential in shaping the human relations theory of HRM which gained popularity in the 1950's. Every practitioner of HRM is aware of Maslow's "hierarchy of human needs" and its relevance for HRM. According to the ideas of humanistic psychology, employees can no longer be regarded as replaceable parts of the productions process. Employees have needs for security, self expression, communications and recognition that must be met by employers in order to achieve a stable and productive workforce. The impact of these ideas was demonstrated by a survey carried out in 302 companies in 1969. Managers in 80% of the companies acknowledged the importance of psychology to productivity and profitability (Goble 1971: 190).

Douglas McGregor was the name that was most familiar to the managers in the survey mentioned above. His book *The Human Side of Enterprise* (1960) is a classic of the human relations school of American HRM. McGregor stated that there are two basic styles of management. One is authoritarian and the other takes into consideration the human needs of employees. He designated these two styles as X and Y respectively. His arguments for the need for the Y style of managers gained wide acceptance.

Work and the Nature of Man (1966) was another seminal book in the development of American HRM. The author Frederick Herzberg argued that "hygiene factors" such as good relations between managers and employees and good benefit factors may make workers happy but the only way to motivate them to work more productively is by giving them responsibility and challenging work. Under the impetus from Herzberg, the analysis of work and the design of jobs to accord with these psychological principles became an important part of HRM.

By the 1970's the rather simplistic ideas of early proponents of the human relations school lost favor. The latest development is the human resource approach which builds on the work of Herzberg and combines elements of earlier theories. Employees are perceived as a resource with needs that are compatible with the needs of the organization. HRM is now defined as "that area of organization life that focuses on the effective management and utilization of people (Walters 1985: 4). The practice of HRM uses the latest scientific techniques in the tradition of scientific management and behaviorist psychology in the search for the enabling organization – an organization manned by motivated and flexible employees – in the tradition of the human relations school and humanistic psychology[1].

---

[1] A number of sources deal with the history of HRM but two that are especially useful because they are edited works which contain a number of writings by key actors in that history are *Human Resource Management and Development Handbook* and *People: Managing Your Most Important Asset*.

2. HRM in the 1990's

2.1 The Environment

The factors that set the parameters for HRM are numerous and subject to a wide variety of interpretations. The five that are selected for mention in this article are selected either because they are perceived to be relatively distinctive to our time or because they are important characteristics of the United States. 1. *Change*, according to one authority on HRM, is the buzz word for our time (Ritter 1989: 30). The United States has always been regarded as a country where change is endemic, but the changes currently taking place appear to be more rapid and disruptive than those in recent decades. Three different forms of change have direct bearing on the function of HRM. One is in the ownership or control of individual firms or corporations. Merger and acquisition activity has never been more intense in the United States than it is in the present time. Both firms that have been taken over and those in fear of a take over have become leaner — shedding both managers and lower level employees. Practitioners of HRM have had to develop skills to "down size" their organizations.

Another change is directly related to the first. In the volatile world inside the corporation today, traditional relationships between managers and employees are changing. Rosabeth Moss Kanter, the new editor of the *Harvard Business Review* and a well known authority on management, wrote recently, "Managerial work is undergoing such enormous and rapid change that many managers are reinventing their profession as they go" (Kanter 1989: 85). Later, in the same article, she wrote, "In the new organization, it's hard to tell the managers from the non managers" (ibid: 88). Peter Drucker, the doyen of American authorities on management, has commented that the organization of the future will be one in which the role of manager is less crucial and less visible than it is today — somewhat analogous to the manager of a hospital. He predicts that twenty years from now firms will operate with less than half the level of management that they have today and that specialists will be the heart of the new information based firm of the future (Drucker 1988: 45). In this volatile organization, practitioners will find that traditional demarcations between job categories will be blurred and traditional channels of responsibility and control will no longer function. Many authorities believe that new forms of management will be essential in this future scenario.[2] Much of the work of practitioners of HRM in the next decade will be directed toward developing the psychological techniques

---

[2] See for instance the article by Kanter cited above.

necessary in order to transform managers and their employees for this new relationship.

The third major change has to do with employment patterns. As we have seen, HRM in the United States developed in the manufacturing industries which were part of the American industrial revolution. Now, however, two-thirds of the work force in North America is in the service sector and 90% is expected to be in white collar or service sector jobs by the year 2000 (World Employment Review: 53). Job categories in many parts of the service sector are highly volatile due, in part, to rapid technological change. For example, an important growth area for employment for women in the post war period was in bank teller jobs. Now, however, the growth in this job category is slowing and the skill requirements are changing due to the introduction of new technology (U.S. Department of Labor 1988: 9 and 229. Also see Strober and Arnold 1987: 121). We have seen the transformation to the automated office and are now considering the home office of the future. In addition, part time work and temporary work are becoming more common. In 1987, 17.45% of employment was part time (OECD 1987: 199). These changing employment patterns make obsolete many assumptions and practices of HRM.

2.2 The Productivity Crisis

The productivity crisis is assuming paramount importance in the United States. As the threat of the cold war diminishes as a public concern, worries about foreign challenges to American economic security are growing. Many state legislatures have considered laws to limit foreign investment and protectionist sentiments in the U.S. Congress are strong. The fear is that American firms have lost their competitive edge. The facts do give cause for concern. Two leading authorities on the topic wrote, "The single most important source of structural change in the United States since 1973 has been the gradual narrowing of productivity levels among industrialized and industrializing economies" (Block and Lennan 1978: 340). The United States had absolute productivity rates far in excess of its leading trading partners in the immediate postwar period, but that lead has lessened in subsequent years due to higher annual growth rates among many of its trading partners. From 1960 to 1987 the average annual growth rate for manufacturing productivity in the United States was 2.8% according to the U.S. Bureau of Labor Statistics compared to 4.5% for West Germany and 7.7% for Japan. Other important trading partners, such as Canada, Great Britain, France and Italy, also had higher annual rates. The result is that the Organization for Economic Cooperation and Development reported in 1988 that unit labor costs in the United States were higher than in many of its

major trading partners. United labor costs declined in Japan in 1988 and
increased only marginally in Germany but they increased by over 4% in
the United States (OECD 1988: 41).

American firms which face increasing global competition are under heavy
pressure to respond to the productivity crisis. Many have responded by
shedding employees or by shedding units that are not cost effective. Others
have been forced into struggles with their workforces in order to win back
concessions given in more profitable times. The most enlightened trend has
been toward "working smarter" by engaging employees and managers in
joint efforts to increase productivity. No matter which course a firm adopts,
HRM is directly involved. No other environmental factor has been more
instrumental in taking the practice of HRM out of personnel offices and
into the offices of managers throughout the organization.

2.3 New Forces in the Labor Pool

New forces in the labor pool is a third environmental challenging HRM.
Demographic changes are having a marked affect on the American workforce. While the workforce is not graying to the extent that it is in Germany,
it is maturing due to falling birth rates. By the end of this century the
average age of the workforce will be 36 which is 6 years older than the
average age at any time in the history of the United States (Hudson Institute
1987: 79). The aging of the workforce was countered by a trend toward
early retirement. That now may be changing, however. In 1948 the labor
force participation rate for men 65 and over was 50%. Today it is 16%
(Parnes and Sandell 1989: 8). Many firms encouraged early retirement with
generous benefit packages. Rethinking is now going on about the desirability
of early retirement. This rethinking is only partly explained by a declining
supply of new entrants. Firms face heavy costs in providing benefits for
retired employees in addition to high training costs for poorly educated new
entrants. Gerontologists question whether early retirement is good for most
individuals. Futhermore, recent research puts in doubt many popular stereotypes concerning problems with older employees (Sonenfeld 1988: 109–
120). In the future many firms will look at ways to retain older workers
and the national trend to early retirement probably will level off or may
even go slightly in reverse. This may raise the average age of the workforce
even above the prediction noted above.

Another major difference in the labor pool will be occur among new
entrants. The proportion of new entrants who are young, white males —
the traditional new hiree for many industries — will decline sharply. Women,
minorities and immigrants will supply five-sixths and the net additions to
the workforce between now and the year 2000 (Hudson Institute 1987: XX.).

The skills and needs which these new entrants bring to the workplace will differ greatly from those of the past.

There is now in the United States a growing incongruity between the supply of labor and the need for labor by employers. The workforce of the next decade will need to be more highly educated than the present workforce. Persons who rank in the lowest level of skills as measured by the U.S. Department of Labor will find that they will be able to fill only 4% of the jobs of the next decade compared to 9% at the current time. In contrast, 41% of the new jobs will require skills in the highest category compared to 24% today (ibid: 98–99). Thirty percent of the jobs of the future will require 4 years or more of university education. Employers are increasingly worried that they will not be able to obtain new employees that match these projected education needs. Studies by the Department of Education support their concern. For example, only 7% of hispanics and only 3% of blacks could understand a bus schedule (ibid: 102). Twenty percent of adults are considered to be functionally illiterate (Training America: 7). "In the 1980's illiteracy moved to the forefront of the American business consciousness", according to Anne Ritter (Ritter 1989: 34). Since a large proportion of the projected new entrants of the workforce are from groups most noted for lower education attainments, it is easy to project that spending on education by American industry will continue to escalate.

The dependence on women in the workforce should increase in the next decade. At the present time 60% of women between the ages of 16 and 65 work. Moreover, women are remaining in the labor force even when they have children (U.S. Congress 1982: 4, 24). A recent study concluded that most women now in the workforce are full-time and career-oriented. This generalization applies across age, race and marital status distinctions (Shank 1988: 5, 8). Women are the only ones in the projected group of new entrants (other than white, males) who have education levels to match projected needs of employers. Women are also an increasing proportion of managers in the United States[3].

2.4 The Legal Environment

The legal environment for HRM in the United States is unique and closely tied to America history and culture. It has significant differences from the legal norms in Western Europe. The laws reflect the individualistic mores

---

[3] Persons interested in the subject of women in management should read the controversial article by Felice Schwartz titled "Management, Women and the New Facts of Life" in *Harvard Business Review* of January – February, 1989 on pages 65 to 79. The article gives us a new term – "the mommy track".)

and the strong free enterprise/capitalistic value system. For example, the United States has no laws establishing worker councils or forms of code-termination. Individualistic American employees have made almost no demand for such group or class oriented rights. American provisions for social security are much more recent and limited than are European social security provisions. Traditionally American employers have and had almost complete discretion on the right to hire and fire under the common law doctrine of employment-at-will. Recent trends are retraining this freedom, however. Most states have started to allow employees to sue employers for wrongful discharge. The growth of such suits has been phenomenal and so has been the size of award given to complainants by sympathetic juries. As a result some firms have established their own process to assure that employees have a fair hearing when they are terminated. However, pressure is growing for a law to assure uniform protection for individuals. A step in this direction was taken in July, 1988 when Congress passed a plant closing bill that requires employers in firms that have at least 100 employees to notify their employees 60 days before a planned closing or a mass layoff. The law exempts firms hit by unforeseen circumstances and it does not require any consultation with the workforce.

American employee law is most rigorous in assuring that employers deal with employees on a fair and objective basis. Personnel decisions must be made on the basis of economic and scientific criteria. This is most apparent in two areas. One is in regard to the instruments of modern HRM. Practitioners must always be careful that test and measures can stand up to a strict test of validity if they are questioned in a court of law. Fear of unfavorable judgments have caused practitioners to limit their use of some tools such as screening tests for job applicants when the validity of the tools may be difficult to prove.

The other area where the law is intrusive concerns discrimination in employment practices. Firms may not engage in unequal treatment or practices which have an unequal impact of employees in regard to sex, race, color, national origin or religion. Separate legislation also prohibits age discrimination. This is a sweeping prohibition applying to all areas of HRM including hiring, firing, promotion, training, and compensation. In addition, firms that have federal contracts also must have an affirmative action plan that compares the number of females and minorities in the workforce and the firm with their presence in the relevant labor market. The plan must also set goals and timetables for bringing the profile of the workforce closer to that found in the labor market and it must set out the actions to be taken. Affirmative action plans have now become a routine part of good HRM practice. No uniform model exists for affirmative action plans so practitioners design their own plans. In many cases the plans have provided statistical studies useful for wider human resource planning efforts. The law does not require absolute equality but rather that firms make a good faith effort. A firm that is found in violation of the law may face a sizeable financial penalty as well as court ordered quotas for women and/or minorities that must be applied in future hiring and promotion decision.

In summary, the main thrust of U.S. employee law is to seek fair play between individual employees and employers. The objective is to assure that the criteria that are used in all aspects of that relationship are economic or market criteria. The burden is on the employer to ascertain that each step in HRM is made on the basis of scientifically valid measures or procedures. Employers must always be aware that their practices may be challenged in the courts in a civil suit undertaken by an employee who believes that he/she has been dealt with in an unfair or discriminatory manner. In this sense the law is highly individualistic with few elements of paternalism or class based rights that are common in employee laws in many countries[4].

2.5 The Industrial Relations System

Industrial Relations is of declining importance in American HRM due to the failure of labor unions to gain members in the new service sector economy. Only 14% of the private sector jobs are held by union members and these are mostly found in traditional industries such as steel and auto manufacturing.

Industrial relations in the United States is characterized by an adversarial relationship between labor and management. Employers association do not play a role in the United States as actors in industrial relations as they do in Western Europe. Rather labor unions and employers meet in direct negotiations on contracts or labor issues. The demands made by labor unions are directly monetary or work related reflecting a tradition of business unionism. American labor unions long ago accepted the values of the free market economy with the accompanying rights of ownership. The law establishes the framework for industrial relations but the government is not an actor in negotiations except in very exceptional circumstances.

In recent years many of the negotiations have been characterized by the term "concession bargaining".[5] Employers, under increasing economic pressure, have demanded the end of concessions granted in more profitable period. Labor unions have attempted to bargain concessions for job pro-

---

[4] For a lucid and comprehensive account of the American employee laws see: Levitan et al. 1986.
[5] For an interesting discussion of the topic see: Kassalow: 1989. Professor Kassalow is a leading authority on comparative industrial relations.

tection. One of the major issues has been over health insurance cost containment. In some cases the issue has lead to long and bitter strikes such as the 1989 strike in the coal industry.

3. The Practice of HRM in the 1990's

HRM today is a much more scientific and broader field than it was in the first personnel office of a hundred years ago. The environmental factors noted above have moved HRM into a central role in modern organizations and put tremendous pressure on its practitioners. Modern psychology has provided tools to create a new relationship between managers and employees. Modern technology has provided the means to standardize and to facilitate the work of HRM. Pressure from the courts has added to the need for uniform procedures that can be scientifically validated. Computers hold great promise for this effort. Personal computers are widely used to compile records and to perform necessary statistical analyses. However, standard software for many HRM tasks is only in its infancy, so most practitioners have to develop their own programs[6]. The 1990's should bring progress in this area because the need and the market is already present in the United States.

Since the scope of modern HRM is so vast, recent and expected developments in key sectors will only summarized in the following.

RECRUITMENT practices are undergoing some changes in the United States. Many firms such as IBM make a practice of recruiting among their own employees for non entry level positions. This is due, in part, for reasons of employee morale and, in part, because the workforce is becoming less mobile (Renders 1989: 2). When recruitment does take place externally the government requires "fair and open" hiring practices (Gatewood and Ledvinka 1976: 15–17). For this reason many firms hesitate to use tests in their selection procedure for fear of court challenges. The structured interview with set questions and a rating scale is frequently used. Although the value of interviews as a selection tool has been questioned, recent research finds that they have validity (Harris 1989: 691). Graphology, which is used in Europe, is not highly regarded in the United States. Many firms conduct cost-benefit analyses in order to assure that their recruitment practices correctly screen applicants to find persons who are both qualified and likely to remain with the firm.

---

[6] Gary J. Meyer: 1984.

JOB ANALYSIS, involving job description, job specification and job evaluation, is a major function of HRM. It is being used increasingly to define new and old jobs. Once used just to regulate jobs, it is now used to provide information for the whole range of HRM activities including job enrichment and career development. Firms may develop their own method or use a standard one such as the Position Analysis Questionnaire or the one developed by the Department of Labor.

Some of the impetus for the use of job analysis comes from the government. Job analysis must be an integral part of any validation study that tries to demonstrate a relationship between a selection device and job performance. The Federal Uniform Guidelines on Employee Selection Procedures (1978) requires that job analyses be performed for all jobs on which validation studies are conducted (Cascio 1982: 49; American Psychological Association 1980).

TRAINING AND DEVELOPMENT is big business in the United States with annual expenditures in the billions of dollars. Four hundred companies have their own training centers (The Making of Managers 1987: 25). Training for non-managerial personnel — as a distinct and specialized activity — has long been a responsibility of firms in the United States. A good training program should utilize the techniques of learning theory such as feedback and "hands on" or active participation by the trainees. The trend today is to keep training courses in-house and closely related to workplace problems. Many training courses involve the use of software packages by the trainee under the direction of an instructor.

Human resource development (HRD) is one of the most exciting fields in HRM today. HRD is "... one of the several human resources specialties in and for work organizations. Its primary focus is developing the key competencies (knowledge, skills, attitudes — through learning — which enables individuals to perform current and future jobs." (Nadler 1985: 4). The term may encompass both the long range planning of the human resource needs of an entire organization and the development of managers who will have the psychological and technical skill necessary for future needs of the organization. Human resource planning in terms of forecasting the future personnel needs of an organization and preparing the necessary personnel is only in its early stages. It is much more ambitious than traditional manpower planning. It should be part of a firm's comprehensive strategic planning bringing together specialist in HRM with senior executives. Few firms make the commitment necessary to carry out such a comprehensive task. However, management succession planning (MSP) is a more limited but useful form of planning. In this case, three reports are prepared. The first is an evaluation of current managers — their skills and readiness for promotion. The second is the forecast of demand — anticipated vacances and/or additions in the managerial hierarchy. The third is the evaluation of the capabilities of possible candidates for openings and recommendations for steps to groom the candidates.

The term HRD is more commonly used in regard to the development of individual managers[7]. Many organizations have made the development of a new generation of managers a high priority. Also many authorities believe that American managers today experience dissatisfaction and frustration in their careers due to high level of change and the resulting insecurity in the corporate world (Roomkin 1989: 57). HRD serves to assist managers to cope with this environment and, therefore, to be more productive. In contrast to training for non-managerial personnel, development implies more broadly based learning — knowledge and attitudes. It frequently involves courses that are designed to make managers better communicators with their employees or better motivators for their employees. It may also involve courses that teach managers how to work together more effectively. Sensitivity training or transactional analysis training are two examples of courses that were widely used. They are not as popular as they were a few years ago but they have been replaced by courses — such as stress management, effective negotiating techniques or cross cultural communications — which are also based on psychology. The primary objective of all of these programs is to develop managers who can function effectively in the new organization where there is less hierarchy and where power and authority are exercised more indirectly.

Assessment centers are an important part of HRD. They first came into prominence in the 1950's (Moses and Byham 1977). Currently about 2,000 assessment centers are in operation. They are used in order to give participants experience in a work related simulation where their behavior can be evaluated by trained assessors. Care must be taken that all of the steps are scientifically valid. The results are used for many purposes ranging from identification by the firm of promising employees to aiding managers in their own individual program of self-development.

A recent variation in HRD is career development systems in which a firm assists its managers in planning their careers (Leibonitz et al. 1986). The firm only facilitates the planning. The responsibility rests with the individual manager. The firm may simply provide career counseling. It may provide managers with new self improvement software programs such as *Discover*, developed by the American College Testing, or *Careerpoint*, developed by Conceptual Systems, Inc. A number of firms offer a comprehensive range

---

[7] For a brief summary of programs actually in use in some firms see: *Innovations in Managing Human Resources* 1984: 13–15.

of services including assessment, performance appraisal and development opportunities. Myron Roomkin argues that there are two trends regarding the use of career development systems in the 1980's. One is for firms to use the process in order to develop an elite group of junior managers. The other is for firms to narrow their expectation of the process and to use it for more limited objectives (Roomkin 1989: 75).

4. Recent Issues in HRM

In addition to the topics discussed above, three issues play important roles in HRM today. 1. Participatory management, which was popular in the early postwar era, is once more on the agenda in the form of employee involvement programs. 2. Every practitioner of HRM is under pressure to design a cost effective benefit package. 3. The right to privacy is a major issue for many employees. In a recent program which the author conducted for labor unions members, privacy issues were the number one concern of the participants.

4.1 Employee Involvement Programs

It is almost a necessity for firms in the United States that want to appear to be modern and progressive to have some type of employee involvement program. Worries about productivity have raised serious questions concerning the appropriate relationship between managers and employees. The military style of management and the adversarial relationship between labor and management that characterized many American workplaces have been blamed for the American productivity problem. The book *in search for excellence* by Peters and Waterman (1982) popularized for the current generation of managers the need to cultivate a closer and more positive relationship with employees.

A large part of HRM today concerns designing and overseeing employee involvement (EI) or quality of work life (QWL) programs. EI/QWL is the "structured, systematic approach to the involvement of employees in group decisions affecting work and the work environment with goals that include reducing product cost, improving product quality, facilitating communication, raising morale and reducing conflict" (Gershenfeld 1987: 124). The challenge for HRM is to link managers and employees into a more productive relationship. This requires not only new institutions in the workplace but also new, cooperative attitudes among both employees and managers.

Probably the most well known form of EI/QWL is the quality circle. The Association of Quality and Participation has existed since 1977 to promote the use of quality circles and to educate people in HRM who are responsible for such programs. The Association has 5,500 members and more than 80 local chapters. A firm that utilizes the quality circle program establishes small work place groups that select and seek to solve issues related to their mutual work. Each group is assisted in its work by a facilitator who is trained in group dynamics. The growth and popularity of quality circles has been phenomenal. Perhaps a million employees in the United States have participated in some form of quality circle. Advocates of the program claim that it results in great improvements in productivity.

Interest in EI/QWL began to grow in the 1970's but gained its current high level of public interest only in the 1980's. Today it is estimated that more than half of the firms listed by the New York Stock Exchange and perhaps 25% of U.S. workers are involved in some form of EI/QWL program (Gershenfeld 1987: 130 f.). Although many of the programs do not last, the total number of programs continues to grow. Moreover, the next generation of managers is learning in business schools that successful management is participatory management.

Many of the early experiments with EI/QWL involved cooperative efforts between corporations and labor unions. The United Auto Workers union has negotiated a number of well known agreements with American car makers. The Communications Workers of America negotiated a program with American Telephone and Telegraph Company. The United Steelworkers of America is another union that pioneered EI/QWL programs in the 1970's. These unions continue to be active on the subject. However, many people in unions are suspicious of EI/QWL programs (see for example Rosow 1986). The tradition of adversarial relations runs deep in the United States.

Most of the EI/QWL programs operating in the United States today do not involve labor unions. The programs are initiated by management in order to improve productivity. Employees seldom demand such programs and are frequently suspicious of the motives of management in establishing EI/QWL programs. This suspicion is fueled by consultants who advocate EI/QWL programs as a means to keep unions out of the work place. However, good EI/QWL programs can fill a void that is left by the decline of unions and by the lack of legislation requiring works councils. The development of these programs is one of the main reasons that human resource managers are spending so much time outside their offices interacting with other managers.

4.2 The Art of Designing an Effective Benefit Package

Benefit packages are important in the United States. Employers voluntarily provide insurance against illness, old age, etc. in order to protect employees against risks that are not adequately covered by the public social security program. These benefits add significantly to total labor costs. These benefit packages are not uniform. They are designed by the individual firm in order to attract and retain good employees but at a cost that the firm can bear. Large firms, manufacturing firms, firms with a unionized workforce and firms with well paid employees are more likely to have good benefit packages than are other firms (Mitchell 1987: 213 – 219).

About 38% of compensation in the United States is in the form of non-wage benefits. About one-third of the non-wage benefits is required by the government largely for social security, unemployment compensation and worker's compensation. The remaining portion is divided among paid leave time, pensions, insurance. Recently a small percent of the benefit package is allocated for profit-sharing (1%) and special programs such as child care that a few employers offer. Employers are free to provide or not to provide these benefits. Paid leave time is the most frequently provided of these discretionary benefits (The United States does not have laws requiring vacations). Health insurance is the second most common. American employers are increasingly concerned by the escalating costs of health care. The United States spends more per capita on health care than other countries. The total has been increasing more rapidly than inflation. General Motors made national news when it informed the public in 1984 that it had spent $ 2 billion the previous year on health care for its employees (which was about $ 430 per car) (Wall Street Journal, Aug. 16, 1984). Today employers are increasingly asking employees to pay part of the cost of the insurance. In addition, human resource managers are designing new alternative packages for health care in order to contain costs. Since 1973 the law requires that if a firm offers health insurance, it must offer an option for a health maintenance organization. The cost of health care continues to be a major problem for employers as well as for the general public.

Private pensions are big business in the United States. The accumulated funds from pensions now provide the largest source of capital. They are also the portion of discretionary benefits most regulated by the government. The law does not require an employer to provide a pension but the law protects against abuse of voluntary programs. About half of the American workforce is covered by a pension plan. However, many employees lose their pension rights by changing jobs before they are vested (Steven 1988: 40 – 49) (Pensions are deemed to have a deterrent effect on mobility in the United States, but still American workers are much less likely to remain in the same firm than are European workers.). The design of pension plans is a function of HRM. No standard form exists. Human resource managers have an infinite range of alternatives from which to select so long as they meet the few protections required by law.

Benefit packages grew greatly in the postwar period. Firms appeared to compete with each other in designing attractive packages. In recent years, however, pressures have grown to contain costs and to tailor the package more specifically for the needs of the work force of the individual firm. The responsibility to design a cost effective benefit package is one of the most important challenges facing American practitioners of HRM today. One of the most innovate variations for benefit packages to appear in recent years is flexible or cafeteria benefits. In this form, the employee may choose among a menu of alternative benefits the ones that most suit his/her needs. The flexible benefit package is popular because it meets the needs of the day in which many families have more than one person employed and in which many women are working. The traditional benefit package was based on the assumption that the employee was a male head of household. Many of the benefits were extended to his immediate family who were assumed not to be employed. Many working women were covered by their husband's health insurance as well as their own. The cafeteria form saves costly duplication for firms while providing coverage that is more suitable for today's workforce. The practitioner of HRM has an important role in designing flexible benefit plans and in advising employees about the alternatives in the flexible plan.

4.3 The Right to Privacy

The right to privacy is the most serious social issue to trouble the American work place in the 1980s. The issue presents a challenge to human resource managers that is just as difficult as containing the costs of benefit packages and much more emotional. The human resource manager is caught between the fear and anger of employees and the public and the concern of employers aroused by the growing costs to the firm of negative behavior by employees. Alcoholism, drug abuse and employee theft constitute the most controversial forms of negative behavior. The costs of these actions to firms is enormous. Drug use was estimated to have cost firms $ 50 billion in absenteeism in 1987. Employee theft is estimated to cost about $ 10 billion a year (Business Week, March 28, 1988: 61). Moreover, every year firms are forced to fire employees for drug or alcohol abuse thus losing millions of dollars that they have invested in these employees. Human resource managers generally agree that more employees lose their jobs as a result of drug and alcohol abuse than as a result of incompetence.

Today many firms in the United States are using tests in order to discover potential or real offenders. These tests have raised a storm of controversy in the United States. Neither their validity nor their legality is universally accepted. An employer may test employees for drug abuse, infections diseases or truthfulness when the information being sought is relevant and necessary and its use is appropriate. However, the line between legal testing and invasion of privacy is unclear and the costs of crossing that line is growing. Jury awards against employers for invasion of privacy increased 2,000 percent between 1985 and 1989. The average award is $ 316,000 (Lips and Lueder 1988: 530).

Polygraph tests have been one of the most common forms of test used by employers despite the fact that their validity is highly questionable. Many firms routinely used polygraph tests for screening potential new employees. Firms also used them in cases of employee theft. However, new state and federal law strictly limit the use of polygraphs and firms, especially in the retail sector, will have to seek another means in order to assure the honesty of employees.

Drug testing is a major issue in the United States at the present time. In March, 1989, the Supreme Court gave government officials the right to order tests for workers in sensitive jobs. This ruling does not directly affect private employers. Issues regarding drug use by employees in private firms include mandatory drug testing, random drug testing, searches of employee lockers and the confidentiality of laboratory reports among others. The problem is further complicated by the fact that studies indicate that the error rate for laboratory reports can run as high as 40%. About 34% of 1,000 firms surveyed by the American Management Association have a drug testing policy despite the legal difficulties associated with such policies (Business Week, March 28, 1988: 65). The responsibility for human resource managers to guide their firms toward an effective but also a publicly defensible drug testing policy is, one of the most difficult challenges that they face in this period which is full of difficult challenges.

5. Conclusion

As HRM in the United States reaches its one hundred birthday, the challenges have never been greater than they are today. The rate of change in the world of work is increasing dramatically. We are moving from the traditional office to the automated office to the home office. We are moving from the blue collar employee to the pink collar employee to the androgenous employee whose collar we never see because we are only linked by a computer. We hire people to process bits of paper, retrain them to punch in data and then remold them to market bank services. We are only beginning to discern the jobs of the future while we already know that the workforce of the future will have serious limitations. At the same time, changes in the environment in which American firms operate have lessened their security and, at the same time, made it more difficult but also more critical to find the proper workforce. Since HRM is the link between the supply and the demand for a workforce, HRM must adapt to changes that are taking place in both supply and demand. These changes affect every function of HRM. Central to every aspect is the productivity crisis and the belief that the solution will arrive through a new relationship between labor and management. Recruitment is affected by the fact that the available labor force will be predominately female and/or minority and will lack the necessary skills. The dynamic quality of modern firms disrupts traditional patterns of employee development and training. Changes in the law and uncertainties in the law narrow the scope for action and increase the risks. The design of benefit packages becomes more complicated due to the changing composition of the workforce and to the growth of costs that are beyond the control of the firm. Costs also limit the utilization of the most modern tool of HRM — the system approach to total human resource development. Finally, the demand of modern employees for a right to privacy which directly confront the demand of modern employers for greater protection against risks arising from the negative behavior of employees provides a challenge for human resource managers which is highly emotional and with serious implications not only for the firm but also for the American society. The tools of HRM are increasingly sophisticated. The status of HRM is improving. But the success of HRM in overcoming these diverse challenges is yet to be determined.

References

American Psychological Association (ed.) (1980): *Principles for the Validation and Use of Personnel Selection Procedures*, 2nd edition, (American Psychological Association, Division of Industrial Organizational Psychology).

Block, Richard N. and Kenneth McLennan (1987): Structural Economic Change and Industrial Relations in the United States' Manufacturing and Transportation Sectors Since 1973, in: Juris Thompson and Daniels (eds.), *Industrial Relation in a Decade of Economic Change*, Madison, Wisconsin.

Business Week (1988): *Privacy*, March 28, 1988.

Cascio, Wayne F. (1982): *Applied Psychology in Personnel Management*, Reston, Virginia.

Drucker, Peter (1988): The coming of the New Organization, *Harvard Business Review*, January – February.

Eden, R. W. and G. R. Ferris (1989): *The Employment Interview*, Beverly Hills.

Gatewood, Robert and James Ledvinka (1976): Selection Interviewing and EEO: Mandate for Objectivity, *The Personnel Administrator*, May.

Gershenfeld, Walter J. (1987): Employee Participation in Firm Decisions, in: Kleiner, Block, Roomkin and Salsburg (eds.), *Human Resources and the Performance of the Firm*, Madison, Wisconsin.

Goble, Frank G. (1970): *The Third Force*, New York.

Harris, Michael M. (1989): Reconsidering the Employment Interview, *Personnel Psychology*, Winter.

Herzberg, F. (1966): *Work and the Nature of Man*, Cleveland, OH – New York.

Hudson Institute (1987): *Workforce 2000* (A report prepared for the U.S. Department of Labor), Indianapolis.

Innovations in Managing Human Resources (1984): New York.

International Labour Office (1988): *World Employment Review*. Geneva.

Kanter, Rosabeth Moss (1989): The New Managerial Work, *Harvard Business Review*, November – December.

Kassalow, Everett M. (1989): *Labour Market Flexibility and New Employment Patterns: The U.S. Case in a Comparative Framework*, (a paper presented to the Eighth World Congress of the International Industrial Relations Association, Sept. 1989, Brussels).

Lips, J. Alan and Michael C. Lueder (1988): An Employer's Right to Test for Substance Abuse, Infectious Diseases, and Truthfulness versus an Employee's Right to Privacy, *Proceedings of the 1988 Spring Meeting*, Madison, Wisconsin: Industrial Relations Research Association Series, March 23 – 25.

Leibowitz, Zandy, Caela Farren and Beverly Kaye (1986): *Designing Career Development Systems*, San Francisco.

Levitan, Sar A., Peter E. Carson and Isaac Shapiro (1986): *Protecting American Workers*, Washington D.C.

The Making of Managers (1987): A report prepared for the British Institute of Management, London.

McGregor, Douglas (1960): *The Human Side of Enterprise*, New York.

Meyer, Gary J. (1984): *Automating Personnel Operations*, Madison CT.

Mitchell, Olivia S. (1987): Employee Benefits in the U.S. Labor Market, in: Barbara D. Dennis (ed.), *Proceedings of the Fortieth Annual Meeting*, Madison, Wisconsin.

Moses, J. and W. Byham (1977): *Applying the Assessment Center Method*, New York.

Nadler, Leonhard J. (1985): HRD in Perspective, in: William R. Tracey (ed.) *Human Resources Management and Development Handbook*, New York.

OECD (1988): *OECD Economic Outlook*, No. 44, December, Paris.

OECD (1987): *Employment Outlook*, September, Paris.

Parnes, Herbert S. and Steven H. Sandell (1989): Introduction and Overview, *The Older Worker*, Madison, Wisconsin.

Peters, T. J. and R. H. Waterman (1982): In Search of Excellence, New York.

Renders, Thomasine (1989): Note to our Readers, *Personnel*, December.

Ritter, Anne (1989): The Way it Was: H. R. in the 1980's, *Personnel*, December.

Roomkin, Myron J. (ed.) (1989): *Manager or Employees*, New York.

60   Beverly Springer and Stephen Springer

Rosow, Jerome M. (ed.) (1986): *Teamwork: Joint Labor-Management Programs in America*, New York.

Shank, Susan (1988): Women and the Labor Market: The Link Grows Stronger, *Monthly Labor Review* (Bureau of Labor Statistics), March 1988.

Sonnenfeld, Jeffrey (1988): Dealing with the Aging Work Force, *People*.

Steven, Beth (1988): *Complementing the Welfare State: The Development of Private Pension, Health Insurance and other Employee Benefits in the United States*, (Geneva: International Labour Office, Labour-Management Relations Series No. 65).

Strober, Myra and Carolyn Arnold (1987): The Dynamics of Occupational Segregation Among Bank Tellers, in: Clair Brown and Joseph Pechmen (eds.), *Gender in the Workplace*, Washington D.C.

Training America: Learning to Work for the 21st Century: Alexandria, Virginia: American Society for Training and Development.

U.S. Congress (1982): *Economic Status of Women* (Hearing before the Joint Economic Committee), Congress of the United States, 97th Congress, February 3.

U.S. Department of Labor (1988): *Occupational Outlook Handbook*, 1988 – 9 edition, April.

Wall Street Journal (1984): August 16.

Walters, Roy W. (1985): HRM in Perspective, in: William R. Tracey (ed.), *Human Resources Management and Development Handbook*, New York.

Human Resource Management in Italy

Hans H. Hinterhuber and Monika Stumpf

1. The Environment of Human Resource Management in Italy

In Italy, Human Resource Management (HRM) takes place in quite a different way than in other industrial nations. *For example*: A large enterprise follows the strategy of restructuring in a particular field and therefore has to close down a decentralized manufacturing division. With regard to corporate policy, no employee will be fired. The managers do not give anyone notice but shut down production, electricity is cut off, telephone lines are disconnected. Wages and salaries are entirely paid out for about one more year; after that all employees voluntarily leave the enterprise. This unusual situation can only be explained by the interplay of circumstances that are *typically Italian* referring to the negotiating mentality of employer and employee.

The Italian *labor market* differs from those of other industrial nations in the way that managerial techniques are more strongly affected by social and institutional factors. In literature one can find a lot of details about the history of managerial techniques and their ideological, political and economical elements (Butera 1988, Costa 1981, Fabris 1980, Rugiadini 1983, Saraceno 1978, Vaccà 1985).

1.1 Historical Dimension of Personnel Management

1.1.1 Political and Economic Influences

The history of Italy has its glorious days, its lows and its periods of downfall which seemed to be unstoppable. The political union came late and was in danger for a long time.

The *Italian unitary state* is characterized by a deep *North-South-Dualism*. There lies the most important national problem — since the turn of the century it has been recognized as such. The task of this century — to get a union between the socio-economically and culturally backward South and the more developped North — was a task that engaged the Italian politics after 1945 in a new and more intensive way. In 1950 the *South money-chest* (Cassa per il Mezzogiorno) was founded which had invested about 150—200 billions DM of today's value in the South up to 1984, the date of cancellation (Petersen 1989, Schinzinger 1970).

When leaving aside the zones of early and intensive industrialisation for the moment (the industrial triangle Genoa—Turin—Milan, Milan—Vicenza—Naples), after the second World War a vast majority of the Italian regions were mainly *agricultural* land. Though with the beginning of the fifties, a big change started. As you can see from table 1, in 1936 half of the working population, in 1951 42,2% of it was employed in the sectors agriculture, forestry and fishery. In 1951 the industry and the manufacturing sectors employed 32,1%, the sectors services and administration occupied 25,7%. From the economic point of view, the primary sector was still quite important. Between 1941 and 1950, the primary sector held 33,7% of the gross domestic product. After 1950, these three sectors had large regroupings. In agriculture, the share of employed decreased from 29,1% (1961) to 17,2% (1971) and 10,6% in 1985. Even in South Italy where agriculture was comparatively the most important sector, the farmer and the agricultural worker become even rarer. This decline during the first two decadess after the war was especially for the benefit of the *industrial sector* which increased from 32,1% in 1951 up to 44.4% in 1971, though from that time on is evidently decreasing. The *tertiary sector* has been growing most for a long time past and has doubled since 1945, today it covers more than 50% of the employed.

If one divides the data according to the *model of formation of classes* (Sylos Labini 1975), it becomes obvious that the working class which was

Table 1: Working Population by Sectors 1936—1985 in %

year	agriculture, forestry, fishery	industry, mining, manufacturing	services, public administration
1936	49,4	27,3	23,3
1951	42,2	32,1	25,7
1961	29,1	40,1	30,3
1971	17,2	44,4	38,4
1981	12,6	41,5	45,9
1985	10,6	37,7	51,7

Source: Petersen 1989

in 1971 quantitatively increasing with 47,8% (1961: 44,6%), since then has decreased relatively and absolutely (1983: 42,7%). This decrease becomes noticeable especially in the sectors industry and building trade.

After a first *"economy miracle"* at the beginning of the sixties, which was in per cent partly higher than in Western Germany, Italy lately got into a heavy *crisis*, which has been overcome only in the beginning/middle of the eighties.

The expansion of the tertiary sector, the measures of reorganisation and restructuring in the industrial sector (Hinterhuber 1988) and the financial aid for the South let the public expenditures climb up to a large extent. The *additional debts* each year have reached until today approximately 12% of the gross national product. Though most of the liabilities of the state are home debts against the own population as treasury loans or similar forms. The Italian *rate of saving* is 22% of the gross national product and therefore one of the highest of the Western World. The public poverty is opposed to private richness which has grown quickly (Petersen 1989).

At the same time, there is a quick rise of the *urban middle classes*, especially due to the new middle class. But the traditional middle classes (manufacturing, trade, transport, 1971: 18,5%, 1983: 20,4%) have an astonishing capability to adapt and to survive (Mammarella 1985).

The *Italian trade unions* have already been linked with *politics* to a great extent − as the trade unions of other European countries, but different from those of the United States. During the first years after the war the two big employees' associations − the Christian Democratic oriented association of Free Trade Unions of Italy (CISL) and the Communist General Trade Unions Association of Italy (CGIL) − have been deeply involved in the disputes between the Christian Democrats and the Communists (La Palombara 1987, Galli 1966, Kreile 1985). One of their main reason was traditionally the *adjustment of the real wage level* to West and North European circumstances.

1.1.2 Social and Cultural Influences

The increasing industrialisation was the reason for one of the biggest streams of movements and *emigration* in Italian history. In the decades after 1945, approximately 5 million Italians from the South were looking for a working and living place in the North of Italy or abroad. Only between 1951 and 1971, South Italy had an emigration loss of about 4 million whereas North-West-Italy gained 2,2 million persons from this movement. In the middle of the seventies, half of the inhabitants of Turin were people from the South, and the *difficulties of adaption* and the *problems of integration* are considerably big.

The problems which result from poverty of a material kind and hunger, are solved today in almost all cases. The aggravated problems of the socio-economic backwardness especially come up in the overcrowded areas in the South where the weakness of the state and illegality of various kinds have led to symtoms of decline in society and to a decrease in living quality.

Taken the *gross domestic product* per head, the South has reached 60% which is national average. The *unemployment rate* of 19,2% (1987) is more than twice the rates of North and middle Italy (8,4%). This unemployment rate mainly refers to the *young people*. Approximately 70% of almost 3 million unemployed in Italy are Youth at the age of 14 to 29, most of them looking for their first job (Peterson 1989).

The *big farmer's family* to which a high number of children meant capital, does no longer exist in its original form, and the number of large families is slowly decreasing; despite all that, relatives hold together as in former times, often over a distance of thousands of kilometers. The Italian spends every free hour together with his parents, brothers and sisters, uncles, aunts, nephews, nieces and grandchildren, and — in case this should not be enough — he invites friends and neighbours. They all help him to solve his daily problems or just pass away their time together. This plays an even more important role in the South than in the North, but in the North of Italy more than in Germany where family ties are largely stunted since the time after the World War II (Schlitter 1977).

Women's movements in Middle Europe and the United States did not meet a lively response in Italy. However, up to now, women have made a lot of steps forward in the public as well as in economy.

1.2 Female Occupation — Women in Management

According to an inquiry that has recently been carried out by Crora, "Centro di Ricerca sulla Organizazione Aziendale" (Centre of Research on Organizational Behavior) of the Management University L. Bocconi in Milan, the share of the *female occupation* in the enterprises was 22%. However, only 5% of the women worked in management positions. Nevertheless, for the leader of the investigation, this is a good start.

Namely there are more scientific investigations which show that the Italian *market of female workers* starts moving and that one can recognize a change in the entrepreneurial personnel policy which, little by little, provides responsible positions to women as well.

The working group "Nuove Tecnologie" (New Technology) carried out an investigation together with Italtel, the Italian telecommunications organisation, concerning the situation of female workers in the area of new technologies. Referring to this investigation, the number of *employed women* has raised, especially in the service sector. On one hand, the researchers explain this fact by a decline of low qualified jobs due to rationalisation;

these jobs were mainly carried out by women. On the other hand, the new technologies would have built working places for women who increasingly have better training. The ambition to acquire more and better knowledge opens the way up to active women in time periods that become shorter more and more (Schmitt 1988).

A *typical female Italian manager* of today has started working at the age of 21, reached a leading position at the age of 37, is now 45 years old and has up to now worked in the same enterprise for 16 years. In general she is married or lives together with her mate (approximately 60%) and has at least one child (53%). Her average income is converted into DM about 95.000, −, and she is quite content with her work.

Frederica Olivares, the founder of "Donne in Carriera" (Women in Management), states: "While the first wave of female careerists has put all the energy into the work, the younger ones today try to join *career and private life*. The female protagonists in America and Northern Europe could possibly learn from us that career and family life can be linked."

But before that, the Italian women still have to think over the *choice of their studies*. A high share of women studying liberal and social sciences makes it hard for the personnel managers in the industry sector to find a woman who is able to become a production manager or marketing manager. An unsuitable diploma need not necessarily close the way up, but it reduces her chances to a great extent (Schmitt 1988).

1.3 Educational Factors

Up to a few years ago, only a small number of graduates were employed in the Italian industry; only lately this number has been raising. As the schedule shows, the *share of university-educated* employees in industry seems to be permanently low, even in highly industrialized areas like Milan and Turino. But more and more people recognize that the growing international competition, a raise in the functions of research and development, financial analyses, marketing etc. requires a certain extent of highly qualified human capital.

Today the big firms also follow this way when getting out of a crisis situation or a phase of restructuring. An inquiry of the Università Cattolica of Milan showed that the phase of putting a total freeze on hirings has generally been overcome. Problems of employment concerning workers of traditional employees have partly stayed the same, yet one looks for *young graduates* to introduce them into innovative functions or trained to change into management in the future. This phenomenon can be seen as an aspect of that tendency to *segment the workers*, a tendency, which is in the

Table 2: Gratuated Engineers and Doctorate per 100 Employed in the Industrie in Selected Italian Cities (over 300.000 Inhabitants)

	Graduated Engineers per 100 employed	Doctorate per 100 employed
Genoa	19,0	4,1
Rome	18,9	4,5
Milan	16,0	3,2
Turin	13,6	2,0
Bologna	13,0	2,0
Napels	11,6	2,0
Venice	11,0	1,0
Catania	10,3	1,5
Florence	10,0	1,4
Bari	9,0	0,9
Palermo	8,2	1,7

Source: Gastaldo 1987

international literature linked with *technical-organizational innovation* of the industry (D'Iribarne 1983, Landsbury 1986, Berger and Priore 1982).

While a huge part of workers stays on the brink of the productive system or is employed in weak sectors or in positions which are temporally limited, badly paid or of bad quality, other professional groups reach a *strategic position* referred to the financial success of the enterprise because they bear innovative know-how or professional knowledge which has not been spred a lot or which is hard to reproduce and absolutely necessary to keep up the competitive power of the firm. Therefore, university education, especially in the technical-sciencial and in the economic fields, is highly required when someone starts working in an enterprise.

The inquiry mentioned above shows that almost all firms *mainly* employ graduates coming out of *engineering sciences*: chemistries, electronics and mechanics. For example, engineers hold also the positions of technical specialists in the factories as well as the main part of management positions. Besides engineers, graduates of the following studies are mostly to be found:

economists who work in all kinds of firms and mainly fulfill the following functions: management planning, finances, administration and marketing;

natural scientists of geology, chemistry and biology work as specialists in functional positions in various firms where they built or complete these positions;

those who have finished studies like *jurisprudence or policy* mainly hold certain positions in staff departments or as experts (mainly responsible in personnel matters) (Colasanto 1988).

2. Management Research and Theory

Although managerial problems in industrial nations are quite the same in the long run, the Italian HRM does have its own characteristics. Managerial research has turned away from uncritically adopting foreign models, especially those of North America. In the past, these models led to simplifications and safeness and did not correspond to the *dualistic economic structure* of Italy and to the *cultural identity* of Italian managers. Approaches seem to become more doubtful; the persons applying them have less confidence in sophisticated, general managerial models. They pay more attention to those models which consider the concrete, specific situations in management.

Compared with other industrial nations, Italian managerial research and teaching contains the following *pecularities*:

(1) Problems of *manual* work in manufactoring processes are discussed in great detail (Costa 1981).
(2) As *trade unions* play an important role in the Italian economic and political systems, factory work is considered to be a central point of managerial problems. This is true even in the case enterprises use modern machines, techniques and automation systems (Rebora 1981, Butera 1988).
(3) Management education is very much influenced by North American schools. US-management techniques are adapted to the industrial conditions of Italy today (Coda 1988).
(4) "Personnel management", "business policy" or other similar disciplines generally are split up into different branches of several economic disciplines.
(5) The Italian expression for HRM is "gestione delle resorse umane". Basically, it contains the following fields:

— Personnel management
— Training systems
— Promotional policy and incentive systems
— Key-people-management
— Outplacing
— Corporate Communications.

In Italy foreign, especially North American developments are quickly adopted, therefore the contents are quite similar to those approaches known from literature. Italian enterprises seem to develop their incentive systems in a different way, therefore this aspect of HRM will be discussed in greater detail later on.

2.1   Approaches to Human Resource Management

The Italian HRM can be divided into the following approaches:

(1) The *book-keeping-administrative approach*:

HRM is reduced to the "administration" of personnel, therefore it only deals with the consequences resulting from certain entrepreneurial decisions that concern the factor of production "labor" (Masini 1977, 1978, Onida 1973).

(2) The so-called *specialized-autonomy approach*:

The personnel area is seen as a differentiated, specialized functional field without decisional authority (Pellicelli 1978).

(3) The co-called *political-autonomy approach*:

It reflects the bargaining power and the behavior of the trade unions versus the personnel department vested with proportionate decisional power (Giannoni 1978, Persio 1978).

(4) The *strategic approach*:

Personnel management is integrated within the strategic process at management level and inspires the strategic entrepreneurial management (Boldizzoni 1982, Hinterhuber 1985, Rispoli 1984, Rugiadini 1983, Saraceno 1978, Varaldo 1979, Vaccà 1985, Golinelli and Panati 1988).

The last conception contains an integral view of the *relations between the enterprise and its stakeholders*, i. e. its employees and managers. This entire, coherent view of the problems of strategic management and personnel policies is, however, *not* seen as the aim of a necessary evolution. The leading supporters of this approach (Costa 1984, Saraceno 1978, Vaccà 1985) adapt it to specific situations that are typical of certain enterprises in which the process of innovation guarantees and requires the preconditions of this integration. The evolution of these conditions develops in a way that entrepreneurial *power* is increasingly restructed by institutional factors and trade unions (Ambrosini 1983, Butera 1983, Nanut 1976). These conditions affect the *organizational structure*. Moreover, existing structures become increasingly inflexible. This evolution which did not lead to a change in relations is still going on in a way that cannot be determined yet (Saraceno 1978).

2.2 Conflict Management

Labor conflicts in Italy are historically connected with the enterprise (Cella 1982). These conflicts have a precise function in the experience of Italian managers. A solution is neither possible nor useful. The labor conflict enables the manifestation of differing interests and economical and social objectives of the employees in a collective, public and organized way (Costa 1984). In Italian literature, this conflict is the precondition to come to an agreement (Biagioli 1982, Costa 1978, Gasparini 1977, Massacesi 1973 Nacamulli 1979, Persio 1978, Pipan and Salerni 1975). This point of view permits three basic ways of handling labor conflicts:

(1) *Atomistic Pluralism*: Conflicts are not institutionalized (Giugni 1976, Vanni 1974).
(2) *Organized Pluralism*: Conflicts are regulated to some extent; it also offers certain methods to resolve conflicts (Pontarollo 1978).
(3) *Neo-Corporativism*: Conflicts are institutionalized (Maraffi 1981, Cella and Treu 1982).

Concerning employees and their organization within the Italian system of industrial relations, there exist both extremes at the same time − the conception of Atomistic Pluralism as well as the conception of Neo-Corporativism. None of it is predominant, nor can a dialectic synthesis be found (Costa 1984).

As far as employers and their associations are concerned, the entrepreneurial behavior is to be found between the integral and the pluralistic conception (Nacamulli 1979). Small and medium sized firms seem to prefer the former. This conception offers a greater scope of managerial initiative whereas large firms tend to gain advantage from the latter. This pluralistic conception only permits consent through complex *negotiations* including high transaction costs and not through authoritarian behavior.

The Italian view becomes even more complex because the state and its great number of public institutions − combined they are the most important employers − want to regulate the labor market. However, their aims are unclear and moreover affected by the changing political influence (Costa 1984, Saraceno 1978).

2.2.1 Legal Environment

The relationship between the employee and the employer is mainly determined by two laws:

Law nr. 604 of July 15th, 1966, regulates the *individual notice*; but there are just two premises left where it is applied (because all the other cases refer to the regulations of the "Statuto dei Lavoratori" − the employees' statute − art. 18):

− enterprises with more than 30 employees,
− but less than 15 persons employed in the establishment (or in the community).

While the *employees' statute* leads to a *really stable working relationship*, law nr. 604 only guarantees an obligatory stability in the case of an unjustified dismissal. In this case, the employer just pays a penalty or forces a reemployment. According to the *employees' statute*, this case cannot be judged as an interruption of the working relationship, therefore, the employer is obliged to continue the normal payment of salary, independent of a reemployment, and also to pay a penalty (art. 18).

The law nr. 300 which came into effect on May 20th, 1970, the so-called *Italian employee' statute* (which can be found in the annex of the "Codice Civile", the Italian civil law) contains the order to ensure the *unionist freedom* within the enterprise which means

— not only the *individual unionist freedom* in the sense that the individual can take part actively and passively in the unionist work without restrictions and danger, nor can he be forced to to unionist work,
— but also the *collective freedom* to organize a trade union itself.

It says nothing about the structure and the sense of democracy etc. within the trade union (Persiani 1986, Suppiej 1982).

2.2.2 Industrial Relations

In 1947 the big trade unions and the employers' associations decided to found by contract the so-called *internal committees* (commissione interne) within each enterprise or within each establishment. They were the *first kind of unionist presence* in the enterprise, not only in the sense of representing the interests of the employees but as well as a representation of political interests. Though, they were not adjudicated the function of a unionist representation and the power to conclude collective labor agreements.

The committee only had the task to control whether the rights of the worker were injured, e. g. control of notices. But in many cases they were dependent on the employers and therefore could hardly fulfill this function. Employees who were uninterested in their trade-unionist work often were the result of it.

In 1970, when the employees' statute was coming into force, they were also provided, even if not by law but by collective labor agreements.

The "Statuto dei Lavoratori" the *employees' statute*, permits the *foundation of unionist representations* in enterprises under the following conditions:

— minimum of 15 employees in the enterprise or in several branches of the enterprise within the same community,
— a connection with one of the federal trade union or with a trade union that signs as well the collective labor agreements on the national or provincial level which are used in this firm.

In case of several firms, these representations can join together by forming the *coordinative organ* (organo di coordinamento) which can then undertake the conclusion of e. g. collective labor agreements.

Each factory can, of course, have *several unionist representations*, namely representations of all trade unions mentioned above. The collective labor agreements now provide to built the so-called "*consigli di fabbrica*" (factory advisers) — where also various unionist representations can be present — to represent the employees in negotiations.

But *by no means*, this committee can be compared with the German "Betriebsrat", defined by German law and called *right of co-determination* (Mitbestimmungsrecht).

As already stated above, Italian law does not explain the structure of the unionist representations in the firm. This is often seen as a *lack of this law*: It does protect the *unionist interests* against the employer but it says *nothing* about a *democratic structure* of the trade union and therefore about the protection of the individual interests within the trade union itself. The law does protect the elected functionary (art. 22, 23 and 24), but it says nothing about the election itself.

The representatives of the trade unions in the enterprise do not need a ratification by the employer. As soon as they fulfill the legal conditions for the foundation, they are authorized by law to conclude *collective labor agreements*. The "contratti colletive" are similar to the German collective agreements. The Civil Law does not contain a corresponding regulation which has been clearly laid down. Therefore, the most important question, i. e. why the collective labor agreement is applied to all employees of the same category, cannot be explained by an explicit law. The *validity* is due to a jurisdiction that has been explained by argument of analogy established in the course of other laws, referring to

— the economic part: art. 36 (Constitution) and art. 2099 C.C. and
— the normative part in a narrower sense: art. 1411 C.C.

In case of violation of the employees' statute, the district judge has jurisdiction; there is no proper Labor Court (Persiani 1986, Ricci 1974, Suppiej 1982).

2.3 Motivation Systems

For traditional reasons, the employee is not able to identify himself with the enterprise nor can he take up the position of an external negotiating party. But these two contradictory tendencies seem to be very much developed within the relationship between the employees (Saraceno 1978): One conception tries to *integrate* the employee whereas the other one tends to let him appear in the role of an *external* negotiating party. The latter seems to dominate in many sectors of the Italian economy, but it does not correspond to the entrepreneurial interests. Enterprises must install effective systems of managing, coordinating, motivating and controlling employees — this depends on how far Italian industry has adopted modern structures of production. The growing interest of enterprises in integrating the employees to a greater extent is confirmed in a large number of publications (Caprara 1982, Coda 1973, Ferrer-Pacces 1974, Lorenzoni 1979, Pellicelli 1978, Rispoli 1984, Rugiadini 1983, Sciarelli 1982, Varaldo 1979, Hinterhuber 1985) which put the stress on systems of payment as a means of motivation.

2.3.1 Financial Incentives

The *system of payment* applied for top management is defined by three parameters (Vanni 1974): *Level* of payment, *structure* of payment and *dynamism* of payment.

The *level of payment* is a function of the corporate strategy and of the corresponding personnel policy (Eminente 1985, Hinterhuber 1985, Rispoli 1984).

Job evaluation as a means to fix the *structure of payment* was first accepted but later on, trade unions strictly refused it because it would divide the labor market into *segments*. However, the strategy of the trade unions aims at a *standardization* of the labor market after discretionary powers and the patriarchal management have nearly disappeared (Pipan and Salerni 1975). Yet one can find detailed description of existing methods of job evaluation despite the fact that they are no longer used except by subsidiaries of foreign firms (Boldizzoni 1982). Companies under Italian leadership take the view that the opposition of the trade unions can change the aim pursued by job evaluation, namely to attain a consent. It could become a reason for permanent conflicts (Costa 1984). In the view of some supporters of this management theory, "Skill Evaluation" seems to be a method to enhance the status of the individual within an economy that is increasingly difficult to plan. It should also increase the flexibility of the enterprise. However, its main advantage is to overcome the unidimensional job evaluation (Baraldi 1982, Biagioli 1982, Costa 1981, Romagnoli and Rocca 1982).

The so-called *classification systems* largely lacks a systematical and theoretical basis till today. They originate from practical experience as far as the connection is concerned between the subjective systems laid down in the course of collective bargaining for different sectors and the requirements of the organization. The normative equality of workers and employees ("inquadramento unico") is an example for the so-called mixed classification system. It was introduced in 1973 under article number 13 of the employee statute.

An interesting approach that may follow the classification systems is the so-called *dynamic analysis and valuation* (Costa 1981). It does not treat the organization and the classification systems as data but as dynamic processes. The approach of *Butera* also tends to define the structure of payment as the main problem of personnel management. The employee is not an isolated individual but a member of a group. He is projected into a certain role within society and holds specific authorities in the organization. Professionality is measured by collective standards (Butera 1977, 1983). These new approaches are even more remarkable because the normative equality of workers and employees is hardly found in real life despite the existing law. Enterprises have developed certain structures of payment that are used whenever control by the trade unions is weak. These structures are based upon subjective systems and cannot be brought in relation to systematic classification systems.

The *dynamism of payment* in Italy is largely built upon automatic operations (principle of seniority and escalator scale) and fixed pay raises (Pontarollo 1978). It offers few possibilities of individual and/or collective incentive systems under the aspect of motivation. The evolution that takes place within the personnel relationship and their work as well as the employees and the enterprise is based upon new laws, regulations and different interpretations of existing laws. It seems to place the normative aspect above payment by improving the working conditions (Saraceno 1978).

Literature generally states that *payment by results* involves less advantages than disadvantages concerning the forms of payment by results (Lombardi 1980). Nevertheless payment by results seems to be more important in practice than one could suggest because of an increase in the mechanisation and the automatisation of the processes of production (Predetti 1980). In any case, arrangements between different sectors and those within enterprises provide detailed regulation of payment by results. Payment by results is more and more replaced by premium pay as is the case in all other industrial nations (Manzolini 1983, Nacamulli 1982).

Referring to the dynamism of payment those forms which provide a long-lasting pay raise become more important these days. This pay raise is based upon the global assessment of the level of performance and/or the performance potential of the individual (Costa 1984): *Performance rating and career planning* are increasingly seen as a means to compensate the flexibility of the organization for a largely reduced dynamism of payment.

Profit sharing of the employees as a special form of the dynamism of payment has never been supported by Italian employees and trade unions. Collective bargaining is clearly preferred when profits are redistributed (Costa 1984). Nor have managers seriously tried to develop effective profit sharing systems; the few known attempts seem to prefer the fostering of the relations to the public rather than the entrepreneurial and sociopolitical

objectives. The accumulation of capital through the profit sharing of
employees is less important (Saraceno 1978). Within the workmen's
cooperatives and the self-governed firms profit sharing can gain some
importance for the future (Costa 1984). Today prevailing opinion states that
equity participation of the employees ("azionariato del lavoro") merely leads
to the creation of a specific group of shareholders who do not have any
influence on the strategic orientation of the enterprise or any other important
function. They are part of the personnel policy and do not have any
decisional power within the enterprise; nor can they be seen as a reform to
the structure of the industrial estate (Saraceno 1978).

2.3.2 Non-financial Incentives

The *organization of work* within the industrial enterprise *traditionally*
delegates all responsibilities exclusively to the lines of the departments of
planning and organisation, without any special orders concerning personnel
management. Starting with an organizational structure according to the
principles of traditional taylorism, it relates to a restructuring of the working
processes when the organisation is developped and its result is a new
definition of the rate of labor division in relation to the internal and external
exchange partners of the enterprise. Proceeding from the aim to increase
directly or indirectly the efficiency of the organization and its members, one
will find all kinds of *job design* − e. g. *job enlargement, job enrichment, job
rotation, work groups etc.* − in the sense of a humanisation of the work
(Butera 1988, Costa 1984, Rispoli 1984).

A lot of additional elements are taken into consideration in the *modern
enterprise* which are important and cannot be renounced of to the sensitive
equilibrium of the enterprise: This refers not only to the decision to be part
of the organization, the quantity and the quality of the work, the creative
contribution that should be part of the work, the sense of solidarity and
working morale against the collegues, but reaches up to the hope for help
and the chance to find a part of his own personal identity out from the role
in the enterprise (Schein 1985, Varvelli 1974).

In all stages of *organizational development* the *non-monetary motivation
systems* are those which create the biggest problems in implementation
because they demand for *specific organizational structures*. At the same time
there is an intrinsic coherence between the main variables concerned −
management style, rate of delegation, rate of task orientation or profit
orientation, rate of automatisation etc. (Nanut 1989).

The analyses of the relations between the individual and the organization
show a kind of *interaction* which is manifested through a mutual influence
and action until the *contract* is *"de facto" stabilized*. Besides, there is a
"psychological" contract which differs from the legal contract concerning

the fact that it is a *dynamic and changing relation* which permanently gets a new definition. Very often, really important aspects of the contract are not discussed formally but, despite that, the "psychological contract" is a *reality* which is of great importance to the productivity and satisfaction of the individual. Two important aspects refer to the principle of the entrepreneurial *authority* and the possibilities of the employees to *influence* it (Schein 1965, 1984, Varvelli 1974).

In general, the organizational reaction is a *reward*, i.e. premia for those who reached the best results, as well as a *sanction*, i.e. penalities for those who did not do a satisfactory job. This link between reward and the working result is also called *"mechanism of praise and censure"* which often includes the following aspect as well. His hidden but has nevertheless a strong influence on the motivation of the employees. In a majority of cases, *tacit agreements* come into effect between the employed and the enterprise itself (which is represented by the upper management level). Those agreements are some kind of reglementation of the rights and duties of both parties. It is a question of *customary law* without a legal basis and even contradictory to existing law in many cases.

This mechanism is deeply embodied in the *Italian management culture*. The employee knows that, for example, he cannot be fired in case of a crisis situation of the enterprise although the management would have the right to do so. However, the employee knows as well that he has to accept a change of his working place when it is required by the enterprise, even though he has the legal right to protest. Actually, this *usage* is *legitimated by tradition*, and both parties accept it as a binding law.

Often, the upper management tries to disregard some of these customary laws, but in general they do regard them because they know very well the *risks* they would take with such a decision. But if the enterprise decides to change rules in favor of its employees — without being forced to by external influences — the employees themselves will often change their behaviors in favor of the enterprise.

This mechanism widens the possibilities of a mutual influence beyond the traditional dichotomy of the situation between employer and employee; consequently it is a matter of *interventions* which demand a high degree of *fantasy and creativity* (Schein 1985, 1984).

3. Human Resource Management in Practice

Various experts have the opinion that compared with all other European economic systems the Italian economy had the strongest development during the last decade. *Development and flexibility of the Italian labor market* was one of the leading subjects of a symposium that recently took place in Paris and which was organized by the French Labor Department (Bertoldi 1989).

According to the view of some French observers, flexibility in *France* is mainly of a *quantitative* kind and has appeared especially in form of a rising precarity of the labor. In *Italy* flexibility has a *qualitative* character as well which refers to the *factor labor* and the *factor capital*. At the end of the sixties, the large Italian enterprises have aimed at a decentralization of the production, with regard to a new allocation of the income and a rising negotiating power of the workers. This *decentralization* of the production has led to a dynamic expansion of the small and mediumsized enterprises. On the other hand, these enterprises succeeded in restructuring themselves, with the aid of an increased income, and have been able to handle the uncertain and diversified demand.

In this way, a *"flexible specialization"* has come up on the *product market* as well as on the *labor market*. This allowed a dynamic adaption to the new conditions of the manufacturing and employment system: A model which is considered to be very difficult to use in France because of its low conformity within the social structure of the local communities, like it is typical for the "Italian case" (Bertoldi 1989).

However, the number of small enterprises has diminished during the very last years in contrast to the big firms which were able to improve the relation of wages and productivity to their favor.

How do the Italians themselves rate their situation today? Is there an *Italian model of organization and management*? A large-scale empiric study of "Crora", the Center for Research on Business Organization in Milan, answered with "yes". The thousand largest enterprises which were in business in Italy in 1987, have been examined. 116 of these enterprises (of which 82% were part of a holding), with a total number of employed exceeding 282.000, gave an answer. With 58%, the most important group are workers followed by white-collars and technicians with 32%, middle management with 6,7%, and upper management with 2,7%.

The result of this study contains a lot of data about strategies, development of the organization and new tendencies in Human Resource Management.

3.1 Organizational Structure

The organizational structure differs according to size and strategy. The model which can be found in most cases, is the *functional* one, with just a few differences caused by the rate of autonomy of several functions (technics, production, trade, administration and finances etc.). The functional segmentation is applied by more than 60% of the enterprises examined (which is 75% of the "smallest"), whereas 23% (40% of the "big ones") apply a divisional structure. The subgroup of the *"magnificent"* enterprises seem to have a proper functional structure as well (60%) or a modified structure (20%), in contrast to firms with a divisional structure (20%).

In this context not only the *mechanism and the upholders* of integration (periodical meetings, task force, sales manager, product manager etc.) play a decisive role, but also the *system of planning and control* which is considered to be developped sufficiently just in 63% of all cases.

It has to be mentioned that those enterprises with the best performance all have a *strategic planning system*, a better developed program's arrangement and supervisions and control compared with the average. All other operative systems like selection and training of the personnel, career planning and motivation systems seem to be very efficient as well.

3.2 Career Planning and Incentive Systems

This sector shows considerable differences to North American and European competitors. A majority of the examined enterprises shows a considerable *"gap"* in the personnel management, especially in regard to personnel planning and training. Going into detail, the matured and formalized systems of *performance valuation* and *career planning* are spred to a small extent (39% of the firms neither have the former nor the latter). Moreover, *the methods of labor valuation* and the monetary incentives are rare and little polished (34% of the enterprises do not have any of these systems or — in case they have one — it is not activated formally). This is an almost inconceivable "backwardness" when considering the fact that the Anglo-Saxon management culture has been generally accepted and managers are given access to a matured Know-How made available by specialized advisers.

But the researchers of Crora refer too, to *another interpretation*, namely that of a *deliberate refusal* which is the expression of a certain *strategy: not to fix* the aims *explicitly*, not to document the parameter and criteria of valuation in order to guarantee a maximum of *"reserves of flexibility"* for the enterprise. The result is in a maximal freedom of action concerning the field of personnel management. This interpretation seems to be confirmed by two facts:

a. The atmosphere of the *industrial relations* is different from the American one, as the trade unions are always prepared to convert the quotas of the income distribution into pay traps and the instruments and parameter of the personnel management into rigid and insurmountable hurdles.

b. the *"gap"* only refers to the *techniques* of motivation and valuation while the systems of personnel selection and training adapt adequately to the needs of the enterprise. 40% of the managers interviewed rated the systems used in their enterprises as highly polished and wide-spred.

But it is possible that this situation is going to change soon: 33% of the enterprises are modifying their career planning system while 35% are working on performance valuation and motivation systems.

3.3 Income Distribution

44,7% of the enterprises provide a bonus; incentives which refer to the total result of the enterprise or the division are very rare, whereas in practice, individual premia for the middle management (58,7% of the firms), for the white-collars (52,8%) and for the workers (49%) are applied more often.

3.4 Continous Training and Career in the Enterprise

The measures of a *continous training* (this is the case in 91% of the firms) refer to beginners (22%) and to employees who have just been promoted with the aim to prepare them for the new position (7%). It refers as well to all other employees (71%). This relates to 72% of the middle management of which each person was trained on an average of 5,8 days in 1987. 51% of the employees result with 9,8 days and 13% of the workers 11 days. 51% of the training programs are carried out *internally* and concentrate on the *technical sector* (with 52%) and on the trade sector (20%).

The *typical Italian manager* differs from his American collegues by the following features: The average age is approximately 48 years and the period of employment is longer than 18 years. In most cases, the leading position is an honoring to the loyality of those who made their career in one and the same enterprise (60% of the cases) and in the same functional area (53%). Within the typical Italian enterprise, managers with professional experience in various operating functions are very scare (18,4%). Even more scarce are those managers who have made significant *experience abroad*. The majority of top managers (75,4%) has never worked abroad and only 5% have built up one third of their career abroad.

In regard to top managers, the situation is different: After graduating from university, 26% attended post-graduate courses (compared with 7,5% of all managers), 55% of them went abroad. The career of top managers has begun in various enterprises and various professional fields in Italy (35%) and abroad (33%). Most of them come from the technical and the

Table 3: Professional Experience of the New Managers (Beginners in 1987)

Professional Experience	Totale of the management	Only Top Management
in one enterprise only	59,7%	40,2%
In several enterprises (same business)	21,9%	25,1%
In several enterprises (different business)	18,4%	34,7%

Table 4: Employment of the New Managers (Beginners 1987)

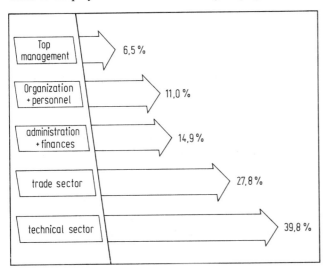

trade sector, followed by administration and finance, organisation and personnel.

The new managers, nominated in 1987, have been recruited from the same firm (43,3%), from other divisions of the holding (18,4%) and externally recruited (38,3%). They are mainly employed in the technical sector, followed by trade, administration and finance, organization and the top management.

Table 5: Career Paths of the Top Managers (Provenance Sectors in % form 380
        Examined Members)

Provenance sectors of the managers (beginners 1987)

technical sector	33,7%
trade sector	33,0%
administration and finance sector	19,2%
organization + personnel	7,2%
no specified sector	6,9%

3.5 Industrial Relations

The percentage of employees of the enterprises included in the sampling
that are trade union members, has increased slightly, starting with 34,5%
in 1986 up to 36,2% in 1987. However, the influence of the united trade
unions has dimished. In 97% of all cases, the unionist representative is the
factory adviser (consiglio di fabrica) but only 76% of the enterprises have
accepted him by contract. Even more obvious is the situation for the middle
management which is represented by a trade union just in 24% of the
enterprises. Middle management as an autonomous category is only represented by contract in 6% of the cases.

More and more *conflicts* are directly connected with a specific working
situation whereas the means of a strike in case of an external issue (including
the renovation of the national labor contracts) is dimishing (Magrino 1989).

4. Prospects

The research report of Crora paints the *Italian model of Human Resource
Management*, alternatively to the Anglo-Saxon one, in the following way:
In case the man (or the woman?) is the resource par excellance which has
to absorb even higher factors of complexity and uncertainty within the
enterprise, then it is necessary to selected him (her) in a very strict way, and

to develop not only competences but also cultural orientations and the micro-values of the social system of the enterprise. This is an integration of the aims and the behaviors of the individual with those of the enterprise not by hierarchical control instruments (valuation schedules etc.) nor by income distribution but by less transparent means of the kind of subtle cultural conditionalities and permanent adaptions of the informal relations and distribution of power.

4.1 Management Theory

Apparently, Italian management thought does not pursue the model of the *"one best way"*, i. e. it does not look for the most suitable of the management models to be compared, which of them would best meet the industrial modernization of the state. Foreign models have been adopted, especially those that have successfully been applied in the United States. This can be blamed for being the reason that management structures become inflexible to some extent. This adoption also hinders the *dynamic interaction between the entrepreneurial subsystem* and different enterprises (Vaccà 1985). Those enterprises that decide to use proved management models cannot avoid to give up their *individual variety* and therefore miss the opportunity to pursue an antonomous innovation or stand out from competition. Italian Management Research recalls to mind its previous values and tradition; it looks for a backing within the enterprise and the *identity* that originates from the national cultural heritage. The rational and the irrational dimension of the strategy and the operative and individual flexibility are emphasized and ought to release personnel energies. Moreover, it should stimulate creativity and spontaneity which both represent the basis to build upon long-lasting defensible competitive advantages.

Italian management research seems to develop towards two different methodical approaches. The former refers to the study of a *"micro-reality"* (Vaccà 1985). This approach rather looks for general laws of evolution, which can be found as weak signals in the microsystem, than for normative statements. The latter analyses the tendencies of evolution of the *macrosystem* which is seen as a dialectic interaction of three subsystems (economy, technology, environment). In this sense management theory becomes part of a more comprehensive discipline which combines the managerial problems of the individual enterprise with the whole economy, the dynamism of the environment and the technological evolution (Vaccà 1985).

Such dynamic management research that resembles a project, results in overcoming the limits between business administration and political economy. At the same time, one does not stress this interdisciplinary approach because of its necessity and its practicality but its contribution to the fact that the understanding and the interpretation of basic fields of management theory horizontally cross micro- and macroeconomy. Considering the complexity of management these days, the limits between business policy, political economics as well as the social disciplines merge into each other. For the future, Italian management research seems to prefer dealing more with the problems themselves than with their limits.

4.2 Human Resources

In times like today where the acceleration of change and the increasing complexity of all the human establishments are the only constant factors, the prospects are very well for the now *fifth-greatest industrial nation* in the world — especially in front of its historical background. Italy has successfully taken the way of the country with the grossest economic contrasts in the whole Europe until the top of the industrial world.

Wieser, an observer of Italy of many years, refers to the *national character* as a deeper motivation. In front of the catastrophes lowering over the centuries again and again, the Italians have developed a high capacity of patience, mobility and improvisation. They have a much higher level of tolerance for the insecurity, the confusion and the contradiction of the things than any other Western nation. Therefore they are able to produce by magic from a maximum of chaos a minimum of order. Over the visible weaknesses and defects, such deeper characteristics are easily overlooked. These characteristics give the country a sturdy psychic force which allows to survive each storm (Wieser 1988).

Thanks to the marked *individualism* of the Italians, there is more *"free style"* in all sectors of life than in the rest of the Western world refering to the economy, bureaucracy and in justice. There also is the strong consciousness of a *minimum of rules* which are to be accepted by all Italians. This atmosphere seems to have the supernatural effect to promote a kind of political and economical *virtuosity* of which each Italian fundamentally is very proud of (La Palombara 1987).

References

Airoldi, G. (1980): *I sistemi operativi*, Mailand.
Ambrosini, M. (1983): *Relazioni industriali e trasformazioni sociali*, Milan.
Baraldi, R. (ed.) (1982): *Fasce di professionalità*, Milan.
Berger, S. and Priore, M. J. (1982): *Dualismo economico e politica nelle società industriali*, Bologna.

Bertoldi, M. (1989): Flessibilità, un prodotto made in Italy, *Mondo economico*, n. 15/89.

Biagioli, M. (1989): *Inflazione, struttara del salario e contrattazione*, Milan.

Boldizzoni, D. (1982): *La direzione del personale*, Milan.

Butera, F. (1977): *La divisione del lavoro in fabbrica*, Venice.

Butera, F. (1962): *I frantumi ricomposti*, Padova.

Butera, F. (ed.) (1983): *La progettazione organizzativa*, Milan.

Butera, F. (1988): *L'orologio e l'organismo*, Milan.

Caprara, G. (1982): *Corso di economia delle imprese industriali*, 2nd. ed., Milan.

Caselli, L. (1966): *Teoria dell'organizzazione e processi dicisionali nell'impresa*, Torino.

Cella, G. P. and Treu, T. (1982): *Relazioni industriali*, Bologna.

Coda, V. (1988): *L'orientamento strategico dell'impresa*, Torino.

Colasanto, M. (1982): *La questione della democrazia industriale*, Milan.

Colasanto, M. et al. (1988): *I laureati e l'impresa — La gestione delle risorse umane tra aspirazioni individuali e contesti organizzativi*, Milan.

Costa, G. (1984): Il lavoro, in: M. v. Rispoli (ed.), *L'impresa industriale. Economia e management*, Bologna: 469–541.

Costa, G. (1978): *Le relazioni industriali*, Milan.

Costa, G. (1981): *La retribuzione. Tecniche e politiche di remunerazione del lavoro*, Milan.

d'Iribarne, A. (1983): Nouvelles technologies qualification, efficience productive et sortie de crise, *Recherches économiques et sociales* n. 8.

Eminente, G. (1985): *La gestione strategica dell'impresa*, 2nd. ed., Bologna.

Fabris, A. (1980): *Storia delle teorie organizzative*, Milan.

Ferrer-Pacces, F. M. (1974): *I sistemi d'impresa*, Torino.

Fortuna, F. (1982): *Tecnica industriale e commerciale*, Milan.

Gagliardi, P. (1986): *Le imprese come culture*, Torino.

Gali, G. (1966): *Il bipartitismo imperfetto. Comunisti e democristiani in Italia*, Bologna.

Gasparini, G. (1977): *Tecnologia, ambiente, struttura*, Milan.

Gastaldo, P. (1987): *La risorsa sapere*, Torino.

Golinelli, G. and Panati, G. (1988): *Tecnica economica industriale e commerciale: imprese, strategie e management*, Rome.

Giannovi, A. (1978): *Autonomia politica*, Milan.

Giugni, G. (ed.) (1976): *Ascesa e crisi del riformismo in fabbrica*, Bari.

Hinterhuber, G. (1985): *La direzione strategica dell'impresa industriale*, 2nd ed., Torino.

Hinterhuber, G. (1988): Sanierung auf Italienisch, in: *Industrie*, 41/1988.

Kreile, M. (1985): *Gewerkschaften und Arbeitsbeziehungen in Italien (1968–1982)*, Frankfurt/M.

La Palombara, J. (1987): *Democracy, Italian Style*, New Haven, London. (German Translation: Die Italiener oder Demokratie als Lebenskunst. Vienna 1988.).

Landsbury, R. D. (1986): *Technological Chance and Industrial Relations*: General report, Intern. Industrial Research Association, 7th World Congress: Hamburg.

Lombardi, E. (1980): *Forme di retribuzione*, Milan.

Lorenzoni, G. (1979): *Una politica innovativa nelle piccole medie imprese*, Milan.

Magrino, F. (1989): La svolta dei mille, *Il Mondo* n. 18/89.

Manzolini, L. (1983 a): *Il caso Alfa Romeo*, Milan.
Manzolini, L. (1983 b): *La politica retributiva*, Bologna.
Maraffi, M. (ed.) (1981): *La società neo-corporativa*, Bologna.
Masini, G. (1977): *Il sistema dei valori d'azienda*, Milan.
Masini, G. (1978): *Lavoro e risparmio*, 2nd ed., Torino.
Massacesi, E. (ed.) (1973): *Inquadramento unico e professionalitá*, Rome.
Momigliano, F. (1975): *Economia industriale e teoria dell'impresa*, Bologna.
Momigliano, F. (1966): *Sondacati, progresso tecnico e programmazione economica*, 3rd ed., Torino.
Mammarella, G. (1985): *L'Italia contemporanea 1943—1985*, Bologna.
Nacamulli, R. D. D. (ed.) (1982): Sindacati e organizzazione d'impresa in Italie, Milan.
Nacamulli, R. C. D. (1979): *Relazioni sindacali in impresa*, Milan.
Nanut, V. (1976): *Strutture organizzative, sviluppo tecnologico e conflitti nelle imprese industriali*, Milan.
Nanut, V. (1989): L'imprenditorializzazione del management, *Sviluppo & Organizzazione*, 112/1989.
Olivieri, W. (1975): *L'inquadramento unico nel settore metal-meccanico*, Milan.
Onida, P. (1973): *Economia d'azienda*, Torino.
Panati, G. (1980): *Politiche di ristrutturazione e decentramento produttivo*, Padua.
Pellicelli, G. (1978) *Le strutture organizzative*, Milan.
Persiani, M. (1986): *Diritto Sindacale, Cedam*, Padova.
Persio, M. (ed.) (1978): *La direzione del personale*, Milan.
Petersen, J. (1989): *Geschichte Italiens*, 2nd ed., Stuttgart.
Petroni, G. (1977): *I quadri dell'imprese. Programmazione e sviluppo*, Milan.
Pipan, T. and Salerni, D. (1975): *Il sindacato come soggetto di equilibrio*, Milan.
Poiani, M. (1986): *La cultura d'impresa*, Milan.
Poiani, M. (1988): *Il mutamento della cultura d'impresa*, Milan.
Pontarollo, E. (1978): *Struttura dei costi del lavoro e contrattazione*, Milan.
Predetti, A. (1980): *L'Automazione dei processi produttivi*, Milan.
Rebora, G. (1981): *Comportamento d'impresa e controllo sociale*, Milan.
Ricci, R. (1974): I rapporti con le rappresentanze dei lavoratori, in: Vanni, L. (ed.): *Manuale di gestione del personale*, Milan.
Rispoli, M. (ed.) (1984): *L'impresa industriale. Economia e management*, Bologna.
Rodota', S. (ed.) (1977): *Il controllo sociale delle attività private*, Bologna.
Romagnoli, G. and Della Rocca, G. (1982): Il sindacato, in: G. P. von Cella and T. Treu (eds.), *Relazioni industriali*, Bologna.
Rugiadini, A. (ed.) (1983): *L'organizzazione nell'economia aziendale*, Milan.
Rugiadini, A. (1979): *Organizzazione d'impresa*, Milan.
Salvemindi, S. (1977): *La progettazione delle mansioni*, Milan.
Saraceno, P. (ed.) (1978): *Economia e direzione dell'impresa industriale*, Milan.
Saraceno, P. (1978): *La produzione industriale*, 9th ed., Venice.
Scamuzzi, S. (1981): *Riforma del collocamento e mercato del lavoro*, Milan.
Schein, E. H. (1965): *La psicologia industriale nella società moderna*, Milan.
Schein, E. H. (1984): Cultura organizzativa e processi di cambiamento aziendali, *Sviluppo e organizzazione*, 84/1984.
Schein, E. H. (1985): *Organizational Culture and Leadership*, San Francisco.

Schinzinger, F. (1970): *Die Mezzogiorno-Politik. Möglichkeiten und Grenzen der Agrar- und Infrastrukturpolitik*, Berlin.

Schlitter, H. (1977): *Italien — Industriestaat und Entwicklungsland*, Hannover.

Schmitt, B. (1988): Italienische Managerinnen, *Mangement-Wissen*, n. 10.

Sciarelli, S. (1967): *Il processo decisorio nell'impresa*, Padova.

Sciarelli, S. (1982): *Il sistema d'impresa*, Padova.

Segatori, R. and Torresini, D. (1979): La professionalità difficile, Rome.

Suppiej, G. (1982): *Il rapporto di lavoro, Enciclopedia Giuridica del lavoro*, Padova.

Sylos Labini, P. (1975): *Saggio sulle classi sociali*, Bari.

Vaccà, S. (1985): L'economia di impresa alla ricerna di una identità, *Economia e politica industriale*, 12/45: 5 – 30.

Vanni, L. (ed.) (1974): *Manuale di gestione del personale*, Milan.

Varaldo, R. (1979): *Ristrutturazione industriale e rapporti tra imprese*, Milan.

Varvelli, M. L. (1974): La motivazione e l'incentivatzione del personale, in: Vanni, L. (ed.): *Manuale di gestione del personale*, Milan.

Vitale, M. (1989): *La lunga marcia verso il capitalismo democratico*, Milan.

Wieser, Th. and Spotts, F. (1988): *Der Fall Italien — Dauerkrise einer schwierigen Demokratie*, Frankfurt/M.

Zanda, G. (1989): *La valutazione dei dirigenti*, Padova.

Zanetti, G. (1979): *Economia dell'impresa*, 2nd ed., Bologna.

Human Resource Management in France

Jacques Rojot

The topic is most interesting, but relatively difficult to cover. In the first place, generalized surveys on the use of practices of human resource management in enterprises do not exist to our knowledge. We do even find few limited surveys on limited samples, whose conclusions may not always safely be generalized. We shall have therefore to draw mostly on data of an impressionistic nature, not supported by hard evidence.

In the second place, France is a country where a massive number of enterprises is of small size, and therefore, in those enterprises, human resource management is likely to be very little or not formalized at all.

However, some elements are available. We have attempted to summarize them below:

1. Brief History

The following development draws most of its elements from a very interesting and original contribution by Jean Fonbonne, a retired personnel director, whom, to our knowledge, is the first to have tried to systematically present an historical overview of the evolution of the personnel management function and the role of the personnel manager in France (Fonbonne 1988).

Industrialization in France develops over the XIXth century. Around 1850, 82% of the labor force is active in agriculture and 10% only is employed in industry. In 1901, these percentages respectively reach 55% and 30% (id.). However, this does not mean that human resource management is, at that time, a concern for enterprises, for not only the prevalent spirit of liberalism, economic and political, brings management to consider labor as a factor of production similar to the others and to be treated in the same way. But foremostly, the actual issues, which could have brought from the shopfloor human resource problems to the attention of management, where hidden from its attention by the system of manpower utilisation prevalent at the times: putting-out, internal contracting, use of "helpers."

In 1896, 472 establishments employ more than 500 employees (1176 more than 200, and 13 more than 5000) (Fonbonne 1988). The size of establishments increases as does the intensivity in capital with more complex and costly technology. Labor law regulating work by children and women, apprenticeship, unions, work related accidents, etc. ... is passed by parliament. All this brings employers to directly employ and supervise more workers. It also signals the beginning of the rule of the foreman. The first appearance of human resource management are under the form of the shop rules, unilaterally established by the employer as he sees fit, covering almost all areas of employee behavior that he wishes within the limits of public order and enforced by the foreman.[1] The law grants them the strenght of statutory law.[2]

Parallely, some large employers in the provinces initiate comprehensive welfare policies which include lodging, medical care, etc. under the influence either of the social doctrine of the catholic church or philantropic ideas issuing of the doctrines of Saint-Simon, Fourrier, Sismondi, Cabet, Owen etc. ... A large number of workers cooperatives also appears. Interestingly, Fonbonne (1988) notes that, generally speaking, endeavours towards improving the lot of the workers are aimed towards life outside of work rather than towards better physical conditions of work or improvement of the place of work. The plant is "a place to produce", and little or nothing is done to make it cleaner, easier to operate in or more convenient for employees, not to mention comfortable or attractive. Its organisation is dictated by the imperatives of production and technology and no thought is given to the human resources implicitly supposed to adapt to it.

Shortly after 1905, selection tests are used in the railways, Paris transport system and Peugeot. Taylorism is introduced and generalized in automobile manufacturing between 1907 and 1919 (Fonbonne 1988). Fonbonne notes that most employers-owners or chief executive officers of firms carry out themselves the personnel function or delegate it to the works manager. Personnel management as such has not yet really emerged in theory or in fact. However, around the 1910's, major banks create a personnel office.

---

[1] Although in practice the two systems do not exactly follow each other in time. Direct employment of a workforce by some employers and inside contracting by others have co-existed, however the first system becomes more prevalent. On this point, for the case of England see Gospel 1983.

[2] The exact legal mechanism is more complex, but as long as he abides by public order and existing statutory law, which was minimal in the time of early industrialization, the employer can freely impose what he wants. The importance of shop rules in French Industrial Relations is paramount. They often unilaterally regulate issues which, in other systems would have belonged to the realm of collective bargaining. Their scope was reduced by statutory law only in 1982.

The Renault automobile company has an existing one in 1915 (Fonbonne 1988).

A second period opens after World War I. Statutory law on all aspects of the employment relationship increases in volume. Vocational training becomes compulsory. The use of testing spreads as well as company's welfare programs. Industrial action is widespread. In answer to these new problems, large companies and plants in increasing numbers create a specialized personnel function, generally with a mixed set of tasks assigned to it. Often called "general services", it is in charge of the care of buildings and grounds, of monitoring entrance and exit of the employees, of time keeping and clocking-in, of guarding the premises to avoid theft and and fires. In some industries, where employment is stable, like banking, elaborate files begin to be kept on individual employees (Fonbonne 1988).

The popular front of 1936 opens a new era with a host of demands led by a powerful and growing labor movement. A wave of plant occupations and strikes violently shakes up ill-prepared and ill-organized employers who had not foreseen these events in the last. They give in with a feeling of defeat. Elected employee representatives, paid vacations, the 40 hours working week, a reform of collective agreements, etc. ... suddenly appear. The need for a specialized service to manage all these new issues and to monitor social affairs and problems is now obvious. Its role is summed up by "hiring, payroll, personnel administration, and relationship with the employee delegates".[3]

After the interruption of the war and occupation, a new wave of statutory laws institutes employment offices, works councils, a comprehensive system of social security, the right to strike is enshrined into the preamble of the new constitution, etc. ...

A host of new ideas spreads as well. The national association of personel managers is created in 1947.

The period of 30 years of extensive growth which follows sees the modern system of French labor relations take shape. The enterprises face new issues such as company run training, regulated by several statutes, in company communication, placement, performance evaluation, promotion systems, wages administration, job evaluation, industrial relations and collective bargaining (mostly at industry level, but with remarquable exceptions company-wide).

A consultant's model for the organization of the personnel function presented in 1953 (Fonbonne 1988) includes the following subdivisions: Statistics, General studies, Training and internships, Labor law, Welfare, Managerial employees, employees' information and secretariat.

---

[3] id quoting Dugué Mac Carthy 1963.

In 1959, a survey finds four types of roles held by personnel managers: a traditional one (hiring, manpower management, job evaluation, discipline and work rules administration, personnel administration, relations with employees), an enlarged one with nex tasks (training, information and communication, organization of the enterprise), a newly added one (social security, welfare and administration of retirement plans, conditions of life at work, medecine at work), and a marginal one, often but not only in small and medium size undertakings (control of time worked by employees, responsability for cash, guards, fire-safety). At the outset of the 1960's, Fonbonne (1988) notes five characteristics of what is still called the personnel function: It is organized in a growing number of enterprises, its scope of action includes business policy issues, it has reached the status of a direction inside the enterprise, personnel directors have a higher level of formal training (45% hold a university degree), initial legal training is no longer the dominant one for them (32%) but it remains important and is always a necessary complement.

In 1962, 1606 enterprises employ 500 employees or more (5415 employ above 200 and 34 above 5000) (Fonbonne 1988). A survey in 1961 carried out on a sample of 281 enterprises finds that all enterprises above 5000 employees have a personnel management direction, as well as 92% of the enterprises between 1000 and 4999, 75% of the ones between 500 and 999 and 72% of the ones above 500.[4]

In May 1968, a new shock wave shakes the French labor relations system, unforeseen by neither employers or government nor unions: Between 9 and 10 millions wage earners go on strike with an estimated 150 000 000 working days lost. New issues are "discovered": immigrant workers, women in the labor force, unskilled and semi skilled workers, students, etc. A general society crisis with interrogations on the role of the major institutions develops.

A formal university degree in personnel management appears for the first time in 1968. Several institutions dealing with the reciprocal roles of the enterprise and its personnel are created in this wake. Job enrichment, control of the multinationals, the social role of the enterprise are the issues of the day. A flow of statutory labor and social law of an unprecedented size follows.

This period ends with the first oil crisis of 1974, which terminates the period of continuous economic growth. The personnel function is now well defined. An analysis of its role[5] defines 3 functions: The social administration of the contract of employment, the management of people (shared with line

---

[4] id. quoting an unpublished MBA thesis by Richert R., Univ. of Texas.

[5] id. quoting Barthod 1976.

management), social development (the analysis of the dissatisfactions needs and expectations of the employees). A new legislative flow follows the arrival of a government of the left to power for the first since 23 years.

A study of 16 large enterprises and groups carried out in 1986 notes that the personnel function is well integrated in the enterprise and its scope is ceaselessly enlarged ... particularly as it regards human ressources management, internal communication, consultant to line management for social development. The personnel manager has become the human ressources manager and its rôle is now considered "strategic". A 1984 survey[6] notes that 74% of the personnel directors interviewed sit on the Management Committee.

Parallely, though, the nature of the function has changed. Galambaud (1983: 57) notes that its future is more uncertain. As its role has grown in importance, the Human Resource Manager has become less of a "professional" and more of a part of the management team. For instance, a lesser percentage of those managers are issued from initial training in personnel, and the technical "personnel" part of their role has less part in their function. At the same time, the ideology of the role of the function produced by the professional organizations of human resource managers is more diffuse. The human resource manager cannot longer be the neutral independant expert specialist in the labor field, that he was up to the 70's. If he is now part of the management team, he has to take sides, and top management hires more a shared ideological position than technical or "professional" knowledge.

Interestingly enough, however, the 1986 study quoted above finds that the human resource management policies of the 16 large enterprises and groups surveyed are "seldom written down and even less often made public", besides, "job definitions are few and, when they exist rarely updated; their usefulness is doubted". This apparent contradiction may be explained by some of the later developments.

2. Objective Specific Aspects of the French Scene which Have an Impact on Human Resource Management

There are several objective characteristics of the French industrial relations system which must be briefly outlined, for they constrain human resource management at the enterprise level:

---

[6] quoted in Liaisons sociales, mensuel, N° 36, February 1989.

As it is already clear from the brief historical development outlined above, but should be underlined, France is a country where in labor law, the foremost source of law is constituted by statutes. Multiple acts accumulated over the years regulate in minute details many issues which, in many other systems, would fall in the realm of collective bargaining. A minimum legal floor of regulation is therefore applicable to all wage earners on issues such as duration of work, lenght of vacation, overtime rates, amount of severance pay, required training, etc. ... Collective agreements, in principle but with a few qualified exceptions since 1982, can only add benefits to that floor. This can be done at several levels: national industry, industry wide, regional, local, corporate, plant, and down to the individual contract of employment which conceivably contain additional individual benefits. All those collective agreements, as well as the shop-rules, whose scope is now limited, are embedded in the individual contract of employment.

This system has the dual effect of tying human resource management in a tight network of legal constraints, theoretically applicable under criminal penalties, and of reducing the scope of collective bargaining. A 1982 effort to revitalize collective bargaining, at both industry and plant level, charac- teristically by making it compulsory under the shape of a duty to bargain (but not to reach agreement), met only with mixed results as it will be discussed below.

This low importance of collective bargaining is not helped by the increas- ing weakness of unions. Wage earners' level of unionization is now estimated between 9 and 12%, down from a post war peak of 28% in the mid seventies.

A second notable characteristic is the influence of the state, materialized by government intervention. Statutory law regulates not only normative matters, such as the relative rights and duties of the parties as social partners, but also substantives issues which would be bargained freely by the parties in other systems. Government intervention has been materialized under many forms besides statutes, such as wages freezes, applicable to the private sector, etc. ... The government is also the main employer in the country, either directly through its public servants, or indirectly through a still large nationalized sector, where it rules wages and conditions directly. Most nationalized companies are tightly controlled by the relevant public au- thorities.

A third characteristic is the centralized nature of the country. A serious effort of the previous governments notwithstanding, most important public decisions are still taken or approved at central level, in Paris. The habit of centralization is hard to break for its dates back to pre revolutionnary days, where the kings "missi dominici" carried his instructions all over the country. Understandably, given the weight of the public sector in the economy and the pervasive presence of the state, the private sector has followed this mode of organization.

A fourth notable characteristic is the existence, in both the private sector and large segments of the public sector, of a complex system of employee representation. Given that unions as such did not get a "de jure" foothold on the shop floor before 1968, a system of elected employee representation had been set up by statutes. Most of those bodies are elected on lists sponsored by the unions at the first ballot, with free candidacy in a second ballot if no majority is reached at the first. Some others are appointed by the elected representatives. In a incorporated company, the following representatives do exist, by statutory law: An elected enterprise committee, which appoints delegates to the enterprise committee if there are several establishments, themselves appointing delegates to the group or holding level consultative group committee; elected personnel delegates at establishment level, a health, safety and conditions of work committee, appointed partly by the establishment committee; delegates of the enterprise committee to the board of directors, with consultative voice only. To this it now must be added union delegates appointed by the union and union delegates near the establishment and enterprise committee. The number of the latter can be multiplied by the number of representative union centres (five at national level, possibly more at local level). Except on mostly minor points, the role of these bodies is mostly consultative or informative. They have no code-termination powers. However, dealing with them represents a significant part of the time of a human resource manager. It should be added that the enterprise committes run a large number of social and welfare activities to the benefit of the employees.

Finally, it should be added that there is an extensive welfare system covering health insurance, old age benefits, unemployment, family allowances, workmen compensation, etc. ... It is run jointly by representatives of employers and unions. The financing is insured by a wage based contribution paid partly by the employer (50 to 60% of the wage paid to the employee) and the employee (18 to 25% of the gross wage received).

3. Subjective Characteristics of the French National Culture Having an Impact on Human Resource Management

Two elements should be underlined here, but they are of a more subjective nature and harder to document in other ways than inference because of the lack and/or inappropriateness hard data.

They are the sociological phenomenon of the prevalence of the French "vicious bureaucratic circle", and the colonization of the all of the top administrative, political and nationalized sector jobs, as well as many of the private sectors ones, by the handful of graduates "summa cum laude" of some elite post graduate schools schools.

3.1 The French Bureaucratic Vicious Circle

It has been evidenced by the remarkable work of Crozier (1963): The notion of vicious circles as conceived as multiple actions of individuals in organizational settings producing unintended consequences is not new and is due to MERTON's analysis of the bureaucracy (Merton 1936), but Crozier develops, enlarges the concept and proposes a model from it, out of which he illustrates some traits which are characteristic of French culture and which have a direct influence upon human resource management ...

Our own understanding of Crozier's model can be summarized as follows: The key to an understanding of the model are the concepts of authority relationships and conflict situations into which they feed-back. The attitude towards authority is determined by basic cultural traits, closely linked to institutional patterns such as class relationship and the educational system. The French conception of authority, by everyone at the top or below, is absolutist, omnipotent. The concept of check and balances, of due process, of institutionalized countervailing power is foreign to it. Combined with the other French cultural value of rationality, authority, seen from the top, seeks to impose substantive rules to bring about order, symmetry and harmony over the environment that it rules. Because of its absolute nature, it cannot be shared or compromised and must remain sovereign, actually and symbolically. Procedural rules are unneccessary because the authority is absolute. Seen from below, such a mode of authority is threatening and to be avoided. Combined with the other French cultural values of independance, individual autonomy, and search for security, the goal of subordinates is to gain freedom from interference and to maintain autonomy. The way to do this is not to have to deal directly with the superior. To do so is inavoidably to acknowledge one's total dependance. Together with avoidance, the only protection is the solidarity of the peer group, where one can hide and enjoy its potential for counter pressure. The only other alternatives to avoidance are total conflicts, which are either destructive or must be negated from above, for its authority is absolute and cannot conceivably be challenged, or absolute submission, which the cultural trait of independance and autonomy prevents from below.

The first characteristic of the French model is therefore the fear of face to face conflict, and perhaps more generally an avoidance of face to face relationships between superior and subordinates.

The organizational solution to this dilemma rests upon the creation of rules: From below, one obeys the rules and thus does not submit to the absolute authority of an individual and as a result protects one's independance. From the top, edicting the rules affirms the capacity of sovereign power. Those rules are impersonal, which from below reinforces the sense of following an abstract order and not bowing to absolutism; and from above follows the rational model of a "one best way" of ruling absolutely over one's domain without having to be bothered to make unnecessary allowances for individual peculiarities. Impersonal rules by necessity imply that people who decide must remain far above those who are affected by their decisions. Thus the power is centralized at the top; and below, the impersonal rules define strata of subordinates with precisely defined borders.

Those values, characteristic of the French culture, can be applied to Crozier's classic model of the Bureaucratic vicious circle, which, when complete, presents the following traits: Impersonality of the rules, centralization of decisions, isolation of strata of employees and development of parallel power relationships.

Theoretically the central power is all powerful, but in each strata, under the conditions of respecting the impersonal rules, individuals enjoy total protection and independance. The only possibility to act from the central power is to add new additional rules, which provide additional shelter inside stratae. The rules need to be impersonal. Therefore the power recedes higher and higher, farther and farther from the knowledge of the elements necessary to take decisions. It must decide without knowing, for it has no primary knowledge of information, and it is in the interest of the subordinates to hide or manipulate information. Its power is hence useless and unavoidably parallel informal power relationship develop.

At the impersonal and intergroup level, there are several other characteristics which accrue from the interpaly of the bureaucratic model and the specific French values, developing trends in organizations which influence human resources management in France: An isolation of the individual, a lack of the development of informal groups, as compared with the US, for instance. This is because in each strata the individual does not need them to be protected, being already under the protection of the impersonal rules applying to his strata. He also knows that such groups threaten the cohesion of the strata and are opposed in principle by its members who enforce control, particularly if such groups cut across strata borders. There is therefore a strong trend towards enforcing strict equalitarianism within strata.

Strata in general tend to favor formal, ritual activities over informal activities. This second trend and the precedent one reinforce each other and result in the absence of cooperation within strata and the repression of attempts within the group at leadership and constructive activities, while producing a general climate of apathy (which helps to escape conflict and to avoid dependance). The exception to the lack of interstrata cooperation is the "delinquent community" aimed at other groups or superiors, which is negative, unstable, not expressed openly, with no leadership in it and strictly equalitarian.

Each strata is isolated, with no overlapping between them, a lack of coordination across them, rigid rules regulating their intercourse.

Devoid of actual power over subordinate strata and protected from interference from superior ones, each strata engages in a struggle for privileges, formal and ritual, with each of the other ones. Real decision making power is concentrated at the very top of the hierarchy.

These factors come into play to the fullest extent in the public sector, sheltered from market pressures and characterized by the statutory nature of the civil service status. However a trend towards them is present in all organizations and affects deeply human resource management. This is particularly true as it regards the interplay of the French cultural traits, present even in situation where various type of constraints prevent a bureaucratic vicious circle to develop.

However, clearly, in the most exposed part of the private sector or in small and medium size business, often family owned, a bureaucratic circle cannot develop and the autocratic rule plays to its fullest extent. This would be specially the case for managers, the more exposed to this authority of top management the higher they get in the hierarchy. This may well extend into large size private companies, where it has been observed that under the spur of the economic development of France and its opening to international competition the traditional trade-off between mid-management and top management had broken down. This old model involved the exchange of unquestioned loyalty and reluctant obedience for safety of employment and guaranteed status.

Schneider (1985) in a review of the literature, around the categories defined by Hofstede (1980) (Uncertainity avoidance, power distance, individualism/collectivism, Masculinity/Feminity), by Kluckholn and Strodtbeck (1961) (Relationship to nature, Human Relationship, Truth and Reality, Human nature, Human activity) and the attitudes towards time and change, finds elements for a significant impact of the French national culture, as compared with the U.S., on strategy formulation by enterprises. Although certain of the conclusions need to be clarified, for the level of conceptualization may be different and the categories not always homogeneous, this confirms that an impact at least similar, if not greater is to be expected in human resource management.

3.2 The French Ruling Elite

The characteristic training of the French elite of administrators and top managers through the highly selective system of the "Grandes Ecoles" is sufficiently well known and has been sufficiently documented in both scientific publications[7] and popular literature[8] to be only recalled here. Let us simply recall that it affects not only the civil service but also the wider area of the public sector and the nationalized companies as well as a significant proportion of the large corporations of the private sector, where a company is "colonized" by a given school and the top jobs reserved for its graduates. Let us also recall that the handful of top graduates of the two or three main schools (ranked among the first few at the exit competitve exam from the school) enjoy an even more privileged status and are virtually guaranteed to finish their career in one of the top positions of the state or at the head of a large public, or even private corporation, through the system of the "grands corps". They move freely from the private to the public sector and/ or into politics, irrelevantly of the majority in power and under the patronage of their elders who guide them along a ladder of carefully selected positions.

A by-product of this system is that a manager rising from the ranks, even with a substantially respectable initial degree, has very few chances to attain the ranks of director, and a civil servant in the same position practically none to reach a similar public job, except for a very few "political appointees", represented by the ruling bureaucracy. In the private sector, Boltanski (1982) illustrates the various career "trajectories" opened to would-be-managers and managers according to their training of origin.

Finally, a perceptive remark of Greyfié de Bellecombe should be kept in mind (1969: 60). He notes that the conception of authority by most of the elite of private and public managers does not change, for the new ones are issued from the same social origin than the old ones and share the same training.

---

[7] See for instance, among many worthwile analysis: Suleiman 1978; Birnbaum 1977; Bordieu 1979.

[8] Among multiple examples see for instance Wickham and Patterson 1983.

4. Changes in the Field of Human Resource Management

4.1 The Impact of the Traditional Features

The precedent remarks should not be constructed as meaning that Human Resource Management in France experiments no change and remains in a time warp set up sometimes in the 1920's. French Society as a whole has experienced tremendous changes since World War II, and unavoidably these changes have had repercussions on human resource management. However, the deep rooted characteristics outlined just above have come to limit and buffer the impact of this change.

For instance, a remarkable study (Trepo 1975 a/b) on the tentative to introduce Management by Objectives in France and the resultant resounding failure[9] puts the blame on the fear of face to face conflict, the way authority is conceived and the mode of selection of top managers. This is illustrated by the fact that on the one hand, subordinate managers who claim for more responsibility, in fact remain passive, look mostly for protection from above and fear to commit themselves on specific objectives. On the other hand, top managers who rule autocratically see the company as a kind of elite school, where to be the boss has to mean to be "the most intelligent one". Therefore subordinates cannot conceivably have valid ideas.

A less theoretical but more recent analysis (Arnoux et Hermel 1985) reports that one of the causes for the failure of quality circles in France is the conflict in values between management which holds traditional ones and the ones underlying the promotion of quality circles: acknowledgement of the expertise of the executants, and their access to information and power as well as the practice of a "micro-negociation" at all levels (which runs contrary, in our interpretation, to the fear of face to face conflict).

Let us also note as a clue that an experienced personnel manager, editor in chief of the journal of the Personnel Managers National Association, when describing the French Personnel Management Scene notes, (Laurioz 1986: 76–79) with may be less theoretical sophistication, but the benefit of a long firsthand experience, the following characteristics: "A quite individualistic national temperament ... A style of management which is fairly

---

[9] This by no means should be understood as meaning that management by objective or evaluation of performance according to a similar system is no longer practiced in France. Only, in many cases the system as practiced is only remotely linked with the objective and the culture that its original promoters foresaw. In other terms in becomes the stake of a different game.

authoritarian and intuitive, preferably cultivating hierarchy and a pyramid shaped organization ... the great lenght enjoyed by the original diploma (of the employee)."

4.2 The Elements of Change

They probably be ascribed to two sources: The legislative changes introduced by the government of the left in 1981 and 1982, after its arrival to power for the first time since 23 years, and a new strategy from the part of the employers and top management.

As far as the first factor is concerned, a general picture has been given of their scope (Caire 1984: 235−57). They were aimed at four areas: regulation of shop rules by restriction of their scope and the disciplanary powers of the employer and right of the employees to express themselves about their conditions of work, reform of the health, safety and conditions of work committees, development of the institutions of employee representation, extension and decentralization of collective bargaining.

A dispassioned and accurate evaluation of the results of the act on collective bargaining has been carried out by Yves Delamotte (1987). The conclusions can safely be more or less transferred into the other areas.

He concludes that at industry level, the act has failed to reinstate collective bargaining in the areas where it had collapsed and that wage agreements both at industry and company level followed governmental and employers associations guidelines (for the first time since world war two, the government managed to contain real wage growth and limit nominal increases at rates below inflation). When agreements were not concluded this gave raise to few conflicts because of the generally low level of mobilisation of the employees.

A new feature is the appearance, made possible by the new act of "concession bargaining agreements", where employment levels stability is exchanged against new and more constraining work schedules. The compulsory negotiation regarding training and the right of employees to express themselves has certainly resulted in an increase in the numbers of agreements, however has had little impact on their substantive provisions besides endorsing the already existing compulsory statutory provisions. The overall summary is that it is probably today the enterprises' social strategy which is the most important factor in the evolution of industral relations in France.

This confirms a relatively widespread[10] impression that the dominant new factor is the appearance of new strategies from the part of employers, jointly

---

[10] See for instance for evidence of that trend in another area than collective bargaining and in another country, respectively: Rojot 1989, as well as an enlarged view in Chelius and Dworkin (forthcoming) and particularly Rojot (forthcoming).

in the field of industrial relations and human resource management. Together[11] with the weakening of unions which we mentioned earlier we believe that this has brought a significant number of top management in companies to integrate industrial relations management within human resources management policies, strategies and tools. Whether this strategy is likely to be successful or not in the long run is another problem,[12] but we consider it a most significant development in the evolution of Human Resources Management. It has taken place within the framework of a renewed influence, an enhanced image and an increased authority of the National Employers Association, the CNPF (see Sellier 1985).

The main elements of this new strategy can be briefly outlined. The key words are probably flexibility and the new justification of managerial authority.[13] Now the emphasis is on the social and economic role of the enterprise as a producer of wealth from which everyone benefits. Galambaud (1983) notes extremely accurately that in the language of the employers' associations and bodies, at least in its public expression, the "owner" (the "patron") disappears and is replaced by the "enterprise" or the "manager". For instance, among multiple other examples, the C.J.P. (Centre des Jeunes Patrons) has become the C.J.D. (Centre des Jeunes Dirigeants). The new managerial practices in the human resource field are therefore legitimized by a new language.

The common denominator of these new practices, flexibility, is imposed by the changes in the environment of business: increased and globalized international competition, the irruption of newly industrialized countries on world markets, the growth of the role of the multinational companies, the shortening of the products' life-cycle and the consequent permanent need for new products, the greater differenciation within product markets, the growing importance of product quality, the volatility in exchange rates and raw material prices, the growth of the services sector, the easy availability of new technology, etc. ...

The new practices issuing from the new strategy can be briefly outlined.

At first there are new practices in manpower management. Even if the extended and systematic applicability of the core-periphery model of management of the work force is questionned[14], there is no doubt that at least

---

[11] There is longer doubt on this point acknowledged by some of the main union centers themselves, however this weakening was questionnable, and questionned as late as the late 1970's and even early in the 1980's, as it was pointed out by Sellier, see Sellier 1989.

[12] For an analysis of the consequence of these new employer and managerial strategies aimed at unions in France see Rojot 1986.

[13] On this second point see Rojot 1986.

[14] See Rojot (forthcoming (b)), on the limits of the core-peripheral model. On the reasons for introducing such innovations at company level see Rojot 1987.

some practices of "externalization", in some sectors of the economy where they were traditonal, have been used increasingly. Such practices include: dismissal for economic reasons, temporary employees, short term employment contracts, part time work, call contracts, subcontracting, contracting out of on site peripheral activities, etc.

Secondly, the agreements related to the duration of work have been multiplied: They include the generalization of shift work, the introduction of night shift, week end shifts, the annualization of the duration of work, modulation of work schedules, etc.

Thirdly, some forms of wage modulation have been introduced. This has taken the shape of profit sharing in many cases, taking advantage of and eventually extending, statutory provisions to that effect, but also of some kind of bonuses or premiums. In the climate of wage moderation described above, wage individualization has also been introduced under various guises: incentives, wage "at risk", etc.

Fourthly, in some large companies this trend towards individualization has been extended to the whole relationship between the employee and the company. Individual career plans have been formulated down to the blue collar level, the relationship employee-manager stressed, the dissatisfaction of the individual employee tracked and eliminated by management, etc.

Fifthly, again in some companies, policies aiming at the better integration of the employee's goals with the objectives of the firm have been devised, using tools like job enrichment and improvement of the quality of life at work, training, pay for knowledge, promotion from within, quality circles (which, in France have known at first a remarkable success, but seem now less in fashion), and now "enterprise projects" which seek to mobilize employees around a single and simple common target, devised by top management (using "just in time", Kanban).

5. Conclusions

Obviously, and as some of the examples pointed out at the beginning of section 4 demonstrate, there is an implicit built-in contradiction between what we have defined as the traditional French values and the value system underlying the use and successful implementation of the new tools of the new human resource management strategy promoted by management.

In the absence of comprehensive surveys of human resource practices, it is difficult to point out towards either the change or the remanence of the traditional values. Individual case studies abound, both of remarkable success of the new strategies, which imply a successful implementation of the new values, and also of resounding failure.

It is, however, possible to point out some interesting elements of evidence. Towards that end we shall briefly review what little, and sometimes contradictory, quantitative evidence is available:

First, the Ministry of Labor issues yearly a detailed and very documented and useful analysis of collective bargaining. The latest one available covers the year 1987 and can be said to confirm the trends outlined by Delamotte and quoted above.

Secondly, the same Ministry issues another analysis of profit sharing agreements. Such agreements are compulsory under a set of conditions, provide for efficient tax penalties when not concluded when those conditions are fulfilled and grant tax advantages to both the company and employees. Therefore their sheer number is not in itself significant of strategic aims by employers. What, however, is significant is the number of agreements signed by companies for which they are not compulsory (mainly those under 100 employees), and the so-called "derogatory" agreements, which provide for additional benefits and more profit sharing and/or employee involvement in profit sharing schemes than the statutory law demands. On December 31st, 1986, 4573 enterprises with less than 100 employees applied a profit-sharing agreement providing results (that is had passed an agreement and had shown enough profit). This represented a percentage of 35,1% of all agreements, in continuing growth (up from 19,6% in 1975). Besides 30,6% of all agreements were derogatory. The law also opens the possibility for another voluntary form of profit sharing by collective agreement with much lesser tax benefits. This is a more flexible form which the parties can shape more easily to their goals than through the cumbersome procedure of "derogatory" agreements. The number of those voluntary agreements had remained low, from 260 in 1974 covering 110000 employees, to 1086 in 1984, covering 335000 employees, and 1303 in 1985, covering 401000 employees. An act of 1986 has facilitated their conclusion and increased the tax benefits. In 1987, a veritable explosion of the number of these agreements took place, 1190 were concluded in this single year, covering 477831 employees. 40% were approved by employees referendum, 34% passed with the work council, and 12% with unions. 85% linked the profit sharing with the yearly income and 14% with productivity.

Thirdly, a survey was carried out in 1987 by the Center for the Study of Income and Costs, on a sample of 100 enterprises employing more than 100 employees, with interesting conclusions (Salaire et Rémunérations 1987). Five industries were covered: automobile, chemicals, textile-clothing, construction and wholesale trade. Some of the results show that, although influenced somewhat by enterprise size, the number of short term employment contracts varied according to industry, from 2,1% in automobile to

10% in wholesale trade. The average turn over was 14%, influenced also by size and industry, from 7 to 22% across industries. Average absenteism was 16 days per year, the smallest in small businesses and wholesale trade and the highest in mid-size enterprises. The percentage of foreign workers varied between 3,5% and 47,1%. Beyond these spot results, the study attempted to draw a typology of human resource management. On the one hand, managers and supervisory staff (cadres) were managed about in the same way across industry, with wage differentials of an individual type, but little differences in averages. The study concluded that they had achieved a "national status" independantly of industry. In all cases, enterprises seemed to aim to fidelize them to benefit from their experience and implication. However, for other categories of employees (workers, white collar, technical staff, foremen, etc. ...), four different types of management strategies were clearly distinguished.

First a "status" one. It was characteristic of large size automobile and chemical and para-chemical companies. They employed a large proportion of managers, engineers and technical staff, a heavy majority of men, few foreign workers. The turnover was low (5%) and unions implanted. Its main features were high wages, low wages differentials, a high level of benefits and welfare and important training expenses relatively equally spread across categories of employees.

Secondly an "organized flexibility" one. It was characteristic of the subcontractors in the automobile industry, smaller firms of medium size in the chemical and industry, smaller firms of medium size in the chemical and para-chemical industry, firms in the textile and wholesale trade. They share some characteristics with the precedent category with a higher turnover and lower, but significant, union presence. Wages are lower with a higher share coming from bonuses and incitatives. Wage differentials are larger, presenteism rewarded, training expenses concentrated on management.

Thirdly, the construction industry is a category by itself. Its characteristics are a high percentage of men, skilled and highly skilled, of foreigners, with a high turnover and low union presence. Wages are relatively low but complemented by benefits and welfare organized at industry level. There are little training expenses.

Finally, the remaining enterprises fit into an "inorganized flexible" category, which contains small size enterprises and some medium size in wholesale trade and textile. It is characterized by low wages, low benefits and welfare, high wages differentials, a heavy turnover, high percentage of women, little union presence.

A fourth element is provided by the publications of the National Agency for the Improvement of the Conditions of Work Directors, considers itself a facilitator, and does gather or publish statistics, it has made public recently (November 3, 1987) a guide containing 500 micro case studies of improvement of Conditions of Work at Plant level, conducted by itself or another organism, of diverse nature and scope. The number itself shows an interest of the enterprises in this area.

A last source out of which we can gather some information from unpublished data has been graciously provided to us specially for the completion of the present paper by the HAYFRANCE company.

The company's field of operations is mostly in the area of consulting on wage systems. A wealth of information can be collected from their studies obtained from surveys of part of their customers.

Two data bases are maintained, one for the managers and managerial staff (cadres), another one for non-managerial supervisory and technical staff and white collar employees. No data concerns blue-collar workers.

The data base for managers covers 220 companies employing more than 65000 managers. The following items are of interest:

In 1987, 37% of the companies sampled granted only individualized wage increases, up from 24% in 1986 and 18% in 1984 (however the trend seems to stabilize in 1988, companies under that system keep it, but few new ones adopt it). 63% grant a mix of general and individualized increases. 3/4 have given bonuses (linked to objectives in 48% of cases) against 2/3 in 1986, among which 32% plan to increase the relative importance of bonuses in wages and 27% to extend the system to non-managerial employees (non-cadres). The percentage of managers promoted was 0 for 33.1%, under 5 for 28%, 5 to 10% for 22%, 10 to 20 for 15.3%.

Seniority bonuses and perquisites, such as company cars, were slowly abandonned, with the exception of employers contributions in a complementary retirement plan, increasingly popular in view of the spectacular fall in the levels of retirement paid amounts (from 70% down to 45% of the wage).

The wage differentials between a top manager (director of a medium size company) and the minimum statutory wage decreased from 17 times to 11.04 times, between the same top manager and a middle manager from 2.66 to 2.57 and between the same middle manager and the minimum wage from 6.4 to 4.3, all from 1968 to 1987.

In general terms, companies sampled foresaw a reinforcement of wage individualization in France, by merit increases for 87% and by bonuses for 51%. Only 1% foresaw an increase in profit-sharing. Regarding flexibility, most companies had pursued or started plans for implementing:

— flexibility in work-time: 63%
— part-time work: 62%
— no change in work time: 22%
— job rotation: 35%
— multi-skilling: 94%

— no change in job content: 11%
— change in mode of pay: 25% (cafeteria approach)
— no change in mode of pay: 75%

74% of the sample declared to have a formalized pay policy. The formalization was effective for managers in 54% of cases, top management only in 14% and all employees in 32%.

38% of the companies had initiated a "company project" around which to mobilize all employees. However, for 24% it was too early to draw conclusions. The rest had noted a result of the project an improvement in the following domains:

— Acceptation by the employees of company's values: 86%
— Absenteism: 52%
— Circulation of information: 63%
— Managerial style: 72%
— Quality spirit: 92%
— Quality of service to customer: 86%
— Speed in answering client's needs: 85%

91% of the sample have a policy of fixing individual objectives to managers. 81% evaluate performance relatively to the objectives and 87% provide for an annual performance evaluation meeting between superior and subordinate.
The following factors are monitored:

— Actual establishment of objectives: 73%
— Actual performance of evaluation meetings: 85%
— company wide level of appreciations: 58%
— division wide level of appreciation: 52%

Finally 28% of companies impose a distribution of the levels of appreciation "under the curve"..

Overall, for 1986, 5% of managers' performance were rated "exceptional", 30% "very good", 56% "normal", 7% "mediocre", and 2% "bad"..

If we consider the non-managerial supervisory and technical staff, together with white collar employees, the following results are to be noted:

84% of companies in the sample granted an automatic yearly bonus of 1/12 of the yearly wage (13th month), 43% a fixed vacation bonus. Seniority bonuses are often provided for by collective agreements for these categories of personnel.

In addition, 45% give variable bonuses. These bonuses were granted upon the following criteria: job-related objectives: 43%, company's income: 33%, productivity: 14%, exceptional work: 52%, other (quality, presenteism, etc.): 29%. The yearly amount of these bonuses varied from a minimum

of 0.8% to a maximum of 12% of the wage. For the years to come the companies (all sample) had the following plans:
increase the variable part of the wage, increase the amount of the bonus in percentage of the wage, apply the variable bonus system to a larger number of employees. For supervisory staff the respective percentages were: 27%, 14%, 86%; for technical staff: 36%, 50%, 60%, and for white-collar employees: 28%, 33%, and 78%.

88% of the sample had compulsory profit-sharing plans and 5% voluntary ones as described above.

All companies but one subsidized the mid-day meal in some way or other, and 76% gave some kind of additonal fringe benefits (among which improved social security contributions: 79%).

76% of companies granted general and individual wage increase and 24% individualized merit increases only (in 1988). 31% plan to systematically increase low wages. In 1987, 98% of companies have globally maintained purchasing power. 13% have systematically done so[15] by general wage increases only, 29% by combining general and individual increases, 50% did it for normal performers only, 2% for high performers only, 6% for low wages only.

Individualized wage increases are linked to performance evaluation in 69% of companies which grant both general and individualized increases and 93% of the ones who give only individualized ones. The criteria are first an evaluation of ability and secondly, by far performance on fixed objectives.

What can be the impact of these new elements on the traditional features of the French model of human resource management?

Indubitably, the new social strategies of enterprises have had an impact: increases in individualization of wages for managers, more segmented modes of manpower management, actions towards improvement of quality of life at work, etc. ... Besides, many enterprises have successfully used the new opportunities opened by the recent changes in statutory law to implement these strategies. For instance, the right to expression, in many cases at plant level, has turned into quality circles, when successfully implemented, and/ or is under the wing of management. Worktime flexibility is another case in point.

On the other hand, a sharp distinction, in the Hayfrance data between what is taking place at managerial and non-managerial level clearly seems

---

[15] Even though there are yearly negociations, they concern only minima the most often. Because of wage drift the actual wages are maintained higher. This has been opposed unsuccessfully by the unions which have seldom succeeded to impose negociated actual wages, but the most often must be content with negociating percentage increeases of minima.

to outline two partially divergent trends in the treatment of the two groups by enterprises. Opinions held by top management in the survey also seem to throw a more realistic light on purely statistical data, as for instance the real meaning of the rise in the number of voluntary profit-sharing schemes in 1987. A distinction could probably also be drawn between a group of more progressive companies and others.

Faced by these contradictory indications, we are bound to conclude that it is still too early to find out if the impact of the new elements in human resource management will significantly transform the traditional French features.

References

Arnoux, J. P. and P. Hermel (1985): Cercles de qualité et fonctionnement de l'entreprise: apports limites et effets pervers, *Direction et Gestion*, no. 6.

Barthod, M. (1976): Structure de la fonction personnel et innovation sociale dans l'entreprise, *Personnel*, no. 192, nov. – dec. 1976.

Birnbaum, P. (1977): *Les sommets de l'Etat: Essai sur l'élite au pouvoir en France*, Paris.

Boltanski, L. (1982): *Les cadres*, Paris.

Bourdieu, P. (1979): *La distinction*, Paris.

Caire, G. (1984): Les lois Auroux, *Relations Industrielles*, vol. 39, no. 2: 235 – 257.

Chelius, J. and J. Dworkin (eds.) (forthcoming): *Reflections on Transformation in Industrial Relations*, New Brunswick, N.Y.

Crozier, M. (1963): *Le phénomène bureaucratique*, Paris.

Delamotte, Y. (1987): La loi et la négociation collective en France, reflexions sur l'espérience 1981 – 1985, *Relations Industrielles*, vol. 42, no. 1.

Fonbonne, J. (1988): Pour un historique de la Fonction Personnel, in: Weiss, D. et al., *La fonction Ressources Humaines*, Paris: pp 1.

Galambaud, G. (1983): *Des hommes à Gérér*, Paris.

Gospel, H. F. (1983): The Development of Management Organizations in Industrial Relations: A Historical Perspective, in: H. F. Gospel and C. G. Littler (eds.), *Managerial Strategies and Industrial Relations*, London: pp 3.

Greytié de Bellecombe, L. (1969): La participation des travailleurs à le gestion des entreprises en France: données de base du problème, *Bulletin de l'Institut International d'Etudes Sociales*, no. 6: 60.

Hostede, G. (1980): *Cultural Consequences*, Beverly Hills, CA.

Kluckholn, F. R. and F. L. Strodtbeck (1961): *Variations in Value Orientations*, Evanston Ill.

Kochan, T. A., H. C. Katz and R. B. McKersie (1986): *The Transformation of American Industrial Relations*, New York.

Laurioz, J. (1989): Specifities of the French Socio-Economic Scene, *Personnel*, no. 306: 76 – 79.

Mac Carthy, O. (1963): *La fonction personnel*, Paris: Editions d'Organisation.

Merton, R. K. (1936): The Unanticipated Consequences of Purposive Social Action, *American Sociological Review*, vol. I: 894 – 904.

Rojot, J. (1986): The Development of French Employers Policies towards Unions, *Labour and Society*, vol. 11, no. 1: pp 1.

Rojot, J. (1987): Accords collectifs et Flexibilité de la main d'oeuvre, *Les cahiers de la Fondation Europe et Société*, January, no. 4.

Rojot, J. (1989): Employers' Response to Technological Change, in: A. Gladstone et al. (eds.), *Current Issues in Labour Relations*, Berlin – New York 29 – 41.

Rojot, J. (forthcoming a): A View from Abroad, in: J. Chelius and J. Dworkin (eds.), opus cit.: *Reflections on Transformation in Industrial Relations*, New Brunswick.

Rojot, J. (forthcoming b): *Report to the OECD's Manpower and Social Affaires Committee*, Paris: OECD.

Salaire et Rémunérations (1987): Doc. no. 87, Paris. Centre d'Etude des Revenus et des Couts.

Schneider, S. C. (1985): Strategy Formulation: The Impact of National Culture: The Case of France, *Pace University Working Papers*, Juli, no. 48.

Sellier, F. (1985): Economic Change and Industrial Relations in France, in: H. Juris, M. Thompson and W. Daniels (eds.), *Industrial Relations in a Decade of Economic Change*, Madison: pp 177.

Suleiman, E. (1978): *Elites in French Society: the Politics of Survival*, Princeton.

Trepo, G. (1975 a): Mise en place d'une D.P.O.: Le role crucial de la direction, *Direction et Gestion*, 1: pp 25.

Trepo, G. (1975 b): Participation: un douloureux constant d'échec, *Entreprise*, mars, no. 1020: pp 46.

Wickham, A. and M. Patterson (1983): *Les carriéristes*, Paris.

Human Resource Management in the Federal Republic of Germany

Peter Conrad and Rüdiger Pieper

1. Introduction

Theorizing about personnel, personnel functions and work behavior (in Germany) comprises both a long tradition and a short scientific history. Current status of the field personnel management and human resource management can only be adequately understood by an overview of its origins. To outline the main characteristics of modern personnel management is no easy undertaking (Gaugler 1988). The number of publications, the diversity of conceptual schemes and approaches on which theoretical and empirical research are based, together with the growing number of research topics and issues on the one hand indicate liveliness of the field and deep interest dedicated to the subject by a growing number of scholars, while on the other hand a comprehensive and unbiased overview of the different theoretical traditions in the field, their presumed contingency factors and the new conceptual inventions and their ramifications is an intricate matter, within the constraints of editorial space. We have therefore confined our analysis to a short historical overview and a description of basic approaches and recent trends in personnel and human resource management in West Germany, plus an enumeration of the most important contingency factors. The main here is mainly to refer to recent reviews and monographs, each of them often containing detailed analyses and quotations of relevant literature, which could be of specific value for more specialized research questions.

The long term domination of personnel management by human relations approaches has decreased drastically during the last 10 years (Staehle 1988 a); the most recent changes from personnel management to human resource management signify changes in concept and practice, apparently theoretical approaches lagging behind the practice of personnel in industry (Mahoney and Deckop 1986). Most appealing seem approaches of integrating personnel management into strategic and cultural frameworks (e. g.

Drumm 1989) also strongly pointing to individual qualifications and personnel development (Thom 1986 b, Weber 1985) as decisive success factors in globalized markets.

In the first section we shall discuss historical and conceptual aspects of personnel functions and management. We shall make abriet outline of basic approaches and recent trends, building personnel management into human resource management. The second section discusses contingency factors upon the development of themes, schemes and practices of the personnel domain.

2. Historical Background

2.1 Early Theorizing

Work and work behavior as central categories of modern personnel management approaches (Neuberger 1985) were discussed in philosophical and theoretical perspectives long before personnel and personnel functions became part of scientific scrutiny in business administration (e. g. Kißler 1985, Eggebrecht et al. 1980). From a historical standpoint, the personnel function − as a specialized activity as well as part of the management process in general − has changed in response to influences from and changes in technology and economy, industrial reorganization, societal factors like prevailing values and philosophical systems on human behavior at work (Tyson 1987, Remer and Wunderer 1977); additionally, at the organizational level, different management styles in handling the human factor must be discerned (for historical examples, see: Eggebrecht et al. 1980: 206−220).

During the (first) industrial revolution, radical changes in the work process and the concept of human work occured. On the one hand, work was no longer considered a slave's duty but a means to human self actualization. Mental work was awarded with higher social status than manual work. Work moral and work attitudes became fully accepted socially. On the other hand, the individual potential to work became a good, negotiable on the labor market. The laborer came into existence (Weitbrecht and Berger 1985). Technologically seen, the building up of the machine-tool industry meant the prerequisite to the production of modern means of production. Technological innovations improved productivity by machine-paced production methods (e. g. cotton and spinning machines), allowed for improved exploitation of raw materials (e. g. coke oven) and better transformation of energy (e. g. steam engine). Economically seen, higher investments into equipment were necessary and a higher cost for stock keeping resulted. Industrial organizations increased in size. High economic pressure was put on organizations to ensure regularity of production. This implied appropriate measures to "fit" the work force into the constraints of factory work. Predictable, rational and comprehensible work behavior had to be procured or created and trained. Insofar as technological innovations and economic constraints demanded changes in behavior, attitudes, and sentiments as well as structural innovations in organizations. This adjustment to the requirements of industrial production, plus the need to establish conformity of personnel, must be considered as starting points of the personnel function in a managerial perspective. Regularity of attendance, presence of duty and adaptation to the mechanical work rhythm had to be ensured through managerial action. Psychological concentration, vigilance and a certain resistance to repetitiveness of task behavior had to be trained and were in need of control. In organizational terms, substitutes of hierarchical leadership integrated control functions into technology (Eggebrecht et al. 1980); the integration of control functions into specific jobs could be observed together with combining control functions by creating supervisory duties. The shaping of sentiments, attitudes and behavior was at least partly built on prior societal experiences from monastic life (Treiber and Steinert 1980) and the evolution of organizational type and structures, typical of historical eras, such as the quilds and crafts (see e. g. Kieser 1984). Different management styles and philosophies in influencing personnel could be observed at the organizational level (Eggebrecht et al. 1980).

High division of labor, miserable working and living conditions, their detrimental effects on the physical, psychological and social well-being of large parts of the work force and the uneven distribution of wealth and power in society ultimately led to the foundation and strengthening of political and social organizations demanding radical reforms. Industrial conflicts became institutionalized with the state being slowly integrated as a third party in the industrial relations system (Weitbrecht and Berger 1985). The young industrial society became the culture medium of modern labor laws and conventions (Rüthers 1973). Legal reforms granting more rights and security to the individual worker were initially implemented to weaken social democratic and trade union movements (Grebing 1976); proving unsuccessful as a means of political manoeuvering: these reforms must be considered decisive in improving working and living conditions. Politically and socially conscious entrepreneurs implemented reforms on the company level (e. g. Franz Brandts, Ernst Abbé), social aspects of the personnel function came to be represented strongly by trade union. The increase in the division of work and tasks and the separation of mental from manual work produced new and higher needs for coordination, resulting in the change of management functions. Externally induced legal reforms had to be absorbed by the single organization and the political, ethical and legal restrictions to further expand average working time lead to the intensified use of human resources. The human work potential and its organizational and psychological integration came under close scrutiny from scientific management approaches and applied psychological research (Hinrichs 1981).

Scientific management integrated industrial engineering (time and motion studies), motivation (pay as motivating factor), organizational and coordination aspects (division of mental and manual work) and ideological engineering successfully to boost individual and organizational outcomes. F. W. Taylor's "shop management" was translated into German in 1908 and the principles of scientific management were popularized by G. Schlesinger. The "Reichsausschuß für Arbeitszeitermittlung (Refa)" — today "Verband für Arbeitsstudien" — was finally founded in 1924.

Psycho-technical and psycho-physiological approaches to the analysis of work behavior developed more or less simultaneously with scientific management. Research on vigilance, individual differences in reaction to work stimuli and strict experimental methods in the analysis of human behavior at work characterized industrial psychology in these days. The "Institut für Arbeitsphysiologie" was founded in 1931, strongly influencing research for almost half a century (Ackermann 1979). The consequences for the personnel function at the turn of the century can be summarized as follows:

- core concepts of job design and re-design are developed
- ancestors of modern motivational theories emerge
- psycho-physiological and mental aspects of work behavior come under close scientific analysis
- selection and training of workers and the development of instruments to achieve these goal become necessary.

Job context and individual differences in work performance develop into domains of scientific and applied management interest. Yet a rather unsystematic compilation of technical, administrative and juridical problems to handle the personnel function prevails, lacking an integrative conceptual basis, already available in more nature scientific disciplines (Remer/Wunderer 1977: 745).

Towards the end of the century, business administration became established as an economic science (Schneider 1985) serving theoretical as well as applied managerial problems (Gaugler 1982). Cost and benefit of human work behavior were emphasized in an organizational perspective analysis of expenditures (Gaugler 1982, Potthoff 1988). At more or less the same time scientific management, profit sharing in industry and the length of the working week were critically reviewed by business administration writers. The development of conceptual schemes to a refined and more adequate analysis of human work as a productive factor progresses (for a comprehensive overview see e. g. Wächter 1981).

Around the turn of the century, personnel managment had obviously become a functional necessity of major organizational relevance. It was identified as a field of practice, requiring specialized attention (Mahoney and Deckop 1986: 224); organizational differentiation of the personnel function remained low as yet, being allocated only a small capacity of independent choice and action. The strong increases in the number of employment contracts and technological innovations made refined hiring practicies necessary; personnel allocation became better organized at the company level and early approaches to procurement and planning of staff were implemented, due to rising labor cost (Remer/Wunderer 1977: 743). Scientifically seen, applied psychological research and scientific management approaches started proving practical utility; the analysis of work in terms of economic theory and as part of the newly institutionalized business administration discipline pointed to intrinsic peculiarities of human work and social interactions in the factory. Human work was no longer analyzed in cost terms only, but as a productive individual and social potential (see e. g. Gaugler 1982, Krell 1988, Niklisch 1932, Wächter 1981), thus laying the foundations for a further integration of behavioral science approaches in later development stages of personnel and human resource management (Ackermann 1979, Ackermann/Reber 1981).

The end of World War I and the constitutional reforms brought about by the Weimar Republic influenced personnel management on different levels. Democratic rights were established in society, labor and working conditions changed (e. g. reduction of the average working week to 48 hours; extension of social security benefits; increase in number of female employees in trade and industry), codetermination was implemented at shop floor level (Betriebsrätegesetz 1920). The industrial relations system underwent modifications with the state guaranteeing and enforcing results of collective bargaining.

Before industrial sociology was applied in empirical research and influenced managerial thinking and action, group production methods were discussed (Hellpach and Lang 1922) and social-psychological concepts were applied in analyzing and smoothening industrial and organizational conflict (de Man 1927). These approaches generally took a critical stance towards scientific management thinking, trying to overcome atomistic perspectives of job and work design by integrating social and cultural factors. It was more than a decade later that industrial sociology was most commonly illustrated through the Hawthorne studies (Roethlisberger and Dickson 1939), addressing issues of social interaction and group functions.

Economic depression and wide spread political and social turmoil strengthend the Nazi party when it came into power. Between 1933 and 1945,

Nazi ideology exploited and partially perverted concepts about social integration like *Betriebsgemeinschaft* und *Werksgemeinschaft* (Gaugler 1982; for a detailed overview see: Hinrichs 1981 and Krell 1988). Leader-follower ideology became predominant and employees were considered "soldiers of work". Political and trade union organizations were liquidated and compulsorily integrated into the Nazi *Deutsche Arbeitsfront*.

Essential theoretical and conceptual developments towards personnel and human resource management as part of business administration started after World War II (Gaugler 1982). Democratic rights were reinstalled, codetermination was implemented at the shop floor level as well as at the board level and the economy developed on an upward trend. Since then, the personnel function and its scientific treatment has been subjected to a variety of developments and changes (for an overview see: Staehle 1989).

2.2 Analysis of the Personnel Function as Part of Business Administration Approaches

After World War II, several journals on personnel and personnel management were founded or re-edited, all of them characterized by a strong practitioner orientation. Systematic and theoretical approaches were rather rare and could only be found in some handbooks and monographs (Staehle and Karg 1981). Separate and independent from psycho-technical engineering approaches, problems of personnel management came under closer scrutiny in business administration. Theorizing was either centered around production and cost theory (Wächter 1981) or integrated into separate analyses on administrative and organizational functions (Ackermann and Reber 1981). Tendencies to institutionalize the scientific analysis of personnel through refinement of conceptions and theoretical approaches improved steadily, while empirical studies into business practice in the personnel domain illustrated the lasting strong ties between personnel management as an applied science and organizational practice (Gaugler 1982).

2.3 Personnel Management as a Business Administration Discipline

Though Schmalenbach had suggested as early as 1947 establishing personnel as a business administration subdiscipline, it took till 1961, when the first chair in personnel management was founded and curriculums were revised, to increase emphasis on personnel administration and management (Chair of Personnel Management and Labor Sciences, A. Marx, University of

Mannheim). Also in 1961, the Academy of German speaking Professors in Business Administration dedicated their annual conference to the analysis of work and pay, with personnel management gaining further credit in the scientific community (Gaugler 1982, Wächter 1982, Ackermann and Reber 1981). In 1973, the Academy established its professional division on personnel (initiated by Gaugler), thus indicating the fast growing number of researchers in the personnel domain. The division allowed for a regular discussion in a wide array of personnel and personnel related problems. Increased emphasis was put on the theoretical contribution to demonstrate and establish conceptual autonomy and on multi level perspectives to integrate relevant research traditions in micro- and macro-organizational behavior (Ackermann and Reber 1981, Staehle and Karg 1981). Numerous textbooks and reviews on personnel management were published (for a comprehensive overview see e.g. Ackermann 1979, Gaugler 1975, 1982, Staehle and Karg 1981). Publications like the "Handwörterbuch des Personalwesens" (Handbook on Personnel), edited by Gaugler (1975), the "Handwörterbuch des öffentlichen Dienstes. Das Personalwesen (Handbook on Public Administration. Personnel), edited by Bierfelder (1976) and the proceedings on personnel and social perspectives in business administration (Linz 1976), edited by Reber in 1977, demonstrated both consolidation of theoretical knowledge and liveliness in controversial and critical discussion in numerous topics.

2.4 Basic Approaches

Personnel management as a scientific field contains numerous approaches for analysing, classifying and synthesizing practical as well as theoretical domains of interest. Although textbooks cannot be considered fully valid indicators, personnel management might be characterized through its high degree of homogeneity, simultaneously lacking uniformity in concepts and approaches, applied to analyzing the wide range of themes (Gaugler 1982: 295; see also Ende 1982, Hentze 1986, Oechsler 1988, Scholz 1989, Wunderer 1975, Wunderer/Mittmann 1983). Main foci of interest are:

— personnel planning
— procurement of personnel, selection and training
— personnel assessment and development
— personnel discharge and displacement
— pay, fringe benefits and incentive systems
— leadership and motivation
— organizational structuring, job design and redesign
— informational aspects on personnel (Staehle 1988 a).

Publications also deal with behavioral and social sciences approaches basic to human and organizational behavior (e. g. Ackermann and Reber 1981), discuss instruments and procedures for organizational manpower planning (e. g. Drumm and Scholz 1983) as well as decision making in and about personnel management (e. g. Hentze 1986, Türk 1978). Research methods are critically reviewed and adapted to the specific constraints and goals of an applied science (Martin 1988).

Selecting between conceptual schemes as analytical tools inevitably implies differential credit to phenomena coming under scrutiny; the selection of a basic framework indicates whether personnel is analyzed, for example, more in a conflict or socially harmonious perspective (Oechsler 1988: 11 – 12).

Three basic approaches can be distinguished (Wächter 1979; for a more detailed partition see e. g.: Hentze 1986, Scholz 1989, Ackermann and Reber 1981):

- work as a productive factor
- applied behavioral sciences approaches
- conflict approaches.

The framework of *work as a productive factor* is closely linked to Gutenberg (1951/1983) and his concept of treating economic organizations in terms of combining input goods, like human work and material resources, into goods and service outcomes. Human behavior at work is modelled in respect with micro-economics, explicitly neglecting behavioral phenomena for reasons of clarity of analysis. The approach is partly based on scientific management thinking by separating manual from mental work activities strictly. This concept was criticized strongly on normative grounds (Staehle 1975), but still remains prominent as a means of theory building and economic analyses of personnel (Oechsler 1988).

The *applied behavioral sciences approaches* nowadays belong to the most familiar and widespread integrating concepts from psychology, sociology, system thinking and macro-organizational behavior into multi-level schemes for exploring and designing managerial and organizational influences on efficiency and effectiveness. Behavioral decision theory (Heinen 1976, Kirsch 1977), inducement contribution theories (Kupsch and Marr 1978), motivational approaches to human work behavior and systems theory as conceptual integrating device are considered of major importance.

Conflict approaches are centered around the description, analysis and explanation as well as management of conflicts and their functional and dysfunctional consequences in organizations. The management of conflict approaches (Marr and Stitzel 1979) analyzes conflicts between individual needs and aspirations and organizational purposes as structural elements in and of organizational life. The mutual adjustment of conflicting interests in organizations is considered to achieve long term individual and organizational success (Marr and Stitzel 1979: 20). The labor-based analysis of business administration ("Arbeitsorientierte Einzelwirtschaftslehre", Projektgruppe im WSI 1974) describes conflicting interests of labor and capital in relation to the organizational personnel function. The role and function of trade unions and their representatives in organizational decision-making, codetermination, quality of working-life and analyzing normative problems in applying scientific knowledge to industrial settings are major areas of interest (see: Chmielewicz 1975, Projektgruppe im WSI 1974, Stoll 1979).

2.5 Recent Trends

Some basic shifts in the orientation of personnel management have taken place during the last 20 years, mainly in the publications of US authors (see e. g. Mahoney and Deckop 1986), which, with a certain time lag, influenced theory building in European and German approaches (Staehle 1988 a). The human resource focus was first elaborated by Yoder in 1959, but only reached broader popularity through Miles, when his famous article on "Human Relations or Human Resources?" was published in the Harvard Business Review in 1965 (see also Miles 1975). This change in terms indicated a shift in perspectives: People were viewed as resources by management and no longer predominantly as cost factors. Human capital theory and behavioral sciences approaches combined into the new breed of frameworks and approaches summarized under the human resource management label (Staehle 1988 a, 1989).

The term "human resource management" should not be used interchangeably with personnel management; mainly because human resource management as a set of different conceptual schemes is symptomatic for the search for over-arching constructs and basic frameworks. Evidently widespread agreements exists about classical research domains in personnel management (Gaugler 1982); controversy remains on the other hand about relevance and scientific fruitfulness of human resource management being more than a fad and a fashion (for several aspects of this controversy see e. g. Ackermann 1989, Krulis-Randa 1987, Marr 1987, Wunderer 1984).

Exogenous factors determining and demanding change in personnel management towards human resource management are:

— increased competitiveness among triadic industrialized nations as well as newly industrialized countries,
— technological innovations and heightened awareness for human qualifications as strategic components of success,
— changes in the demographic composition of the work force,
— changes in value systems and individual life styles,

- modified aspirations toward work and work life,
- forseeable shortages in labor supply,
- stagnating productivity and quality of goods and services,
- codetermination in multi-national subsidiaries in the Federal Republic of Germany.

Endogenous factors producing a shift in perspective are:

- more mature theoretical approaches for analyses and design in personnel management,
- strong trends towards integrating strategic, organizational structure and human resource thinking,
- highly sophisticated and skilled personnel managers trying to turn theoretical knowledge into applied wisdom

(see e. g. Bühner 1987, Nkomo 1980, Staehle 1988 a, Staffelbach 1986/1987, Wohlgemuth 1987).

Recent approaches in human resource management stress three aspects:

- personnel function and personnel management become closely integrated into strategic framworks,
- organizational and cultural factors become strongly tied to personnel management,
- personnel management itself becomes a top management priority.

The human resource management approaches elaborated by Remer (1978) and Berthel (1979/1989) belong to the first and most comprehensive, to outline and promote the idea of integrating strategic, organizational and personnel dimensions; the former integrates theories of the firm, macro-organizational approaches and general management concepts with personnel administration and hierarchical leadership. The latter views personnel management in terms of intra-organizational systems design and behavior modification for improving individual and economic outcomes. Human resource management is seen as a cross-functional task implying the structuring of organizational systems for coordinating human activities and leadership to influence attitudes and behavior towards work directly.

Bleicher (1984, 1985, 1986, 1987) outlined the integration of strategic personnel management into strategic management with organizational culture as the social integration device for harmonizing conflicting interests. Changes in conventional perspectives on personnel management are specified and basic trends are portrayed: from administration to strategic relevance, from cost factor analysis to resources planning, from social engineering to sense making processes and the abundance of the human qualifications to their scarity in the near future.

The work of Ackermann (1987, 1989) is mainly based on empirical research. It examines contingency factors upon the elaboration of human resource strategies, thus elaborating and revising former research by the Michigan group (Tichy et al. 1982) and Evans (1984, 1986) at INSEAD. A comprehensive overview indicates that human resource management strategies tend to follow business strategy and be largely independent of environmental pressures, company size and resource availability.

3. Applied Concepts

Whereas for the scientific discourse on management a growing importance of the human factor can be identified, empirical research paints a different picture of management practice within companies. According to Wunderer (1984), the personnel management department has very often but a low status in the company. In addition, top managers in the personnel management department often have not made their career in this field, but have gained practical experience in other functional areas. Lattmann (1985) argues that the top managers in the personnel management department have but limited influence on the company's strategic decisions. Furthermore, he mentions that a number of tasks have shifted to other departments, thus leaving mainly administrative tasks to senior managers in the personnel management function. As a result of this, the portion of people being employed in this field has shrunk to a level that companies had in post-war years. Wächter (1987) makes similar observations: he states that many companies tend to decentralize and de-professionalize their personnel management, thus re-integrating personnel management tasks into the line functions. This, however, can also be seen as an integration into general and strategic management.

Similar to this discrepancy between theory and practice with regard to the importance of the human factor is the difference between the tendency in the scientific discourse on personnel management and tendencies in practice. Whereas the scientific discourse shows a tendency in conceptualization and a clear shift from concepts of personnel administration to strategic personnel management and HRM, applied approaches in West German companies still differ very much. The degree of diversity in applied approaches is shown by various company reports published by German management journals and — systematically — by a survey made by Ackermann et al. (Ackermann 1987, Wührer 1985, Ackermann and Wührer

1983). This survey which includes 80 large German and Austrian companies, identifies four different personnel management strategies:

— development strategy
  intensive development activities, long-range planning, sophisticated selection strategies
— assessment strategy
  assessment with regard to performance is the prime task
— research strategy
  intensive internal and external research, sophisticated selection strategies
— administration strategy
  traditional personnel administration

Ackermann argues that various internal and external factors have an influence on a company's decision about which type of strategy they are going to select. However, the relation between these factors, the type of strategy being chosen and the economic success of a company has not yet been examined sufficiently.

Taking such differences into account in the practice of personnel management, it can be argued that in fact there is *nothing like the* German approach to human resource management but that a number of diverse strategies and approaches are being used by West German companies.

4. Contingency Factors of HRM

Like other management functions, HRM is influenced by a number of external factors. This is true not just for the choice of personnel management strategies (Ackermann 1987), but also for the translation of a selected strategy into action. In the sixties, traditional contingency theory research demonstrated the impact that an organization's environment has on its structure and emphasized the importance of a fit between structure and environment. Since then, such external influence has been proven for other management activities such as planning, strategy formulation and also personnel management. In addition, the list of constraining factors has been widened and rendered more specific. However, the early argumentation that those external factors have a determining influence has been neglected. On the contrary, management is now being seen as having a certain scope of choice within those constraints (Khandwalla 1977, Kubicek 1980, Miles 1975, Sydow 1985, Miles/Snow 1978). Thus, strategic choices (Child 1972) are not just seen as possible but as necessary for all management functions and, accordingly, for HRM, too.

Although the importance of external factors on any management activity is no matter of dispute, there are various kinds of enumerations of those factors. Luthans (1976) e. g. distinguishes between three levels of constraints:

- general external factors, i. e. social, economic, political, legal and technological factors,
- special external factors like competitors, clients and suppliers,
- internal factors like structure and technology.

Carlisle (1976) also names political, technological, sociocultural, and economic forces and institutions as the major external constraints. Kieser and Kubicek (1983) make a distinction between internal and external dimensions. Within the list of external constraints, a global environment (societal and cultural dimensions) and an environment that is specific to the organization's tasks (competition, clients, technology) can be distinguished.

With regard to personnel management in particular, similiar enumerations of contingency factors can be found in management literature. Most authors name external factors solely. Bisani (1976), Eckardstein and Schnellinger (1978) and Remer (1978, 1985) e. g. list society, economy, technology, law, science, culture, politics and employees as such dimensions. In addition to this, Remer (1985) also mentions the importance of internal constraints namely general management ideas. Ackermann (1987) also lists both external and internal contingency factors of HRM: business strategies, organization structure, company size, availability of researchs, and the environment of the organization.

Since ideally and by definition[1] HRM is both the result and a part of the organization's strategy, business strategies have to be seen as major determinants of HRM. For international comparisons, however, such intra-organizational factors are of slight importance since to a certain degree they too are influenced by external constraints or − if not − they are characteristic just for the organization in question. Thus they cannot form a starting point for general international comparisons but for comparisons between single companies only. Internal factors such as strategy and general management ideas may explain differences between personnel management strategies actually being used by German companies, but cannot serve in enlightening differences between Germany in general and other nations. Consequently, in his international comparison of HRM, Gaugler (1988) restricts himself to environmental dimensions. He distinguishes between cultural, economic, and technological factors, labor availability and the industrial relations system. Similarly, Hossain and Davis (1989) list cultural,

---

[1] Many authors argue that the difference between personnel management and HRM consists of just this integration of personnel management functions into strategic management (e. g. Tichy et al. 1982; Cascio 1986).

educational, technological and labor factors as the most important environmental forces that pose as potential barriers for HRM. In the following, we shall use a very similiar catalogue, i. e.:

— economic factors
   (type of economic system, natural resources, market conditions, technology)
— industrial relations system
— demographic and educational factors
   (labor availability, education and training system, general level of education and training)
— cultural factors.

4.1 Economic Factors

A major — if not the most important — constraint of management in general is the economic system. In planned economy systems, most decisions will be made centrally by the government or government agencies. Companies have to fulfill a given plan. Since strategic choices are rare or almost non-existent, HRM too is largely determined by external (political) goals. In a free enterprise economy like the Federal Republic of Germany (FRG) however, the success of a company depends on its own strategy and its ability to compete with other firms. Thus HRM ideally becomes an instrument to increase an organization's competitiveness. The major constraint — and also the driving force — for HRM that results from this type of economy is the survival and the financial success of a company.

A special factor of the economic system of West Germany is the openness of its national market and its strong export orientation. In comparison to other free enterprise economies like Japan, France and the United States of America with protectionist trading policies in certain areas, there are but limited restrictions to importing and exporting goods and capital. Thus German companies meet a strong competition with foreign firms in the domestic market. Since Germany has only a limited number of natural resources and thus has to import most of them, the country has to have a strong export orientation. Traditionally, German companies produce many more goods than they are able to sell on the domestic market. Often, more than half of a company's sales is made abroad[2] with markets in Western Europe dominating. Furthermore, with the establishment of a single European market in 1992, competition on the German domestic market will

---

[2] Export shares of more than 50% are common in the chemical, the automobile and the mechanical engineering industry.

grow and European companies will be forced to think and act even more internationally. Protected national markets will then no longer exist.

Present and still growing competition forces German companies to concentrate on technology and on the only natural resource Germany has to offer: its people. As Gaugler (1988: 27) mentions this situation forms a great challenge to HRM:

... HR management must stimulate the employees to be very flexible and highly motivated. They must encourage the employees to accept innovations which are intended to improve the company's competitive strength. HR management must also promote the creativity of the staff through suggestion systems, especially quality circles, and other techniques, so that as many employees as possible may contribute to improving the company's market position.

This challenge is enlarged by the fact that West Germany is a country with one of the highest wage levels worldwide. Thus, German companies have to maintain high productivity levels in order to remain competitive. Two factors are important for maintaining high productivity levels: the skills of the employees and the technology being used. Consequently, German companies tend to concentrate on the types of production and service that demand skilled workers and high technology. Other types of production are often moved to countries with lower wage levels to decrease production costs. Whereas some production technologies lead to an elimination of human work — at least to a high degree and especially in fields that traditionally demand only low qualifications — most computer-based technologies demand even more skills. Thus, in general, the need for skilled workers both in factories and offices is actually increasing (e. g. Baethge and Overbeck 1986, Kern and Schumann 1984). In addition, these new technologies require major capital investments which can only be returned by using such technologies more intensively. Means for intensification are new types of shift work, additional shifts during weekends, and flexible working hours (e. g. BMW in Regensburg). In the end, this trend towards flexibilization may also lead to a major shift in German labor relations that are nowadays characterized by a high degree of standardization.

4.2 Industrial Relations System

Whereas economic factors only form a very general but external framework for HRM, a country's industrial relations system has to be seen as both an external and internal constraint since it arranges and determines the nature of the relationship between a company's management and the employees.

Any industrial relations system is made up of the relations between three groups of actors: the state, the companies represented by their owners and their management, and the employees and their representative organizations (Dunlop 1958). An important factor for HRM is the degree to which the state may interfere in labor relations and in which labor relations are regulated by state legislation. In general, it can be argued that in comparison to other market economies, the FRG has a high degree of state regulation (Fürstenberg 1985).

Within an industrial relations system, five levels of state regulation and of interaction between the three actors can be distinguished (Bauer 1985):

- state level
- collective bargaining level
- company level
- plant level
- individual workplace and work contracts

On the *state level*, the West German constitution provides a very general framework for the country's industrial relations system since it gives guidelines for detailed legislation. First of all, it guarantees several individual rights such as the free choice of profession and work-place and the protection of private property. Secondly, it guarantees collective rights, especially the right of employees and employers to form representative organizations and to bargain freely about wages and working conditions without any state interference. Thus the German state guarantees trade unions and employers' associations freedom in concluding collective labor contracts and does not interfere actively in day-to-day-activities. This non-interference can be seen as characteristic for the *collective bargaining level* (so called: Tarifautonomie). Collective agreements may cover compensation, benefits, working conditions, working hours and all other questions that are seen as important by unions and/or employers. They form the framework for HRM within each company. However, existing state regulations are superior: what has been regulated by the law cannot be changed through collective agreements although state regulations that lay down minimum requirements may be improved through additional private contracts. Minimum requirements e. g. exist for vacations, working hours and safety regulations. In addition, there are numerous laws for labor protection that are absolutely binding.

Collective agreements are made on regional levels (Tarifbezirke) for whole branches of industry. Representative organizations of employees and employers are structured according to this with branch organizations split up into regional divisions. Since the representatives of both trade unions and employers' associations are full-time functionaries, it can be said that Germany labor conflicts are managed professionally (Fürstenberg 1985: 10).

Whereas the degree of unionization is approximately 42% (in 1988), almost all companies (90%) are members of an employers' association. More than 80% of unionized employees are members of a branch group of the Deutsche Gewerkschaftsbund (DGB, 7.8 million in 1988, 17 unions). Other trade unions limit themselves to certain professional groups like the Deutsche Angestellten Gewerkschaft (DAG, 0.5 million) to white-collar workers and the Deutscher Beamtenbund (0.8 million) to permanent civil servants. Where different trade unions are involved in bargaining processes, they usually have some kind of coordination. Thus companies do not face numerous simultanous conflicts with various unions as they do in other industrialized countries. In practice, agreements being made cover both unionized and non-unionized employees if the company is a member of the relevant employers' association. If not, special agreements have to be made. Collective agreements are as binding as law on the members of both sides. Thus on the company level, only additional, more detailed agreements may be made by the management and the shop stewards. For managers, individual contracts have to be made since this group is not covered by collective agreements.

To a certain degree, the mood of collective bargaining is fixed by state regulations and previous labor court decisions. As a consequence, strikes and other forms of open labor conflicts are rare (e. g. 1986: only 28000 work days in total). Industrial action may only occur when the representative organization negotiate about collective agreements and after negotiations have failed. Even then, however, an arbitrator has to be brought in first[3]. If arbitration fails, several bodies of the unions and the unionized workers themselves (with a majority of 75%) have to approve the decision to go on strike. The companies may answer with lockouts. Since the state remains neutral in labor conflicts, neither locked-out workers nor strikers receive unemployment money. Only unionized employees are paid some financial support out of strike funds.

On the *company and the plant level*, the system of legally guaranteed *codetermination* is characteristic for the German industrial relations system. Historically, this system goes back to 1920 when for the first time state legislation created the possibility to set up worker representations in all companies. On the company level the employees may exercize their influence through representatives in the supervisory council (Aufsichtsrat), a control organ[4] that is obligatory for all joint-stock companies. Numerically, the employees' representatives have a parity in this organ, but practically they are in a minority position because the chairman, who, because of the electoral system is a representative of the stock owners, has the casting vote. In smaller companies (500 to 2000 employees), the employees only elect one third of the supervisory board's members. For large mining and steel

---

[3] For details of the arbitration process, see Keller 1985.
[4] The supervisory board elects and controls the executive board. It also has to approve major managerial decisions like large investments and new strategies.

companies with more than 2000 employees, there is a special codetermination system. Here, too, employees and capital owners each elect half of the supervisory board. In addition, they have to agree on a further member who has the casting vote in conflict situations. Furthermore, there has to be a labor director on the executive board who cannot be appointed against the will of the labor representatives. In general, because of this representation in the supervisory council, German employees have an impact on strategic management and other major decisions. Practically, various labor conflicts are already tackled, and sometimes even solved in these organs.

On the *plant level*, the employees may exercise their influence through elected works councils. In each company or shop-floor with more than five employees, works councils may be formed if the employees wish to do so. Their members are under special protection from dismissal. In general, they exercise their office outside their normal work duties. In companies with more than 300 employees, however, some of them have to be released from working responsibilities. Works councils have almost no rights in the economic management of the company[5] but have various options in influencing a company's HRM policy. Whereas in some matters they only have to be consulted, they may participate in the decision-making process in others (participation rights) or even have to approve management decisions (genuine codetermination rights) (Gaugler 1985).

$$\text{Codetermination} \nwarrow \text{Works Council} \nearrow \text{Participation}$$

Codetermination	*Participation*
working hours	manpower planning
payment methods	dismissals
hirings and transfers	work procedures
social amenities	operation changes
training programs	job desciption
regulations for vacations	design of work places
safety regulations	
regulations for selection	
and assessment	

In general, employees exercise their rights through works councils. However, there is also a number of additional rights on the *individual work contract level* that has an influence on HRM; e. g. employees are entitled to read their personal file and be informed about how their pay is calculated.

---

[5] Through special committees (Wirtschaftsausschuß) however they have the right to get a number of information about the economic situation of the company.

They may also demand information about the type of work done and its place in the overall production process. In cases of complaints or conflicts with the management, employees are entitled to the support of the works councils. This however often leads to a mediating and peacemaking function of the works councils (Richter 1985: 154), especially since German law obliges works councils and management to cooperate peacefully; means of labor conflicts such as strikes are not admitted except for the annual collective bargaining procedures. Consequently, on the individual work contract level, open labor conflicts are relatively rare, while conflict management on both the plant and the individual work contract level is highly formalized by the law.

In summary, the German industrial relations system can be described as highly standardized, extensively organized by state regulations, with a high degree of formalization of labor conflicts and a high degree of codetermination (Fürstenberg 1985, Wächter 1981). All factors combined make it a very special case in the Western industrialized world that has a vital role in determining HRM strategies within German companies.

4.3 Demographic and Educational Factors

With regard to HRM, the most important demographic factor is *labor availability*. In the immediate post-war period, there were high unemployment rates. This situation changed in the 60s with the so-called *Wirtschaftswunder* (economic miracle). During the sixties there was practically no unemployment but additional workers had to be searched for abroad to make further economic growth possible. At first, hundreds of thousands of refugees from East Germany filled the gaps in the West German workforce. After the building of the Berlin wall in 1961, which put an end to the exodus, West German companies began searching for additional workers in the Mediterranean area. Nowadays, about 8% of the West German workforce is foreign. Simultaneously, more and more women have joined the work force, in the beginning primarily as part-time employees, nowadays often with the same career orientation as men. In 1986, women accounted for 38% of the work-force; more than half of the women between the ages of 15 and 65 was in employment.

Momentarily, West Germany is facing a very mixed labor market situation: although there are almost two million unemployed people in the country, there is also a growing shortage of skilled workers and professionals. Most unemployed people largely lack the skills, training and experiences that the companies require. At the same time, job demands are often on the encrease because of new technologies. Kern and Schumann (1984) are even talking about a Renaissance of the skilled worker. A study done by

Baethge and Overbeck (1986) indicates similiar tendencies for the office area. As Gaugler (1988: 29) mentions,

this situation has ... a major impact on HR management. HR must continually seek new ways to attract and retain employees who have those skills and experience that are in particular demand and short supply. In countries where the shortage of qualified workers is particularly acute, HR management has an additional function. By means of employee development programs, including extensive occupational training, the companies strive to qualify previously unskilled people for jobs that they are otherwise unable to fill.

In West Germany training is usually provided by a joint cooperation of companies and state schools, the so-called dual system. First of all the state is in charge of the school and university system. There are but very few private institutions that are all under state supervision. Attendance at state schools is free of charge. In some regions, even study materials are provided free. School attendance is compulsory from the age of six to 18. Full-time attendance is required for nine years and part-time attendance at vocational schools for another three years thereafter. There are three basic general forms of school education: the basic secondary school (Hauptschule, nine or ten years), the intermediate school (Realschule, 10 years), and high school (Gymnasium, 13 years), which is the prerequisite for study at university. More than 90% of those who end their general schooling at either the junior secondary school or the intermediate school go into vocational training. The German system of vocational training combines on-the-job-training within companies with theoretical learning in vocational schools. Large companies usually have their own training centers, whereas trainees of smaller companies often attend intercompany training centers. Private enterprise and government are jointly responsible for this dual system. Momentarily there are more than 400 various programs that all lead to a formal degree (e. g. *Facharbeiter*). In accordance with the German craftsman tradition, these degrees serve as the basis for further qualification. The German chambers of commerce (*Industrie- und Handelskammern*) and companies jointly offer additional training programs that lead to a foreman's qualification (*Meister*). A foreman is usually the lowest management level in West German enterprises. Most middle and top managers have an academic degree, either in business administration or engineering.

Almost 20% of an age group attends a university program. This number has increased dramatically during the last two decades. Whereas in 1970 there were only about half a million students at West German universities, there a more than 1.7 million nowadays. Business Administration has become extremely popular in the last couple of years. With only four exceptions, universities are state owned but have the right to govern themselves. Attendance is free of charge; special financial support is given to students from low-income families.

The state also provides various options for adult education. First of all, most of the municipalities have adult training centers (*Volkshochschulen*), which offer both professional training and courses that people attend just for fun or because of a general interest. Registration fees are very low. There are some 860 adult training centers in West Germany that offered about 360 000 courses in 1986, attended by 5.2 million students. Training programs that are intended to improve the employment prospects of employees and — especially — of the unemployed are offered by Federal government agencies and are paid by them. In 1985, more than half a million people attended such long-term programs. They all receive financial support for their participation from state funds. In some parts of West Germany the local government offers additional special support to those citizens who intend to participate in short term adult education and training programs. In Hessen, for example, employees are entitled to a special (paid) one-week holiday for attending an educational program that they may choose freely.

In addition to state agencies and state sponsored adult education and training programs, most of the larger companies run their own training centers and programs for their employees. Often they do not only provide special training programs for higher vocational qualification or management development but also general courses that range from language courses to sport programs. Employees may attend such courses whenever they are interested, often without paying anything and sometimes even during their regular workday. More important however are specialized training programs. In 1987, Germany companies spent more than DM 26 billion for training and development programs (vocational training not included). However, most of the money is used for management development programs that are usually organized as off-the-job-training (Bardeleben and Böll and Kühn 1986). Because of this Staehle (1989: 811) argues that companies tend to use government programs and agencies for the training of unskilled workers — and increasingly even skilled workers — and to provide their own programs for managers and most of the office staff. This is understandable insofar as the dual system provides German companies with skilled staff that are of full use from the very beginning, whereas academics (i. e. managers) have only received some general education in their professional field. Additional special training to prepare them for work within a company has still to be provided by the company itself. Hence most German companies offer special trainee programs for university graduates and an elaborated system for management development.

This system of education and training, especially the dual system of vocational training, can be seen as a uniquely German feature that has no parallel worldwide (with the exception of the other German-speaking countries). It certainly forms a strong constraint for HRM in German companies.

As a recent survey of the Institut der Deutschen Wirtschaft (1989) shows, it is also seen as a major strength of the national economy by a vast majority of German companies.

4.4 Cultural Factors

In comparative management research, culture is often treated as the single most important factor influencing management activities (e. g. Hofstede 1980, Ronen 1986, Terpestra and David 1985). For HRM, Steers (1989) even sees a cultural imperative. However theoretical concepts that might serve in giving a general framework to distinguish the various existing cultures are non-existent. Even the definition of culture is a matter of controversy (Adler 1986, Kroeber and Kluckhohn 1952, Whitely and England 1977). Empirical studies usually restrict themselves to comparisons of either a very limited number of cultures or nations (often just two), to single elements of culture like certain values, or they try to examine whether a behavioral theory is universal or culture-bounded. Studies that have tried to combine these interests (e. g. Hofstede 1980, Haire and Ghiselli and Porter 1966, Ronen and Kraut 1977, Sirota and Greenwood 1971) are rare and, in addition, can either demonstrate but single dimensions in which cultures differ or are too general for giving an in-depth view into a single culture. Even Hofstede (1980) whose empirical study of cultural dimensions of forty countries is the broadest and most important that has been made up to now, can give only vague information about German culture[6]. According to the four dimensions[7] that he used for his analysis, German culture (like Austria and the German speaking part of Switzerland) is low in tolerance for risk, low in power distance, high on the masculinity index and moderately high in individualism. As Ronen (1986: 181) mentions, other studies show that in German culture self-realization, leadership, and independence are emphasized as life-goals. When Sirota and Greenwood (1971) studied the work goals of employees in a large multinational company, they found that Germany was high on security and fringe benefits and one of the highest in "getting ahead". Furthermore, several studies demonstrate that Germans are highly competitive, while little regard is placed on reliability and patience.

---

[6] Hofstede (1980: 25) defines culture as a mental program, as "the collective programming of the mind which distinguishes the members of one human group from another".

[7] The four dimensions are: power distance, uncertainty avoidance, individualism and masculinity.

In addition to such surveys, there are numerous assumptions and popular views about Germans. Folk tales describe Germans as very task-oriented, relatively formal and with a high status orientation. Germans are often also viewed as bureaucratic and as both authoritarian and strong believers in authority. The latter view goes back to the last century's empire but became empirically evident in the Third Reich. With Adorno's famous study about the authoritarian character (Adorno et al. 1950) — which actually was a study about the German character — this image of a typical German found some scientific proof.

However such general findings and views about German culture offer but limited explanations. Sometimes they have more the character of prejudices than descriptions of today's reality. First of all, there is a cultural diversity in Germany. This is true for the various parts of the country since it still is very decentral. With the exception of the empire and the Weimar Republic, there was never any dominant cultural center in Germany (like e. g. Paris in France and London in Great Britain). The different parts of Germany have their own traditions, i. e. at least partly their own culture. In addition, during the time of the German economic miracle in the sixties, there was a large immigration of foreign workers into Germany, primarily from the Mediterranean area. Today there are about five million foreigners living in the country, most of them with a very different cultural background[8]. Besides this kind of growing ethnic diversity there are changes in the value system, too. Several studies indicate that since the seventies German culture has changed profoundly. Various stereotypes of typical Germans no longer seem to be valid: for many Germans, the traditional task-orientation has shifted to a leisure orientation; obedience and conscientiousness have changed to self-realization, and bureaucratic views to a desire for autonomy. However, the former homogeneous "German" value system has not changed in a single direction but has given place to a pluralization of values, norms and life-styles (e. g. Klages 1984, 1985; Kmieciak 1976, Strümpel 1977, Klages and Kmieciak 1981). This pluralization is especially true for work values (Pawlowsky 1985, von Klipstein and Strümpel 1984, 1985; Noelle-Neumann and Strümpel 1984). A growing number of Germans no longer defines individuality and social status in terms of profession and professional status (Dahrendorf 1982, Matthes 1983, Offe 1984). Even within management, divergent work attitudes and value orientations can be found (von Rosenstiel

---

[8] Whereas most of the immigrants from Eastern and Western Europe have been assimilated to a certain degree, the Turkish immigrants which form the largest group of foreigners living in West Germany (about one million) tend to preserve their cultural traditions. The most important reasons for this is that the Turks have a different religious background. They are muslims, whereas the other immigrants from the Mediterranean area are Catholics.

1983). Thus within the German culture there are nowadays various subcultures with sometimes even contradicting value systems (Pieper 1988: 16 – 37). Often, a subculture has more in common with a similiar subculture in Britain, France or the United States than with other subcultures in Germany or with major cultural streams in the country. Furthermore, values are changing relatively fast now. Consequently, studies that were made in the seventies (like Hofstede's) are partly out of date. Of course, all of this makes HRM more complicated. Instead of creating a single strategy for all employees of a company, various HRM-strategies for the varying groups have to be formulated. Managers who are in charge of HRM do not only have to know something about German culture in general, but they have to find out to which subculture the single employee or the work group belongs before he/she is able to search for appropriate HRM instruments.

5. Summary and Outlook

In summary, it can be argued that HRM is neither a new concept for practice within German companies, nor for the theoretical discussion. However, there is a number of national peculiarities, especially the industrial relations system with the German type of codetermination and its high degree of formalization by state regulations and the dual system of vocational training. Since people are the only natural resource that the country has to offer, HRM traditionally plays an important role for most companies. Several trends indicate that the importance of HRM might even increase in the future:

- new technologies both in manufacturing and the office and a growing speed of technological changes
- a growing number of people with an academic education and consequential new demands for working conditions
- a growing number of women in the work-force, especially in management
- a shortage of skilled workers and professionals in several professional fields
- continous changes in the value system and a growing pluralization of German society

Because of these trends, administrative approaches to HRM in practice and views like Gutenberg's factor approach in the academic discussion will no longer be able to solve the practical problems that German companies are facing in this field. Thus both practitioners and business school researchers are focusing on concepts that integrate the personnel management function into strategic management. New issues, such as ethics in HRM, are arising (Drumm 1989). Taken together, these trends and the long tradition of HRM in Germany will ensure that in the future HRM will be an even more important topic, both for practitioners in companies and theorists in the academic world in Germany.

References

Ackermann, K. F. (1979): Hauptströmungen und gegenwärtiger Entwicklungsstand der Personalwirtschaftslehre an den Hochschulen in der Bundesrepublik Deutschland, in: F. Bisani and H. Friedrichs (eds.), *Das Personalwesen in Europa*, Teil 1, Königstein/Taunus: 18 – 70.

Ackermann, K. F. (1986): Konzeptionen des Strategischen Personalmanagements für die Unternehmenspraxis, in: H. Glaubrecht and D. Wagner (eds.), *Humanität und Rationalität in Personalpolitik und Personalführung*, Freiburg/B.: 39 – 68.

Ackermann, K. F. (1987): A contingency model of HRM-strategy. Empirical research findings reconsidered, in: Lattmann, Ch. (ed.), *Personal-Management und Strategische Unternehmensführung*, Heidelberg: 65 – 83.

Ackermann, K. F. (1989): Strategisches Personalmanagement auf dem Prüfstand – Kritische Fragen an ein zukunftsorientiertes Konzept der Personalarbeit, in: K. F. Ackermann, G. Dannert and P. Horvath (eds.), *Personalmanagement im Wandel*, Stuttgart: 1 – 29.

Ackermann, K. F. and G. Reber (eds.) (1981): *Personalwirtschaft*, Stuttgart.

Ackermann, K. F. and G. Wührer (1983): *Ein Fragebogen zur Messung der Unternehmens- und Personalpolitik*, Stuttgart.

Ackermann, K. F. and G. Wührer (1984): *Personalstrategien in deutschen Großunternehmen. Ergebnisse einer empirischen Untersuchung*, DBW-Depot 84 – 3 – 1. Stuttgart.

Adler, N. J. (1986): *International dimensions of organizational behavior*, Boston, Mass.

Adorno, T. W. et al. (1950): *The Authoritarian Personality*, New York.

Baethge, M. and J. Overbeck (1986): *Die Zukunft der Angestellten*, Frankfurt/ M. – New York.

Bardeleben, R. von, G. Böll and H. Kühn (1986): *Strukturen betrieblicher Weiterbildung*, Berlin – Bonn.

Bauer, J. P. (1985): Zuständigkeit der Akteure, in: Endruweit, G. et al. (eds.), *Handbuch der Arbeitsbeziehungen*, Berlin – New York: 145 – 167.

Berthel, J. (1979): *Personal-Management*, Stuttgart.

Berthel, J. (1989): *Personal-Management*, Stuttgart (2nd. ed.).

Bierfelder, W. (ed.) (1976): *Handwörterbuch des öffentlichen Dienstes. Das Personalwesen*, Berlin.

Bislani, F. (1976): *Personalführung*, Wiesbaden.

Bleicher, K. (1984): Unternehmenspolitik und Unternehmenskultur: Auf dem Wege zu einer Kulturpolitik der Unternehmung, *Zeitschrift für Organisation*, No. 53: 494 – 500.

Bleicher, K. (1985): Zur strategischen Ausgestaltung von Anreizsystemen für die Führungsgruppe in Unternehmungen, *Zeitschrift für Organisation*, No. 54: 21–27.

Bleicher, K. (1986): Unternehmenskultur und strategische Unternehmensführung, in: Hahn, D. and B. Taylor (eds.): *Strategische Unternehmensplanung*, 4th ed., Heidelberg–Wien: 757–797.

Bleicher, K. (1987): Strategisches Personalmanagement. Gedanken zum Füllen einer kritischen Lücke im Konzept strategischer Unternehmensführung, in: H. Glaubrecht and D. Wagner (eds.): *Humanität und Rationalität in Personalpolitik und Personalführung*, Freiburg/B.: 17–38.

Block, R. (1988): Das Klischee vom Bedeutungszuwachs der Weiterbildung, *Die Mitbestimmung*, No. 12/1988: 704–708.

Bühner, R. (1987): Strategisches Personalmanagement für neue Produktionstechnologien, *Betriebswirtschaftliche Forschung und Praxis*, No. 3/1987: 249–265.

Carlisle, H. M. (1976): *Management: Concepts and situations*, Chicago.

Cascio, W. F. (1986): *Managing Human Resources*, New York.

Child, J. (1972): Organizational structure, environment, and performance: The role of strategic choice, *Sociology*, Vol. 6: 1–22.

Chmielewicz, K. (1975): *Arbeitnehmerinteressen und Kapitalismuskritik in der Betriebswirtschaftslehre*, Reinbek.

Dahrendorf, R. (1982): Arbeitsgesellschaft am Ende, *Die Zeit*, Nr. 48/1982: 44.

De Man, H. (1927): *Der Kampf um die Arbeitsfreude — eine Untersuchung auf Grund der Aussagen von 78 Industriearbeitern und Angestellten*, Jena.

Drumm, H. J. (1989): *Personalwirtschaftslehre*, Berlin.

Drumm, H. J. and C. Scholz (1983): *Personalplanung*, Bern–Stuttgart.

Dunlop, J. T. (1958): *Industrial Relations Systems*, New York.

Eckardstein, D. von and F. Schnellinger (1978): *Betriebliche Personalpolitik*, 3rd ed., München.

Eggebrecht, A., J. Flemming, G. Meyer, A. von Müller, A. Oppolzer, A. Paulingyi and H. Schneider (1980): *Geschichte der Arbeit — vom Alten Ägypten bis zur Gegenwart*, Köln.

Ende, W. (1982): *Theorien der Personalarbeit im Unternehmen*, Königstein/Ts.

Endruweit, G., E. Gaugler, W. H. Staehle and B. Wilpert (eds.) (1985): *Handbuch der Arbeitsbeziehungen*, Berlin–New York.

Endruweit, G. and G. Berger (1989): The functioning of institutionalised forms of workers' participation — seen from a science perspective, in: Gladstone, A., R. Landsbury, J. Stiefel, T. Treu and M. Weiss (eds.), *Current issues in Labour Relations*, Berlin–New York: 87–104.

Evans, P. (1984): On the importance of a generalistic conception of human research management: a cross-national look, *Human Resource Management*, 1984, 23: 347–363.

Evans, P. (1986): The Strategic Outcomes of Human Resource Management, in: *Human Resource Management*, Vol. 25, No. 1: 149–167.

Fombrun, C. J., N. M. Tichy and M. A. Devanna (eds.) (1984): *Strategic Human Resource Management*, New York.

Fürstenberg, F. (1985): Kulturelle und traditionelle Faktoren der Arbeitsbeziehungen aufgrund der Sozialstruktur, in: Endruweit, G. et al. (eds.): *Handbuch der Arbeitsbeziehungen*, Berlin–New York: 3–27.

Gaugler, E. (ed.) (1975): *Handwörterbuch des Personalwesens*, Stuttgart.

Gaugler, E. (ed.) (1979): *Ausbildungskonzeptionen und Berufsanforderungen für das betriebliche Personalwesen*, Berlin.

Gaugler, E. (1982): Gegenstandsbereich und Erkenntnisstand des Personal-Managements, *Betriebswirtschaftliche Forschung und Praxis*, 1982, 34: 285–301.

Gaugler, E. (1985): Mitbestimmung in Betrieb und Unternehmung, in: Endruweit, G., E. Gaugler, W. H. Staehle and B. Wilpert (eds.): *Handbuch der Arbeitsbeziehungen*, Berlin–New York: 169–186.

Gaugler, E. (1988): HR Management: an international comparison, *Personnel*, August 1988: 24–30.

Grebing, H. (1976): *Geschichte der deutschen Arbeiterbewegung – ein Überblick*, 7th ed., München.

Gutenberg, E. (1951/1983): *Grundlagen der Betriebswirtschaftslehre*, Band 1: Doe Produktion, Berlin–Heidelberg–New York (1983: 24th ed.).

Haire, M., E. E. Ghiselli and L. W. Porter (1966): *Managerial thinking: an international study*, New York.

Hartmann, H. and P. Meyer (1980): *Soziologie der Personalarbeit*, Stuttgart.

Heinen, E. (1976): Industriebetriebslehre als Entscheidungslehre, in: Heinen, E. (ed.). *Industriebetriebslehre*, 5th ed., Wiesbaden: 25–78.

Hellpach, W. and R. Lang (1922): *Gruppenfabrikation*, Berlin.

Hentze, J. (1986): *Personalwirtschaftslehre*, 3 volumes, 3rd. ed., Bern–Stuttgart.

Hinrichs, P. (1981): *Um die Seele des Arbeiters. Arbeitspsychologie, Industrie- und Betriebsoziologie in Deutschland 1871–1945*, Köln.

Hofstede, G. (1980): *Culture's consequence*, Beverly Hills, Cal.

Hossain, S. and H. J. Davis (1989): Some thoughts on international personnel management as an emerging field, in: Need, A., G. F. Ferris and K. M. Rowland (eds.), *Research in Personnel and Human Resource Management, Supplement 1: International Human Resources Management*, Greenwich, Conn.–London: 121–136.

Institut der Deutschen Wirtschaft (ed.) (1989): *Qualified in Germany – Ein Standortvorteil für die Bundesrepublik Deutschland*, Köln.

Keller, B. (1985): Schlichtung als autonomes Regelungsverfahren der Tarifvertragsparteien, in: Endruweit, G., E. Gaugler, W. H. Staehle and B. Wilpert (eds.), *Handbuch der Arbeitsbeziehungen*, Berlin–New York: 119–130.

Kern, M. and H. Schumann (1984): *Das Ende der Arbeitsteilung?*, München.

Khandwalla, P. N. (1977): *The design of organizations*, New York.

Kieser, A. (1984): *Zur Evolution von Organisationsformen I, Zunft, Verlag, Manufaktor*, Arbeitspapier Lehrstuhl für Allgemeine Betriebswirtschaftslehre und Organisation der Universität Mannheim, Mannheim.

Kieser, A. and H. Kubicek (1983): *Organisation*, 2nd. ed. Berlin–New York.

Kirsch, W. (1977): *Einführung in die Theorie der Entscheidungsprozesse*, 2nd ed. 3 volumes, Wiesbaden.

Kißler, L. (1985): Arbeitswissenschaft für wen? Die Antwort der arbeitsorientierten Wissenschaften von der Arbeit, in: Georg, W., L. Kißler and V. Sattel (eds.), *Arbeit und Wissenschaft: Arbeitswissenschaft? Eine Einführung*, Bonn: 9–36.

Klages, H. (1984): *Wertorientierungen im Wandel*, Frankfurt–New York.

Klages, H. (1985): Empirische Bestandsaufnahme des Wertewandels, in: Bertelsmann-Stiftung (ed.): *Unternehmensführung vor neuen gesellschaftlichen Aufgaben*, Gütersloh: 24–39.

Klages, H. and P. Kmieciak (eds.) (1981): *Wertwandel und gesellschaftlicher Wandel*, Frankfurt–New York.

Klipstein, M. von and B. Strümpel (1984): *Der Überdruß am Überfluß*, München–Wien.

Klipstein, M. von and B. Strümpel (1985): *Gewandelte Werte – Erstarrte Strukturen. Wie die Bundesbürger Wirtschaft und Arbeit erleben*, Bonn.

Kmieciak, P. (1976): *Wertstrukturen und Wertwandel in der Bundesrepublik Deutschland*, Göttingen.

Krell, G. (1988): Organisationskultur – Renaissance der Betriebsgemeinschaft?, in: Dülfer, E. (ed.): *Organisationskultur-Phänomen – Philosophie – Technologie*, Stuttgart: 113–126.

Kroeber, A. and C. Kluckhohn (1952): *Culture: A critical review of concepts and definitions*, Cambridge, Mass.

Krulis-Randa, J. S. (1987): Strategie und Personalmanagement. Konfusion über einen unternehmenspolitischen Wandel, in: Lattmann, Ch. (ed.). *Personal-Management und strategische Unternehmensführung*, Heidelberg: 3–12.

Kubicek, H. (1980): Bestimmungsfaktoren der Organisationsstruktur, Potthoff, E. (ed.). *RKW-Handbuch Führungstechnik und Organisation*, Essen: 1–62.

Kupsch, P. U. and R. Marr (1978): Personalwirtschaft, Heinen, E. (ed.). Industriebetriebslehre, 6th ed., Wiesbaden, 525–659.

Lattmann, C. (1985): Die Personalabteilung, *Die Unternehmung*, No. 3/1985: 192–211.

Luthans, F. (1976): *Introduction to management: A contingency approach*, New York.

Mahoney, T. A. and L. D. Deckop (1986): Evolution of concept and practice in personal administration/Human Resource Management, *Yearly Review of Management of the Journal of Management*, Vol. 12, 1986: 223–241.

Marr, R. (1986): Technologie und Personalmanagement, *Die Unternehmung*, Vol. 40, No. 2: 103–117.

Marr, R. (1987): Strategisches Personalmanagement – des Kaisers neue Kleider? Kritische Anmerkungen zum derzeitigen Diskussionsstand, in: Lattmann, Ch. (ed.). *Personal-Management und strategische Unternehmensführung*, Heidelberg: 13–23.

Marr, R. (1987): Entwicklungstendenzen in der Personalwirtschaftslehre, in: H. Glaubrecht and D. Wagner (eds.), *Humanität und Rationalität in Personalpolitik und Personalführung*, Freiburg/B., 387–400.

Marr, R. and M. Stitzel (1979): *Personalwirtschaft – ein konfliktorientierter Ansatz*, München.

Martin, A. (1988): *Personalforschung*, München–Wien.

Matthes, J. (ed.) (1983): *Krise der Arbeitsgesellschaft?*, Frankfurt/M.

Miles, R. E. (1975): *Theories of management*, New York.

Miles, R. E. and C. C. Snow (1977): *Organizational strategy, structure, and process*, New York.

Mohr, A. (1977): *Personalplanung und Betriebsverfassungsgesetz*, Köln.

Muszynski, B. (1975): *Wirtschaftliche Mitbestimmung zwischen Konflikt- und Harmoniekonzeptionen*, Meisenheim am Glan.

Neuberger, O. (1985): *Arbeit*, Stuttgart.

Niklisch, H. (1932): *Die Betriebswirtschaft*, 7th. ed., Stuttgart.

Nkomo, S. M. (1980): Stage three in personnel administration: Strategic Human Resource Management, *Personnel*, July/August 1980: 69–77.

Noelle-Neumann, E. and B. Strümpel (1984): *Macht Arbeit krank? Macht Arbeit glücklich?*, München.

Oechsler, W. A. (1988): *Personal und Arbeit – Einführung in die Personalwirtschaft unter Einbeziehung des Arbeitsrechts*, 3rd ed., München–Wien.

Offe, C. (ed.) (1984): *"Arbeitsgesellschaft" – Strukturprobleme und Zukunftsperspektiven*, Frankfurt–New York.

Pawlowsky, P. (1985): *Arbeitseinstellungen im Wandel*, München.

Pieper, R. (1988): *Diskursive Organisationsentwicklung*, Berlin–New York.

Potthoff, E. (1988): Rechnen im Personalwesen – von der Lohn- und Gehaltsabrechnung zum Personal-Controllingpersonnel Beckerath, P. G. von (ed.), *Verhaltensethik im Personalwesen*, Stuttgart.

Projektgruppe im WSI (1974): *Grundelemente einer Arbeitsorientierten Einzelwirtschaftslehre*, Köln.

Remer, A. und R. Wunderer (1977): Entwicklungsperspektiven im betrieblichen Personalwesen, *Zeitschrift für betriebswirtschaftliche Forschung*, 1977, 29: 742–761.

Remer, A. (1978): *Personalmanagement: Mitarbeiterorientierte Organisation und Führung von Unternehmungen*, Berlin-New York.

Remer, A. (1985): Vom Produktionsfaktor zum Unternehmensmitglied. Grundlagen einer situations- und entwicklungsbewußten Personallehre, in: W. Bühler et al. (eds.), *Die ganzheitlich-verstehende Betrachtung der sozialen Leistungsordnung. Ein Beitrag zur Ganzheitsforschung*, Wien–New York: 375–391.

Richter, M. (1985): *Personalführung im Betrieb*, München–Wien.

Roethlisberger, F. J. and W. J. Dickson (1939): *Management and the worker*, Cambridge, Mass.

Ronen, S. (1986): *Comparative and multinational management*, New York.

Ronen, S. and A. I. Kraut (1983): Similarities among countries based on employee work values and attitudes, *Columbia Journal of World Business*, Vol. 12, No. 2: 89–96.

Rosenstiel, L. von (1983): Wertwandel und Führungsnachwuchs, *Personalführung*, 11/1983: 214–220.

Rüthers, B. (1973): *Arbeitsrecht und politisches System*, Frankfurt/M.

Schneider, D. (1985): *Allgemeine Betriebswirtschaftslehre*, 2nd. ed., München–Wien.

Scholz, C. (1989): *Personalmanagement. Informationsorientierte und verhaltenstheoretische Grundlagen*, München.

Sirota, D. and J. M. Greenwood (1971): Understanding our overseas work force, *Harvard Business Review*, Vol. 49, No. 1: 53–60.

Staehle, W. H. (1975): Die Stellung des Menschen in neueren betriebswirtschaftlichen Theoriesystemen, *Zeitschrift für Betriebswirtschaft*, Vol. 45: 713–724.

Staehle, W. H. (1988 a): Human Resource Management (HRM) – eine neue Managementrichtung in den USA? *Zeitschrift für Betriebswirtschaft*, Vol. 58: 576–587.

Staehle, W. H. (1988 b): The changing face of personal management, in: Dlugos, G., W. Dorow and K. Weiermair (eds.), *Management under differing labour market and employment systems*, Berlin–New York: 324–333.

Staehle, W. H. (1989): *Management*, 4th ed., München.

Staehle, W. H. and P. Karg (1981): Anmerkungen zu Entwicklung und Stand der deutschen Personalwirtschaftslehre, *Die Betriebswirtschaft*, Vol. 41: 85–90.

Staehle, W. H. and K. Macharzina (eds.) (1986): *European approaches to international management*, Berlin–New York.

Staffelbach, B. (1986): *Strategisches Personalmanagement*, Bern–Stuttgart.

Staffelbach, B. (1987): Skizzen strategischer Personalpolitik, in: Lattmann, Ch. (ed.): *Personal-Management und strategische Unternehmensführung*, Heidelberg: 47–63.

Steers, R. M. (1989): The cultural imperative in HRM research, in: Need, A., G. R. Ferris and K. M. Rowland (eds.), *Research in Personnel and Human Resources Management*, Supplement 1: International Human Resources Management, Greenwich, Conn.–London: 23–32.

Stoll, E. (1979): *Industrielle Arbeitslehre*, Köln.

Strauss-Fehlberg, G. and H. Wächter (1980): Langfristige Entscheidungen im Personalbereich und Einflußmöglichkeiten durch Mitbestimmung, in: Koubek, N., H. D. Küller and I. Scheibe-Lange (eds.), *Betriebswirtschaftliche Probleme der Mitbestimmung*, Köln: 127–145.

Strümpel, B. (1977): *Die Krise des Wohlstandes*, Stuttgart.

Strümpel, B. (1985): Arbeitsmotivation im sozialen Wandel, in: Bertelsmann-Stiftung (ed.), *Unternehmensführung vor neuen gesellschaftlichen Aufgaben*, Gütersloh: 65–81.

Sydow, J. (1985): *Organisationsspielraum und Büroautomation*, Berlin–New York.

Terpestra, V. and K. David (1985): *The cultural environment of international business*, Cincinnati.

Thom, N. (1986 a): Personalentwicklung in deutschen Mittelbetrieben, *WISU* No. 8/9: 418–425.

Thom, N. (1986 b): *Personalentwicklung als Instrument der Unternehmensführung*, Stuttgart.

Tichy, N. M., C. Fombrun and M. A. Devanna (1982): Strategic human research management, *Sloan Management Review*, Vol. 23: 47–61.

Treiber, H. and H. Steinert (1980): *Die Fabrikation des zuverlässigen Menschen – über die "Wahlverwandtschaft" von Kloster- und Fabrikdisziplin*, München.

Türk, K. (1978): *Instrumente betrieblicher Personalwirtschaft*, Neuwied.

Tyson, S. (1987): The management of the personnel function, *Journal of Mangement Studies*, Vol. 24: 523–532.

Verband der Hochschullehrer für Betriebswirtschaft e. V. (ed.) (1962): *Arbeit und Lohn als Forschungsobjekt der Betriebswirtschaftslehre*, Wiesbaden.

Wächter, H. (1979): *Einführung in das Personalwesen*, Herne–Berlin.

Wächter, H. (1981): Das Personalwesen: Herausbildung einer Disziplin, *Betriebswirtschaftliche Forschung und Praxis*, 1981, 5: 462–473.

Wächter, H. (1987): Professionalisierung im Personalbereich, *Die Betriebswirtschaft* 2, 1987: 141–150.

Weber, W. (1985): *Betriebliche Weiterbildung*, Stuttgart.

Weitbrecht, H. and G. Berger (1985): Zur Geschichte der Arbeitsbeziehungen Deutschland, Österreich, Schweiz, in: Endruweit, G. et al. (eds.), *Handbuch der Arbeitsbeziehungen*, Berlin—New York: 483—510.

Whitly, W. and G. W. England (1977): Managerial values as a reflection of culture and the process of industrialization, *Academy of Management Journal*, Vol. 20, No. 3: 439—453.

Wirtschafts- und Sozialwissenschaftliches Institut des Deutschen Gewerkschaftsbundes (WSI) (1981): *Mitbestimmung in Unternehmen und Betrieb*, Köln.

Wohlgemuth, A. C. (1987): Human Resource Management aus unternehmenspolitischer Sicht, in: Lattmann, Ch. (ed.), Personal-Management und strategische Unternehmensführung, Heidelberg: 85—103.

Wührer, G. (1985): *Strategien des Personalmanagements*, Krefeld.

Wunderer, R. (1975): Personalwesen als Wissenschaft, *Personal — Mensch und Arbeit im Betrieb*, 1975, 27: 33—36.

Wunderer, R. (1984): Strategische Personalarbeit — arbeitslos?, *Zeitschrift Führung und Organisation*, Vol. 53: 506—510.

Wunderer, R. und J. Mittmann (1983): 10 Jahre Personalwirtschaftslehre — von Ökonomie nur Spurenelemente, *Die Betriebswirtschaft*, No. 4, 1983: 623—655.

Yoder, D. (1959): *Personnel principles and policies*, Englewood Cliffs, N.J.

Part II
Key Problems of Human Resource Management in Socialist Countries

Human Resource Management in Yugoslavia: Problems and Perspectives

Danica Purg

1. Introduction

Human resource management is emerging as a crucial factor in the turbulent environment of the socialist countries, where the aspirations for political democratization are closely linked with the efforts to establish a market economy, privatization and similar trends. In the majority of these countries political reforms are now well ahead of economic reforms and there is a real danger that the process of reform and transformation will be too slow if the economic reforms lag behind the political reforms. The same is true for the reform of the individual enterprises, which must also keep step with the reform processes.

Although the countries of Eastern Europe and Yugoslavia are suffering from a lack of capital, it is a fact that the speed of future development, its nature and quality, will depend above all on human resources and knowledge.

In socialist ideology, all legislation and philosophical theory were centered on the individual and his work. However, practice has shown that the system did not bring a release of human energies and talents, that the employees were not imbued with the entrepreneurial spirit, and that they were not motivated to do their best. The excessive intervention of politics in the enterprise is certainly one of the reasons for this situation, and excessive politization of the positions and operations in the enterprise, which should have a primarily professional character, is another. If we add to this the excessive formalization and regulation in the processes of work and decision making, we have a fairly clear picture of the mosaic of causes for the failures in the area of management development.

Centralization and bureaucratization at various levels were characteristic for the countries of Eastern Europe, while Yugoslavia had 40 years of self-management, of decentralization of the decision-making process at all levels — from the individual company to the commune, the republic and the

Federation. However, despite considerable differences in historical development, there were nevertheless some very similar characteristics, especially as regards the value systems in these societies: equal opportunities for development, a large measure of social security for the employees, protection of the standard of living of the whole population by both the enterprises and the state, glorification of physical labor, the principle of equal remuneration, etc.

The reform processes will certainly change some values. Human resource management and the creation of a new management model, which is slowly emerging in individual countries, is certainly an area which will have a decisive influence on the future course of events in this part of the world. In the present contribution an attempt will be made to present the basic problems and trends of developments in this area in Yugoslavia.

2. Postwar Developments

The present situation in Yugoslavia must be seen against the background of postwar developments. The system of self-management, which has constituted the basis of Yugoslav economic and political life for over 40 years was a response to the economic blockade of Yugoslavia by the socialist countries in 1948. The new system introduced the participation of employees at all levels of the decision-making process, not only within the enterprise, but also at the level of the local community, the constituent republic and the Federation. It safeguarded the rights of the employees, protecting them against unjustified dismissal and similar.

In the fifties, the development strategy of the country was based on the theory of industrialization common to all socialist countries: Import substitution, internal criteria of development, controlled prices, administrative allocation of capital. Between 1955 and 1965 the Yugoslav model appeared to be a very successful one; this was a period of high productivity growth (4.8% annually), capital efficiency and economic growth (8.8% average annual growth of GDP). During this time Yugoslavia developed significant industrial capacity, technical knowledge, research infrastructure and management competence. However, particularly after the reform of 1965 — an unsuccessful attempt to open the national economy to international competition — intervention by the state prevented the qualitative and structural transformation of the economy. The result was above average growth of real wages, more rapid growth of imports (15.1%) than exports (10.0%) and a decline in new investments. Furthermore, inappropriate development

criteria led to duplication of production capacities in the individual constituent republics and provinces. Unprofitable investment projects raised production costs, the Yugoslav economy became increasingly indebted, while
exports declined steeply.

In the 1980s, the Yugoslav economy was thus characterized by above
average consumption of energy, raw materials, capital and labor per unit
of production, obsolete technical standards and lack of know-how, insufficient investment in marketing, low quality of goods and services, low rates
of domestic savings, inefficient use of knowledge and human capital,[1] a
negative balance of payments, a negative balance of trade, subsidization of
weak industries to preserve employment and to maintain the standard of
living, and an accelerating rate of inflation, which reached 1,500% in 1989.

In 1989, after a long and unsuccessful series of endeavours to effect the
necessary institutional changes, a radical economic reform was launched by
the Markovic government. The reform has transformed the Yugoslav economy into a market economy and is providing a highly conducive environment for joint ventures and other forms of cooperation with foreign countries. Over thirty new laws (on foreign investment, on enterprise, tax policy,
etc.) provide a broad and solid framework for the new economic policy and
for changes in management structures. The crucial feature of these changes
is the new role of human resources management, which in the past had an
ad hoc self-management function but which is now becoming a professional
management activity.

3. The Economic Reform and Changes in Mangement

Although self-management constituted the ideological and legal basis for
the society, there has always been a latent conflict in the relationship between
the state and the system of self-management in enterprises (and at the lower
levels of the administration in general) — a conflict between centralization
and decentralization. In order to achieve its economic and social goals, the
state regularly deliberately intervened in the operations of the companies,
through price controls on raw materials and finished products, controls on
imports of raw materials, technology and spare parts, controls on exports
and on wages. Management was also constricted by the self-management

---

[1] 80% of R & D experts work in the universities and institutes, i. e. they are not
directly involved with the production process.

system within the company itself. Despite very extensive normative regulations, there were many unclear elements in the system, mainly due to the
confusion regarding the division of competences between management and
the self-management bodies in the companies. The position of manager in
a self-managed company is an *office* rather than a profession.[2] The manager
is chosen and appointed by the workers' council (for a period of 4 years,
reappointment is possible) and is responsible to the workers' council.[3]

Under the system of self-management, managers are expected to ensure
conditions which permit full and effective participation of the employees in
the decision-making process. The law has tended to be very concerned with
the interests of the companies. The employees' interests were furthermore
mainly confined to the satisfaction of basic needs such as housing and
pecuniary remuneration, and the realization of short-term goals. And,
because of the dominant position of the workers' council in the area of
general strategy and policy, the management function was limited to day-
to-day operations and to keeping up good relations with the local authorities.
Consequently, the most important functions of the management were: first,
to fulfil the basic needs of the employees and to attain short-term goals;
and second, to secure support (from banks and government) at times of
crisis.

Until recently, there was practically no competition among producers.
Thus the structures and organization of companies tended to be inflexible
and the employees became passive and unprofessional. Recent research has
revealed that on average top managers in Yugoslavia stay with a company
twice as long as their counterparts in the U.S.A. The risks of entrepreneurship have been transferred from the company to the State, the Party and
the banks.

---

[2] Because executives were seen as officials, until recently there was no special school
   or educational institution in Yugoslavia for managers. The establishment of the
   first management school, the Executive Development Centre, at Brdo near Kranj
   in 1986, was the first step towards recognition of management as a profession.
   A second step, a new school, is now about to follow.
[3] The question whether the manager is an official or a professional reveals a series
   of dilemmas with regard to the management function in self-managed organizations. In the self-management system two things are expected of a good executive:
   he has to be a good businessman and he must be able to get on well with the
   authorities. The idea that the executive is an official is primarily based on the
   theoretical analysis of self-management. If the employees work at workplaces
   which are social property, then they also have the right to decide what should be
   done with the fruits of their labours and how their work should be organized.
   That means that there is an integration of the organizational functions of leadership, management and administration and there is no longer a special group
   of professional managers. (Kavčič 1987: 209–213).

Confronted with rapid technological changes, the Yugoslav economy will have to effect changes in the legal structures, in industrial and political relations, and particularly in the attitudes of all those involved (employees, managers, politicians).

The changes introduced by the economic reforms and the new legislation in 1989 are providing the necessary conditions for the development of the entrepreneurial spirit in Yugoslav enterprises. In fact, we could see this as a new model of socialism. Its success will depend primarily on whether the basic propositions underlying the new legislation can be fulfilled:

1) All enterprises (whether they are social, private, mixed or cooperative property) will operate under the same conditions.
2) New criteria for incentive and motivation of employees and executives will be introduced. In the new environment executives will have more responsibility and this calls for better educated and more entrepreneurial executives.
3) There will have to be change in the corporate culture[4] if Yugoslav companies are to succeed in a market economy. Every interest group in the company must start to think and to behave differently (become consumer-oriented, develop marketing skills and orientation, strengthen the links between marketing, R & D and consumers, make the organizational structure of the enterprise more flexible, change the "image" of the employee, i.e. eliminate anti-intellectualism and boost teamwork). These necessary changes will confront Yugoslav society with the need for new skills to solve new problems, for example: how to manage conflict, particularly conflicts of interests within the organization how to undertake collective bargaining;[5] how to operate and manage a company based on capital (and not only on labour, as has been the case up to the present); how to define the role (rights and duties) of executives under the new conditions, and their relationship with the other groups in the production process — supervisory boards, workers' councils, unions, etc.; and how to undertake management development and human resource development under the new conditions.

---

[4] Only very recently have some of the best, internationally-oriented companies (e.g. the Gorenje concern and some others) begun to consider the concept of corporate culture and made efforts to involve all employees in the shaping of a corporate culture and its integration into company strategy.

[5] The trade unions are only new becoming acquainted with this model of labor relations and are still learning the procedure.

4. Human Resource Management — From Social to Professional Activity

Up to the present, personnel management has been, at best, a peripheral activity in Yugoslav companies. Decisions on such matters as employment, dismissals, recruitment, motivation and remuneration were in the competence of various commissions, committees and other self-management bodies, whose members for the most part knew nothing, or very little, about personnel management. The experts in the field were required merely to report and to propose solutions. As a result, decisions regarding personnel were neither well-considered nor appropriate. Not only were there various self-management commissions, in most companies there were also a number of influential individuals who meddled in the affairs of the personnel department, giving directions, making proposals and sometimes even demands. Thus in point of fact, human resource management really had a social function and the personnel managers were no more than administrators of this socialized personnel policy (Zrismek 1989: 81).

Beside the internal factors which made professional personnel management impossible, there were also different bodies and institutions outside the company which greatly curtailed the independence of the personnel services. For example, the Self-Management Court, the communes, the socio-political groups, the unions, the Party, etc. Decisions were not taken on the basis of knowledge.[6]

There were practically no dismissals, nor was it possible to transfer an employee from one workplace to another (if he was needed elsewhere, or if it was thought that he would do better at another workplace). This considerably limited the scope for flexibility within the company. Once an employee had a workplace, he stayed there, no matter what happened.

4.1 The Personnel Department

A low level of expertise, lack of coordination and smallness are typical for personnel departments in Yugoslav companies. Hitherto, they have been concerned mainly with social problems, with things which were in essence

---

[6] Practice and research have shown that problems with regard to the influence of external agents on the work of the management arise above all in cases where the cooperation between the supervisory board, the workers' council and the employees breaks down. It is typical for successful companies that all actors in the process cooperate in mutual efforts to achieve the common goal, the success of the organization. (Glas 1985).

within the competence of trade union organizations. They had, above all, as has been mentioned, *a social function*. The economic reform, and with it the reform of the enterprise, has also provided the right framework for the transformation of the structure and competences of the managerial and self-management bodies in the company. The self-management bodies are losing the right to decide on concrete personnel matters — such as the engagement of new employees, their deployment in the organization, transfers, promotions, dismissals, remuneration, etc. In future these matters will be regulated by collective agreements and other legal provisions.

With the new legislation there will be greater opportunities for motivation and remuneration — where there had been a tendency to political egalitarianism, to level downwards on the principle that: "we are all equal, and so we must all get equal pay."

The right to work brought all the other rights — the right to housing, schooling, health care and social protection. Thus the employee usually received a wage which was determined more by his needs (a big family, for example, needs a bigger apartment, etc.), than by his contribution to the productive process. This policy had still stronger roots in other socialist countries (in some countries such principles led to severe discrimination, for example the selection of people who were allowed to study on the basis of social criteria and not school results; the development of the children of intellectuals or members of higher classes was impeded — which was never the case in Yugoslavia).

In the self-management system the employees assessed each other's performance, and all assessments were made on the basis of the "systematization" of jobs, a document which was adopted in the self-management bodies after long discussions by all employees. This document was usually a compromise between the different interests of the employees in the company, a result of: "I'll vote for you, if you vote for me" deals, and not of planned and professional work in a personnel service, with the involvement of the employees in the preparation of the document.

With regard to remuneration, for example, Yugoslavia had reached a ratio 1:3 between the lowest and the highest wage in a company; but when the economic crisis struck in the seventies and eighties and the lowest-paid employees were very close to subsistence level, many companies changed this ratio to 1:2. Since the companies in Yugoslavia are organized on the principle of self-management and are thus to a large extent autonomous, we cannot say that the situation was the same everywhere. Some successful export-oriented enterprises were able to remunerate the employees in such a way that those at the bottom of the wage scale had a respectable living wage, while the salaries of the personnel with higher qualifications were such as to motivate them to stay with the company and make their contribution to its development.

4.2 Problems in the Educational Structure of the Workforce

Not only is the professional level of the personnel departments low, so is the professional level of the workforce. For example, in Slovenia, the economically most highly developed republic in Yugoslavia, 40.3% of the workforce have no professional training of any kind, 27.5% have completed three years of vocational training (following 8 years of elementary schooling) and 20.9% have secondary education. Only 11.1% of the workforce have college or university education and only a quarter of these graduated from a technical faculty (this is obviously a big problem for the development of high technology and of industry in general.[7] Comparative studies show that Yugoslavia is lagging 20 to 30 years behind the developed countries as regards the education of the workforce (Zrismek 1989: 75−77).

The improvement of the existing personnel structure is thus one of the priorities for personnel departments in enterprises. Here it should be noted that in Slovenia, more than a third of the employees do not have appropriate training for the work which they are doing. The figures are similar for the whole of Yugoslavia, except that in the less developed republics the problem is still more acute because of the lack of people with technical skills.[8]

The economic crisis in Yugoslavia is the result not only of an ill-advised educational policy (which has its deeper roots in the ideological paradigm that in a socialist society every citizen has the opportunity to study whatever he likes), but also of the unwise investment policy of the past twenty years (investment in large systems, in high technology in areas where conditions would suggest labour-intensive, rather than capital-intensive industry). Further, there is the egalitarian philosophy mentioned above, which has led to a drain of the best trained personnel through emigration, and the fact that

---

[7] With the Associated Labour Law passed in the mid-70s, Yugoslavia equated productivity with material (physical) production and the quality of work was not a criterion for the promotion and remuneration of employees. The quality of work was not even the basis for employment or dismissal. As a result, education and knowledge were devalued and both companies and individuals lost their motivation for education. The 1980s saw a significant decline of interest in further study, but the economic reform of 1989 heralded a new, more encouraging era for the acquisition of knowledge at all levels. (Kranjc 1984).

[8] One of the biggest problems of the underdevelopment in the province of Kosovo is in fact that with the awakening of Albanian national consciousness, the younger generation concentrated on the study of Albanian literature, music, etc., but there is a lack of engineers specializing in metallurgy, machine building and similar areas. In view of the fact that the Kosovo region has great potential in primary industry (mines, iron and steelworks, etc.) this problem is crucial.

the enterprise has had primarily social and political functions. While in some countries progressive parties are making efforts to ensure that the factories are not only places where people work, but also places where they learn and develop cultural and social interests of all kinds, Yugoslavia — and in my view other socialist countries too — have gone to extremes in this respect.[9]

The social security of the individual was the foremost consideration, and complete job security meant that the labor market did not develop and that there is now a great immobility of the workforce within the individual company and in the economy in general and a considerable amount of concealed unemployment, which constituted, and is still constituting a heavy burden on the economy and leading to the collapse of factories the moment they are exposed to economic laws, to a market economy.

4.3 New Trends in the Area of Human Resource Management in Yugoslavia

The economic reforms and the reform of the enterprise have opened new opportunities for the development of personnel, motivation, remuneration, and similar. The new legislation permits the transfer of employees as the company requires and permits rather more flexibility, but many things are still unclear, that is, they are left to the discretion of the individual company. Where the management of the company has been able to convince the majority of the people that their strategy is right, the climate for the introduction of change is very different from that in companies where the cult of physical labour is still predominant and where the concept of the individual's contribution is conceived in terms of hours, and not as the employee's contribution to the creation of new value in the widest sense.

It is therefore very difficult to speak of any minimum standards and of a model of the situation as regards human resource management in Yugoslavia. In the past two years some of the most progressive companies (e. g.

---

[9] Up to the present Yugoslav companies have been operating in a significantly different environment than that of companies in developed countries. Firstly, the companies are set in systems which ensured them of almost complete economic safety (the solution of economic problems with the help of high prices set by the companies or by the state administration and support from reserve funds which loss-making companies receive — irrespective of their business perspectives); secondly, the legislation gave employees almost complete job security; and thirdly the employees did not accept the entrepreneurial role, but preferred the traditional areas of trade union activity, such as pay rises and job security, irrespective of the performance of the company. (Svetlik 1987: 255).

the pharmaceuticals factory Krka, the Gorenje concern) have, despite the fact that the old system was still in operation, already begun planned development and monitoring of personnel development. Such companies (e. g. Gorenje, Elan, Lesnina, Rotomatika and others) have also restructed their enterprises in all areas — they have begun to send larger groups of people for external training, they have begun to build up a corporate culture, etc. They have, on their own or through the first management school in Yugoslavia, initiated the transfer of knowledge from well organized companies in other parts of the world into their companies, adapting it to suit their own conditions. Companies with really progressive managements have, for example, already begun to send their executives and young managers in transition to study in other countries.

The transitional period is naturally painful and often appears at first to have technocratic features. This is rather like the issue of the concept of the market and the market economy or that of political democracy in the countries of eastern Europe. The strongest support for the free market, for a radical curtailing of social benefits, for pure professionalization of human resource management, for the dissolution of the communist parties, etc., often comes from countries hitherto characterized by very little market, a dearth of political rights (here Yugoslavia was an exception) and a multitude of social benefits.

It will probably not be long before a synthesis between these two attitudes is reached and new models of human resource management are developed on the basis of the traditions of the countries and the companies, and parallel to this will be the introduction of a model of a more professional attitude to work, more quality and also more flexibility. And perhaps then the model of self-management, which Yugoslavia has very successfully developed for almost forty years, will be transformed and improved. Perhaps it will become less a formal system and more a concept, a way for people to work and live. Perhaps the employees will not have as many rights as they used to have when decisions on big investments (which they never understood anyway) are taken, but more rights in matters concerning their own immediate environment, at work and in the community — rights which directly concern them and their own development.

The term "management of people" has never been accepted in Yugoslavia, because of its negative ideological connotation. The term "human resource management" is now being introduced, but at a time when people are beginning to look at this area with different eyes, emphasizing that people are not resources, not human capital, but that the capital is the people's knowledge and talent, and that consequently we should be speaking of "managing people's talents."[10]

---

[10] In this connection there was an interesting discussion published by Pierre Casse in the IMEDE Perspectives for Managers, Lausanne, No. 5, 1989.

It is true that one swallow does not make a summer, but nevertheless we see that a large section of the (developed) Yugoslav economy is becoming aware of the importance of a qualitative shift in the conception and significance of personnel development. And that the market — however we understand it — plays a positive role in this regard by putting a price on people and knowledge.

References

Casse, Pierre (1989): *Perspectives for Mangers* (No. 5), Lausanne. IMEDE.

Glas, Miroslav et al. (1985): *Notranji dejavniki poslovne uspesnosti organizacij zdruzenega dela v SR Sloveniji* (Internal factors contributing to the success of self-managed organizations in Slovenia), Ljubljana.

Kavcic, Bogdan (1987): *Tehnologija in samoupravljanje* (Technology and Self-Management), Socioloske teme, Ljubljana.

Kranjc, Ana (1984): *Sodoben razvoj izobrazevanja odraslih* (Contemporary development of adult education), Zavod za tehnicno izobrazevanje, Ljubljana.

Svetlik, Ivan (1987): *Zaposlovanje: Uveljavljanje znanja pri delu* (Employment: Application of knowledge at the workplace), Socioloske teme, Ljubljana.

Zrimsek, Zdravko (1989): *Naloge kadrovskih sluzb v novih pogojih. Kadrovska funkcija in podjetnistvo* (The Tasks Facing Personnel Departments under the New Conditions, the Personnel Function and Entrepreneurship), Symposium of Personnel Managers, Bled.

Human Resource Management in Czechoslovakia — Management Development as the Key Issue

Ondrej Landa

1. Introduction

As many other industrial nations, Czechoslovakia and its economy and the whole society face an acute challenge of radical increase of efficiency, international competitiveness and far-reaching changes in traditional economic as well as social structures. This requires steering the economy from the course of extensive (i. e. capital and labor consuming) growth to an intensive mode of development that is based on increasing productive power of science and high technologies combined with efficient social organisation, international co-operation and innovation-oriented patterns of social behaviour.

These concepts are the springboard of the current socio-economic reform that has been under way in Czechoslovakia for the past two years. The declared goal of this "Czechoslovak perestroika" is to release all innovative forces in the society that have been hampered by the old administrative-bureaucratic system of economic planning and social control.

Czechoslovakia's only resource for this demanding programme of societal change is the good educational standard, ingenuity and inventiveness, rich cultural tradition and workmanship of its people. Hence the crucial role of the "human factor" for the success of our reforms and the focus on human resource management as the cornerstone of the renewal of corporate competitiveness and efficiency.

2. Tradition and Current Problems of Human Resource Management in Czechoslovak Companies

Four decades of socialist societal system have created a new tradition of HRM of its own right, a distinctive HRM culture, indeed. Since the late forties the Communist-Party-governed state has tried to offer tangible proofs that socialism is a historically superior system as far as the social well-being of the working people is concerned.[1]

In the name of greater social security new labor laws were adopted to protect the rights of employees to such an extent as made it almost impossible to fire people even for permanently sloppy performance. The corporate management was put under strong political and social control of the Communist Party and Trade Union organisations. As a consequence, it gradually lost its independence and action-readiness. Heavy and strenuous manual work was celebrated as the main source of societal wealth. The importance of intellectual work was often underestimated.

2.1 Social Planning

The redistribution of societal wealth through a range of social benefits offered to the employees of socialist organizations is one of the characteristical features of the Czechoslovak HRM system whose tradition goes back to the late 1940s. The enterprises have assumed an important role of providers of various social services that improved material well-being of employees and created better conditions for the satisfaction of their developmental needs.

Material benefits typically include the provision of company flats or substantial financial help for individual construction schemes, free children care in creches and nursery schools, extensive company- and trade union-sponsored recreation, spa vouchers, interest-free loans for major household purchases, or subsidised household services (to-the-door order shopping, transport service and deliveries, reparations, car rentals etc.).

Intellectual and cultural development is supported by free in-company and external educational and training programmes, company-sponsored

---

[1] The authoritarian aberrations of the Stalinist regime should be clearly distinguished from the progressive and often rather generous working-class-oriented welfare and social policies that were pursued at the same time.

participation in distance study on secondary, college and university levels, subsidised or free theatre and concert tickets, art exhibitions on company premises, collective excursions to places of historical or cultural interest, local trade union libraries. Larger companies even constructed their own Houses of Culture — large establishments with a numerous professional staff.

Physical fitness care is provided for, too. Many companies have their own amateur clubs where hundreds of thousands employees practice recreational sports. Free access to public sport and recreational facilities is offered by the majority of Czechoslovak organisations. Large companies have their own excellent facilities.

A major part of these social benefits and developmental activities is covered from Cultural and Social Needs Fund (CSNF) that is established by every company by law. An equivalent of 2% from the organization's overall payroll fund has to be allocated to the CSNF every year. All employees are entitled to enjoy the benefits of the scheme. Company branches of the trade union organization play the key role in the administration of the corporate social and cultural programmes. These programmes had been run as a separate, consumption-oriented part of the organisations' activities until the end of 1970s. They were only partially linked to the performance of individuals and were not considered to be a particularly important factor for the enhancement of the company's productive potential.

Only in the beginning of the 1980s when it became increasingly obvious that the traditional model of extensive economic growth had reached its limits, the corporate social benefit programmes begun to be transformed into an integral part of the company planning systems. Heretofore loose social programmes were linked to other company programmes geared to the improvement of the quality of the working life and to the enhancement of the role of the human factor in increasing the organisation's productivity and innovation potential.

Comprehensive plans of social development were introduced by a few most progressive companies at first. In 1986, however, a special Governmental Decree on the Planning of the Personnel and Social Development (the so called Social Planning Decree) was passes that made it obligatory for all enterprises to formulate a comprehensive social plan as an integral part of the organization's planning system. The key feature of this concept was an emphasis on the content linkage of the comprehensive plan of social development with other mid-term and long-range plans of the company (financial, production, R & D, investment, personnel). The general purpose was to put corporate social programmes into service of the accelerated development of enterprises, of increasing their productivity and innovative potential. The pivotal role of the "human factor" in corporate strategic planning was thus acknowledged and the full use of the social driving forces of the enhanced performance and innovation was to be strived for.

The bureaucratic-administrative approach to redefining the social dimension of the corporate planning systems undermined the efficiency of the new legislation, however. Only a few companies were farsighted enough to recognize the crucial importance of strategic human resource management for the sustained development and long-term economic success. In far too many cases the norms of the Social Planning Decree were implemented rather formally within basically unchanged organizational structures as another regulatory measure imposed by the state authorities. They were left in the discretion of personnel departments that lacked both the necessary authority and the expertise to prepare and carry out comprehensive socially-based strategic plans. At the same time, the capacities of external professional consulting services were limited and only rarely available for the in-depth structural revision of the corporate planning systems. Competent and appropriately staffed strategic planning units and/or conceptual teams that would work closely with the corporate top management were clearly very much needed.

Comprehensive plans of social development have been most effective when they were elaborated as a part of total reconstruction and innovation projects that assured their close linkage with other structural parts of organisation's strategic plan. Such capital-intensive projects are usually subsidised from the state budget and get the logistical support from branch applied research institutes. In the majority of Czechoslovak companies, however, the challenge of comprehensive social planning and strategic human resource management is still to be met.

2.2 Remuneration and Incentive Systems

The prevailing egalitarian socio-economic appreciation of work was reflected accordingly in pay systems and resulted in the remuneration levelling between highly qualified/skilled and unqualified/unskilled work. Such a misinterpretation of the concept of the socialist collectivism also tended to foster egalitarian tendencies in remuneration within the same job categories regardless of the individual performance resulting in the subsequent loss of motivation for top-level performance. An unwritten social norm of more or less equal pay for everybody in the same work group had been established in a great number of Czechoslovak organisations. To a large extent, management lost the basic stimulaton tool.

The roots of the loss of effectiveness of the pay systems can be traced back to the early fifties. Their underlying social and economic patterns are very resilient. In spite of several reforms of pay tariff systems that were intended to increase the management's leverage in this domain, the remuneration levelling as an economic and social phenomenon still exists.

Only 21.5% of 3610 managers, engineers and technicians from more than 700 companies that have taken part in a recent survey did point out that the above-average performers are significantly better paid in their organizations than those employees whose performance is under-average.

Czechoslovak socialism traditionally learned toward moral stimulation of the top-level performance and innovation activities. The post-war enthusiasm that accompanied the initial build-up period of the socialist society in Czechoslovakia supported the illusion of unexhaustive sources of working people's energy and inner drive to work for the better future of all. Gradually, however, the management tended to take this initiative for a moral obligation of every employee. Extra working hours, rising target quotas and appeals to employees' co-responsibility of the overall performance of the company were almost routinely recurred to wherever the problems to fulfill the plan were encountered. Often employees' involvement and self-sacrifying efforts were to compensate for the incompetent management or unreliable deliveries. Consequently, the impact of moral incentives has decreased to a great extent. The renewal of the stimulation power of both material and moral incentives is one of the big issues of the current Czechoslovak economic reform.

2.3 Employee Education and Training

General approach to employee qualification development has been rather generous in Czechoslovak organizations in the past decades. It is a standard practice that employees apply for further studies under various distance schemes with the company's backing. If they obtain the company's support they are automatically entitled to the distance studies scheme benefits that offer up to 30 days of the paid leave each year to attend the classes that a part of the particular educational programme or to take part in the ecaminations. The distance student is entitled to 80 days of the paid leave to prepare the diploma dissertation, too. This scheme in anchored in the present Labor Codex and covers all types of graduate and post-graduate studies. Usually all material costs of distance study (tuition fees — if involved, travel and board, in some instance even study materials), are covered by the sponsoring organisation as well.[2]

---

[2] In Czechoslovakia all secondary, pre-graduate and graduate studies are free. No tuition fee is collected. All expenses of schools, colleges and universities are coverted by the Ministry of Education from the state budget. Only for special post-graduate courses the tuition fee is required. Also the majority of learning/ training programmes offered by branch management development institutes and other educational and training institutions collect the tuition from the participants.

In order to secure the benefits from the new knowledge and skills acquired by their employees organizations usually tie their support of distance studies under the above conditions with the signature of the "fidelity contract" by the employee. It is usual that the employee has to agree not to quit the sponsoring organization for as many or twice as many years as he or she enjoys the organization's distance study support. Companies also try to secure the steady inflow of young talents by offering scholarships to the college and university students. In consideration, the students sign an agreement to join the organization in question upon graduation and stay with it for the stipulated number of years.

An integral part of companies' educational and training schemes is a number of in-company training programmes led by invited specialists from the universities, research institutes and/or govermental administrative bodies. The corporate specialists also participate in professional meetings, conferences, seminars and training programmes run by the Czechoslovak Scientific and Technical Society and other professional associations.

3. Management Development — Its Tradition and Current Practice in Czechoslovak Organizations

Management development activities represent the key element of the Czechoslovak human resource management system. Management education and training programmes are an important agent of the fundamental improvement of the corporate management and leadership that is a necessary precondition of the renewal of organisational efficiency, innovativeness and competitiveness.

Czechoslovak management development is very interesting, too, because it is an institutionalized system with a specific tradition. Management development has been an object of great attention and support from the state in the past twenty years. There were several reasons for this effort to raise the level of leadership skills and management performance of Czechoslovak executives and managers:

- recognition of the key role of efficient corporate management as an agent of innovation and development,
- far-reaching revamping of management in the years 1969 – 1971 as a consequence of political changes in Czechoslovakia,

— introduction in 1971 of the binding general principles of cadre and personnel policy that postulated that life-long cyclical development and training was a basic qualification requirement of every manager regardless of his or her seniority,
— attention given to management development in other socialist countries and the challenge of international managerial know-how and teaching methods.

3.1 Comprehensive performance appraisals and assessment of the leadership potential

The universality and comprehensiveness of Czechoslovak system of personnel management and management development may be presented as the two advantage points that created an opportunity for the smooth development of efficient strategic human resource management in the very beginning of the 1970s. All executives, managers and other "cadres" — virtually the entire professional staff of any organization — were included in the scheme by administrative decrees of the highest political and governmental bodies.

According to these decrees every "cadre" and "cadre reserve" (those who did not yet hold managerial positions but were being prepared for them) were to pass a periodical — once in every two to five years — comprehensive commissional review of his or her managerial/professional performance and growth potential. The core of this procedure is

— a rigorous appraisal of the attestee's performance and results produced in the preceding period,
— an assessment to what degree the personal developmental goals that had been set by the previous appraisal session were met,
— evaluation of the attestee's political profile and activities,
— an assessment of the attestee's developmental potential and of his or her suitability for the present or proposed position,
— the formulation of the key goals of the personal professional growth for the following period.

The results of the comprehensive appraisal of managerial/professional performance and leadership potential are subsequently elaborated into an Individual Plan of Personal Development. On this base specific learning and training activities and programmes are to be selected and/or devised to meet the manager's developmental needs. This process is schematically represented in the Figure 1.

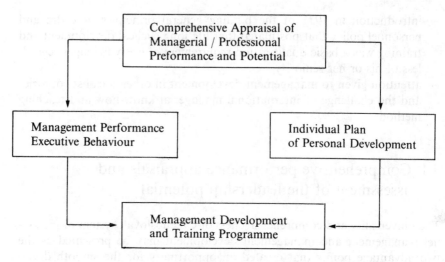

Figure 1: Management Development Cycle in Czechoslovak Organisations

The above system has been in use in Czechoslovak organizations since the early 1970s. Its potentialities have not been fully exploited, however. The system suffers from the typical ailments of centrally imposed administrative measures. It looks fine on paper but it has been implemented rather formally and it is rarely fully integrated into the day-to-day management practice. Comprehensive appraisals of the managerial/professional performance and leadership potential have often degenerated into one-shot campaigns that al parties involved wish to run as smoothly as possible and whose practical purpose is to rubber-stamp the status quo. Individual Plans of Personnel Development tend to be rather formal documents that may have a formidable appearance but lack the real commitment from both the subject himself and his superiors. Many managers resign themselves without any real interest and conviction to the participation in the recommended or obligatory management development and training programmes. They may have a good reason sometimes because the practical value of some of these programmes is rather dubious.

3.2 The Cyclical Management Development Scheme

Management development and training programmes did, in fact, enjoy even greater support from the central governmental and Communist Party bodies than the introduction of universal management appraisal system. An enormous effort and huge sums of money were invested into creating an universal training system that would take comprehensive care of managers' developmental and Communist Party decrees inaugurated the so called Cyclical Management Development Scheme that encompassed some 340.000 Czechoslovak managers "from the shop-floor steward to the minister". The ambitious idea was to create an institutional system that would make up for largely insufficient management education during regular graduate studies and provide a career-long re-training of all managers in Czechoslovak organizations.

A network of management development and training institutions was established. At the top of the institutional pyramid are the Institutes of Management in Prague and Bratislava that are commissioned — together with the Institute of the State Administration — to train the chief executive officers of the largest Czechoslovak corporations and the senior governmental and public administration officials. Similarly, each ministry founded its own branch management development institute responsible for the training of the senior managers of companies, R & D institutes and other organisations within the administrative jurisdiction of the respective ministry. Also many large corporations and companies established well-equiped management training centres that served their middle and lower-level managers.

It was the ambition of the Cyclical Management Development Scheme (CMDS) to involve all Czechoslovak managers in the Basic Management Development Programme in the first "cycle" (1972—1977). The Programme was to provide the fundamentals of management sciences. It was conceived as a series of 5-day or 10-day off-the-job seminars (altogether some 280 teaching hours grouped into five to ten entensive sessions stretched to one year or one year and a half period). During the second part of the Programme all participants elaborated on a dissertation project geared to the application of the acquired knowledge and skills to the solution of a selected problem of their job. The graduation from the Programme depended on the successful presentation of the dissertation before the commission of experts and representatives of the organisation concerned.

The participation in the Programme was obligatory as a fundamental part of the career planning of all "cadres". Once a manager was nominated by the personnel department of his company, only the most urgent personal or working reasons could elicit the postponement of his or her participation. The whole scheme was backed by the authority of the Communist Party and its implementation was closely monitored by the highest CP organs. The active involvement in the implementation of the CMDS was one of the key appraisal criteria of the chief executives of Czechoslovak organisations. The exemption from the Basic Programme was possible only when the particular manager was personally involved in the officially recognised proxy developmental activities such as research projects or CMDS lecturing.

A great effort was exerted to ensure the structural compatibility of individual learning/training programmes run by various management development institutes and training centres within the CMDS. For the purpose of the mass-scale implementation of the CMDS, executives and managers were grouped into several categories:

Cat. 1   — ministers of federal and state governments, presidents of regional administrations
Cat. 2   — CEOs of corporations and largest companies, senior governmental officials
Cat. 3A — managing directors of companies and large plants, heads of ministerial departments corporate senior staff officers
Cat. 3B — senior staff officers on the company level, lower levels of corporate staff management
Cat. 4A — plant managers, lower-level staff managers on the company level
Cat. 4B — junior line managers (foremen, shop stewards, etc.)[3].

For each executive/management category there was a specially designed learning/training programme that took into account the specificities and needs of management on that particular level: in case of categories 3 and 4 these programmes responded to the conditions of the particular industry, too. Sponsoring management development and training institutions had to submit for approval by supervising CMDS board a formal project and scenario for each type of CMDS learning/training programme they planned to inaugurate. The Master Projects of the Basic Management Development Programme for individual executive/management categories were prepared by teams of experts to provide guidance to individual management development institutes and training centres.

This formidable management development scheme had several weak points that proved to be of crucial importance:

1. The broad frontal approach to the implementation of the CMDS strained the human resources of management development institutions. To build new training facilities was easier than to staff them with competent instructors and lecturers. Too many training programmes were started at

---

[3] The management development and training responsibilities for the above executive/managerial groups were assigned to the following institutions:
   Cat. 1 The University of Political Sciences of the Central Committee of the Communist Party of Czechoslovakia
   Cat. 2 Institutes of Management in Prague and Bratislava, Institute of the State Administration
   Cat. 3 branch management development institutes
   Cat. 4 corporate training institutes, company training centres

the same time and many an organiser found it impossible to get the first-class instructors. Therefore, many specialists without any previous teaching or facilitating experience were quickly turned into lecturers. Only a small part had enough pedagogical talent to master the specific skills needed for successful management training. In most cases the quality of management development programmes suffered.

2. The content of the first CMDS cycle was too heavily theory-oriented. The conceptors of the scheme felt that the participants should master not only the basics of the general management theory but the broad cross-cut of economic, political, psychological, sociological, organisational and informatics foundations of management and business administration as well. Kaleidoscopic, rater superficial course programmes resulted from this approach. Usually there was neither time enough for in-depth exploration of the key management problems nor for training of practical management and leadership skills. Lectures prevailed: participative teaching methods were only rarely used. Managers and executives taking part in the CMDS programmes found little or no relevance to the practical issues of management in many teaching units. Consequently, management development and training lost much of its credit.

3. Management development was conceived as a mass process of training managers as individuals, not as members of specific management teams. At senior management levels (CMDS categories 2 and 3) the CMDS programmes addressed only general needs of managers at that particular hierarchical level, never specific management problems of a concrete company. As a consequence, the practical relevance of the CMDS programmes was questioned by the participants.

4. The Dissertation Projects that were to provide the practical focus of the whole programme for each participant suffered from the administrative-bureaucratic approach, too. The procedure was too formal, rigid and cumbersome. For the majority of participants, to write a dissertation was just another task to be fulfilled. The CMDS programmes were so disconnected from both the operational and the strategic problems of most organizations that only rarely somebody cared whether the particular Dissertation Project did bring innovative ideas or whether these ideas were implemented. Therefore, most managers treated their Dissertation Project as a writing exercise with little practical value.

5. All these features of CMDS programmes contributed to the emergence of the problems of study motivation and discipline. A great part of managers who were more or less arbitrarily nominated to the CMDS programmes lacked the necessary commitment and determination to learn. They mostly regarded the participation in the management development programme as one of many nuisances that accompany the management profession and not as an opportunity to enhance their own managerial competence. With such an attitude it was extremely difficult to reach significant results.

3.3 Management Development in the 1980s

The obvious problems of quality and efficiency of the training programmes and courses of the first cycle of the CMDS, while its costs — both financial and human — remained high, led to the loosening of the central control and to gradual abandonment of the whole scheme. Several years of decentralised management development system followed when companies were free to send their personnel to the training programmes offered by professional management development institutions or not. They continued to do so, but senior executives only rarely did participate themselves.

Therefore, in mid-eighties the Czechoslovak government decided to introduce a new centrally administered management development programme (MDP) for the top echelon of corporate managers. This system was far less ambitious than the CMDS a decade ago. Only about eight thousand corporate presidents, vice presidents and managing directors were included into this management development system. Its emphasis has been on personal study projects geared to the specific needs of individual participants. Each project is focused on the preparation of an important innovation for which the particular manager is responsible. Management development institutes supervise this process and enroll the participants in suitable topical seminars that are designed to provide methodological know-how for the successful completion of the individual innovation projects. Some institutes also offer limited consulting support for both preparation and implementation of the individual projects.

Although the whole system was designed to fit the needs of individual senior executives, the administrative approach to its implementation backfired again. Many participants lack inner motivation and drive that are necessary for the success of any innovation project. In far too many cases the participation in the MDP is considered to be a duty, not an opportunity to launch the process of personal and organizational change.

The very concept of individual development scheme is often inappropriate. The nature of managerial and organizational innovations requires the team approach to management development programmes. Participants find it often impossible to implement the MDP-inspired concepts in unreceptive, unprepared organisational setting. The MDP effectiveness suffers not only when the MDP-motivated individual innovation project does not grow out of the real development needs of the particular organisation but also when its solution and implementation is not organically woven into the company's life.

It is obvious that the current management development system cannot continue unchanged. It does not reflect the changing needs of business management and entrepreneurial challenge called forth by the Czechoslovak economic reform that is to leave its experimental stage in 1990. Vis-a-vis this 'Czechoslovak perestroika' challenge new management development concepts and forms have already emerged.

3.4 Recent Developments

The last two years brought several fundamental changes in the system of central planning, in standing economic mechanism as well as in labor legislation. These developments have a profound impact on the whole area of strategic human resource management, too, although it is not easy to make a reliable of the extent and sometimes even of the nature of these changes.

The new State Enterprise Law increased the economic independence of the companies and corporations. Direct administrative methods of central planning and control of economy gave place to a more market-based economic mechanism. Profit replaced the index of fulfilment of plan target quotas as the criterion of company's success and the base for funding its developmental needs.

The State Enterprise Law made the employees co-responsible for the management of their company: the job of Managing Director is elective by the Assembly of Worker's Delegates. The Company Workers' Council as the executive body of the new participation scheme has to approve all major decisions of the company's management (e. g. plan target quotas, key investment projects, profit distribution). Its representative takes an active part in the meetings of the company's Management Board, too.

The new laws on cooperative and private service activities deregulated some restrictive barriers that blocked entrepreneurial initiatives. The opportunities for cooperative or private management consulting and management development thus opened are being aggressively pursued by enterprising individuals or teams who offer original management training programmes and process consulting services. The transfer of advanced human resource management concepts and know-how has been facilitated. The progressive companies begin to respond to the available 'parallel' options of external HRM and management development expertise.

Czechoslovak management development, management research and management consulting institutions also begin to bridge the gap separating them from the current international theory and practice of management. The traditional isolationism is being speedily abandoned. International guest lectures appear more and more often in management development programmes. Special seminars with Western management professionals offered to the broad management public are becoming a commonplace. In October 1990 Prague is going to host the Second European Management Congress sponsored by CECIOS — European Council of Management. The Congress focus will be on Strategic Management and Innovation in International Perspective — Management Development and Consulting for the 1990's. A great seminal impact on the practice of human resource management in Czechoslovak organizations can be expected from the Congress.

The enhancement of entrepreneurial functions and market orientation of the state companies creates an urgent need for a new model of management education, development and training. Several institutes have introduced so called 'Socialist Entrepreurship Programmes'. The universities are experimenting with postgraduate studies in business administration that are designed to emulate the programmes of Western business schools and international management development institutes and their East European (Hungarian, Soviet, Polish) offsprings. New options for managerial education are being actively sought.

The current practice shows, however, that the ambitious domestic projects are not so easy to implement. The major subjects that make up the Western management development programmes, such as strategic management and policies, international marketing, innovation management, financial management, strategic human resource development have been absent from the curricula of the Czechoslovak management education institutions in the past two decades. There is a lack of competent teachers in these diciplines. Most institutes are not capable to get rid of their traditional training concepts that are theory-ladden, general methodology-oriented and predominantly psychological in skill training. The new 'socialist entrepreneurship training programmes' or 'management schools' do only a lip-service to modern business administration education so far.

The solution to this problem has been sought in partnership with Western partners. Several co-operation projects with international management schools are under discussion. The much needed transfer of modern management expertise occurs also within the framework of intergovernmental agreements of cultural, educational and scientific co-operation with the EC countries, USA and Canada. In 1990, the first groups of executives will take part in international management development programmes in United Kingdom, Sweden, FRG.

3.5 Czechoslovak Management Development Experience — Lessons for the Future

The in-depth excursion into the tradition of management development and training in Czechoslovakia permits to infer several general lessons that may be of some value to those countries or institutions that are seeking their own model of management education.

Beware of administrative approaches to management development! It is possible to press managers and executives into participation in management development and training programmes. It is impossible, however, to induce their high study motivation by decree. To be effective, the whole management development system has to be an organic part of a growth-oriented, constantly innovating and learning organisation. It must be supported by personnel policies that highly value managerial competence, creativity, entrepreneurial spirit, and ability to grow.

This organisational and managerial environment is a vital prerequisite of the full commitment of the company's staff to formal education and training programmes as well as to permanent informal self-development. I call the management development system that has been fully integrated into the organisation's permanent self-renewal the *organismic management development system.*

Too intricate system does not work:

The effects of management development and training programmes are achieved in the course-room and in the working place, not at the distant planner's desk. It does not have much sense to insist on perfect project that gets polished in several rounds of expert reviews (and sometimes not-too-expert reviews, too) if the programme staff lacks the means and know-how that are necessary for its successful implementation.

Match your resources with your ambition:

The idea of frontal involvement of the whole body of management staff at all hierarchical levels into a comprehensive management development scheme does have a lot of attraction. Czechoslovak experience shows that such mega-project may be sustained financially for a number of years. It is only a matter of investment priorities. The effectiveness of any management development system depends more on people than on funds available. It is extremely difficult, if not impossible, to staff too many management development and training programmes with top teachers and facilitators. It is better to have less management development but of high quality rather than to have everybody involved in poor programmes. The managers' attitude to development and training is too important to be sacrified to the overambitious management development schemes.

Do not sacrify highly effective intensive training forms for the sake of extensive training campaigns!

This is another aspect of the previous adage. The Czechoslovak government's decision to introduce the extensive Cyclical Management Development Scheme in 1972 forced several management development institutes to drop or unnecessarily revise their traditional − and in some cases rather successful — training programmes in order to cope with the heavy load of CMDS training activities.

The same fallacy tends to occur on the company level, too. It has become a commonplace that innovative companies invest heavily in the training of their employees. The top management of renewal-oriented organizations finds it sometimes convenient to emulate the mangement development and training policies of leading-edge companies by taking the decision to intro- duce an extensive "renewal" training programme designed to involve all core comployees. If such a priority is single-minded enough it may virtually wipe out rather input-intensive management development activities in the company no matter how vital they may be for the enhancement of the organisation's innovation potential.

Build the training programme around specific needs and management problems of the particular training group:

Avoid the pitfalls of the would-be efficiency of implementation of the universal master projects elaborated by ivory-tower experts that are not familiar with the specific problems and needs of the participants. Focus the teaching and training process on the real-life developmental problems and innovation projects of the participants. Use the problem-solving process as a framework for the transfer of the relevant body of knowledge as well as the stage for the development of the necessary conceptual, problem-solving and social skills, for the training in the implementation of appropriate methods. Treat each study group as unique.

Use the team approach to management development wherever feasible:

It is all right to provide individual managers and executives with excellent opportunities to study at the leading management development institutes. Though the impacts of such training on the individual's managerial potential are sometimes remarkable, the better part of its effects often gets lost in an unreceptive and resistent organizational environment. In our experience, the innovative management depends as much on creative teamwork as on competent leaders. If the top executives — no matter how well trained — are not supported by teams of atuned and committed people who share the common vision, the company will lack the necessary vitality, innovative thrust and determination.

An appropriately conceived problem-solving/training programme offers an excellent opportunity to develop such a teamwork and shared vision. At the same time, demanding objectives in the areas of skill training, innovation generation and strategic problem solving may be reached.

Use management development programmes for idea generation, innova- tion search, and strategic problem solving:

Do not "waste" the creative efforts of the participants by solving unrelated case studies and simulations. Focus on the imminent strategic and innovation problems of their own organisation(s). Let them feel the creative potential of the collective mind and effort. Facilitate their problem-solving activities and guide them to produce tangible results for the enhancement of innovation processes in their own organisation(s). Have the output from creative problem-solving activities printed and make it available to the participants on the spot.

Design special development programmes for young managerial talent; use management training to identify and commit the high-calibre young people:

Early management development and training is vital for the acceleration of the professional growth of the young staff members. If properly designed, it permits to assess the potential of individual participants, too. Often it triggers off the heretofore unmanifested leadership talent, creativity, responsibility and action-readiness. The successful participation in the specially designed programmes for the "cadre reserves" and "young managerial talents" shortened the career path of quite a few Czechoslovak managers to senior executive jobs.

Make management development competitive:

Do not press everybody to participate in a dull, unattractive training scheme. Design top-level management development programmes, advertise them throughout the company (industry) and let people compete for admission. Enhance the value of the programme by rigorous selection procedures.

Consistently support your management development system by the integrated HRM and personnel policies:

The first-class performance in a demanding management development/ training programme attesting to the high managerial potential should accelerate the career advancement. On the other hand, the human resource management system of the company must include a permanent and reliable search mechanism for the talented people to be nominated for participation in the special management development and training programmes.

Personal support and commitment of the CEO is crucial for the full effect of management development in any organisation:

The ambitious management development schemes failed to produce the intended results in many Czechoslovak organisations just because they were considered to be the responsibility of the functional departments (personnel, HRD, management development and training). Managing directors for whom management development is the top priority are a rarity. Without a

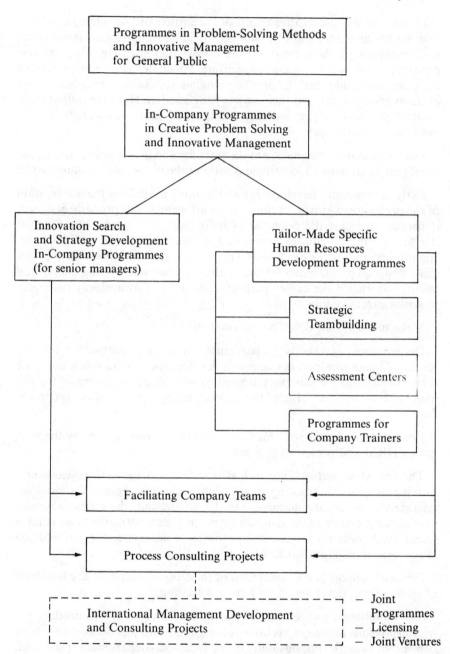

Figure 2: Modular System INVENTA — from General Management Development
and Training to Process Consulting and International Projects

determined support of the CEO the senior line managers feel free to relieve their subordinates from the training sessions that are a part of various management development programmes. As a consequence, management development and training quickly degenerates to an activity of secondary order that may be included into when there are no more pressing tasks and problems to be dealt with. Without CEO's unfaltering support management development can never become the prime agent of organisational renewal, nor the practical source of innovative ideas and activities.

Combine the management development and training activities with the process consulting:

The management development and training programmes that are limited only to the demonstration of efficient methods and approaches to strategic management problem-solving and innovation-generation tend to be sterile in the on-the-job practice of management. For instance, the creativity stimulation techniques that have been a part of management development programmes in Czechoslovakia for decades have not really found way to the corporate problem solving. The lack of professional follow-up consulting support proved to be crucial.

On the other hand, the results of the author's INVENTA Modular Management Development/Consulting System attest to the smooth transfer and organic diffusion of the methodological know-how in the organisations involved. The key factor of the success is the gradual transformation of the management development programme into a process consulting project. See the Figure 2 for the schematic illustration of the transition of the INVENTA Modular Management Development System to the process consulting projects.

4. The practice of Management Development in Czechoslovakia — Recapitulation and Prospects

For the purpose of clarity I will summarise the state of affairs and perspectives of Czechoslovak human resource management in a sequence of brief reviews. The Tables 1 and 2 recap the main assets and liabilities of the present HRM and management development system. An outline of the key factors that will have a definite impact on the future set-up of the management development and training in Czechoslovak organisations follows. The

Table 1: Human Resources Development Situation in Czechoslovakia —
          The Positives

- new awareness of the key role of the "human factor" for the innovative development and prosperity of the company
- growing importance of the Human Resource Management and Human Resources Development functions in the system of the corporate strategic management
- regular periodical management performance appraisal and assessment of individual leadership potential
- obligatory individual plans of personal development
- management development established as a matter-of-fact part of the manager's job
- management development system for senior executives in force
- institutional infrastructure of management education, network of management development institutes, good training facilities
- availability of some original management development and training concepts and programmes
- emerging competitiveness and entrepreneurship on the supply side; new HRD, HRM and management development expert and consulting services
- awareness of the pressing need of the change of traditional approaches to management development, willingness to learn on the part of the management development organisers
- legislative incentives for distance, on-the-job graduate and postgraduate studies

Table 2: Human Resources Development Situation in Czechoslovakia —
          The Negatives

- pay levelling regardless of performance and/or real contribution prevails in most organisations
- loose ties between qualification growth and pay check
- bureaucratic formalism affecting
    - performance appraisal
    - personal development plans
    - nomination and selection procedures for management development and training programmes
    - employee suggestion schemes
    - institutionalized intra-organizational competition
  as well as many other developmental activities
- non-innovative organizational culture in a great majority of organisations
- scholastic management development programmes prevail
- considerable international isolation blocked the transfer of the state-of-the-art management development know-how

main transition trends in the field of management development and training that will determine its landscape in Czechoslovakia in the 1990s are subsequently outlined. The last table reviews the consulting and expert services in the area of human resource development that begin to fill in the gap on the supply side of professional management consulting in Czechoslovakia.

5. The Major Changes Affecting the Future of Human Resources Development. Human Resource Management and Management Development in Czechoslovakia — Some Enigmas

Economic reform:

How will the companies respond to the increased economic pressure on the profit generation? How will those organisations that have the liquidity problems react?

Will they tend to cancel their management development programmes as a part of the cost-saving measures in order to improve the profit-ratio? Or will they consider the investment into people to be an important renewal factor?

Appointment by election:

Will Managing Directors who are subject to re-election in five years pursue determinedly the long-range policies or will they pay more attention to the short-term political climate in the company?

Workers' Councils:

Will they support innovative, high-risk, "tears-and-blood" management strategies, or will they press for conservation of the traditional workers' prerogatives and benefits even if these are not substantiated by the organisation's productivity and competitiveness?

Political situation:

What will the model of Czechoslovak political and economic reform look like? What degree of deregulation and decentralisation will be politically acceptable? What will be the role of the market mechanism?

International co-operation:

Will Czechoslovakia be an attractive partner for the joint business activities and for the transfer of the top management development and management consulting know-how?

Various scenarios, some of them mutually contradictory, are plausible for the above questions. In 1989, it is impossible to make a reliable forecast of the development of the macro-economic and political environment in which the human resource management, HRD and management development will take place in the 1990s.

It is possible, however, to outline the main trends that will characterise the future transition from extensive to intensive mode of management development (see Table 3).

Table 3: Management Development in Czechoslovakia: a Transition from Extensive to Intensive Mode

TREND Nr.	TRANSITIONS
1	From general programmes for wide management public to specially designed IN-COMPANY PROGRAMMES
2	From problem simulation to the JOB-RELATED PROBLEM SOLVING (current real-life problems)
3	From theory and methodology to INNOVATION SEARCH and STRATEGY GENERATION
4	From skill training to CHANGE OF ORGANISATIONAL CULTURE
5	From training of individuals to TEAM BUILDING (particularly top management team development programmes)
6	From individual management development programmes to MODULAR SYSTEMS
7	From hit-and-run training programmes to permanent STRATEGIC COLLABORATION in management development with external experts
8	From traditional management development to IMPLEMENTATION PROCESS CONSULTING
9	From functionally-sponsored programmes to CEO INVOLVEMENT AND SPONSORSHIP

Human Resource Management in the German Democratic Republic: Problems of Availability and the Use of Manpower Potential in the Sphere of the High Qualification Spectrum in a Retrospective View

Hansgünter Meyer

1. Introduction

The experience of the GDR is in full accordance with the wide-spread programmatic statement that the human factor and, as such, personnel policy strategies, i. e. human resource management, is becoming a key factor for economic success — both for individual companies and for entire economies. I deem it worth intensely scientifically discussing whether and in what way a growing degree of similarity of the technological and economic systems in the world will lead — or at least contribute — to an increasing comparability of the problems of human resource management in countries with differing political and economic structures.

2. Labor Availability

2.1 Some Peculiarities of Labor Availability in the GDR

As for the GDR's manpower potential, this country is obviously faced with a situation that — worldwide — at least should be very rare and atypical if not unique.

1) The percentage of employees in the total residential population is particularly high.
   International comparison to illustrate this (percentage of employees, 1983 figures):

FRG	40.1		Canada	43.1
CSSR	48.4		Poland	31.6
GDR	50.6, in 1986: 51.3		Sweden	50.7
France	38.4		USSR	47.5
UK	42.2		Hungary	46.3
Italy	36.4		USA	43.3
Japan	48.1		total number of employees in the GDR: 8.45 million	

In the GDR this high recruiting rate of employees includes a high percentage of women (48.1 per cent of the employees are women, this means 88 per cent of the women at working age, including apprentices, schoolgirls, and students that come to another 8.5 per cent of the female residential population). There were virtually no available resources in manpower since there was no unemployment in the GDR. Even the release of labor due to the modernization of production is very small in spite of the planned reorganization of an annual number of 250,000 to 260,000 work stations and in spite of the increasing use of robots and automated plants. The reason for this was that the introduction of new technologies − as in other countries − is a hybridization process, a curious growing together of latest, recent, and old technologies whereby the innovative cells or islands remain surrounder by a more or less broad and relatively labor-intensive technological periphery.

What, above all, considerably adds to increasing the investment expenditure per work station is swiftly modernizing this periphery. Small countries and such ones of minor export power are faced with additional difficulties − compared with big countries realizing high export surplus.

Despite this fact, the country's economic management time and again refered to the urgency of the task to find adequate solutions to release workers thus making them disposable. However, there was not much success. In addition, there has been a downward trend in the birth rate since the early 1970s. In contrast to the FRG where the number of young people starting their working life reached a peak at the end of the 1980s, this downward trend already becomes apparent in the GDR. It will reach the rock bottom in 1993/'94. The decrease in the birth rate was approximately 20 per cent. Some remarks about the reasons: The so-called "Pillenknick" (birth-rate slump caused by the pill) was very vehement in the GDR. Sociologists have found out that this is connected with the fact that women go out to work whereby — apart from the high percentage of employed women — there is another peculiarity: 85 per cent of the young women pursue ambitious careers, i. e. more than 50 per cent of them are trained to be skilled workers, and 30 per cent of them acquire even higher qualifications. The interruption of employment due to the women's giving birth to a child — which hardly leads to loss of earnings — means undesirable loss of qualification and disruptions in the career progression although the mothers are given generous material support by the society.

In the GDR — in contrast to many other developed industrial countries — employment of women means that women identify themselves with a lifelong occupation, a habit that no longer differs from the men's attitude; and their employment only occasionally means an additional contribution to the family's budget. As for the expectations of most of the women, their employment is the realization of an ambitious career progression (in this or that way). Last but not least this was also since a long time a constituting component of the family's standard of living and their way of life, thus an essential aspect of their intellectual-cultural sphere. Sociological inquiries revealed that, nevertheless, 99.1 per cent of the young women want children of their own. 92 per cent of women in th GDR give birth to at least one child, which is a very high rate even on an international scale.

Another peculiarity of the manpower potential in the GDR was the reduction of the working life due to long periods of training as well as generous exemption from work for post-graduate qualification courses, extramural studies and evening classes, exemption from work after giving birth to a child, which comes to more than 40 million paid working days a year, exemption for activities in the artistic sphere and in the field of competitive sport. The annual amount of available working hours was also reduced through relatively generous exemption in case of illness, through a large number of prophylactic measures as well as due to many regulations concerning the reduction in working hours for acceptable private reasons.

2.2 The Impact of Social Policy and Incentive Systems

What was discussed in the GDR was the question whether all these socio-political privileges — which undoubtly come in useful for the quality of life of the population — are just about to go beyond what is permissible in view of the requirements of the economic rationality. Of course, this is a basic question of any human resource management, namely: how large must or may the social expenditure be in order to reduce the burdens of work without diminishing the economic result? Certainly, the economic efficiency increases more rapidly if the working people's interests do not have to be shown much consideration for. A general social stress situation crops us which makes it possible to exert enormous pressure to do well, and experience bears it out that the respective performance is really accomplished then.

The alternative, a socio-political conception of consideration and avoidance of ahrdships combined with growing demands on capacity, is more difficult to manage. The goal cannot be reached through pressure to do well but only through effective motivations, through improved qualification, professional ambition in the special field, social and technical acceptance of the working conditions, sense of social responsibility.

One thing is certain: the decision has been made in favour of the GDR citizens' extensive relief of hardships and fear for their existence and in favour of the reduction or elimination of pressure, and this decision will be effective in the long term. Attempts are made to bring this strategy in line with the requirements of the economic efficiency. This puts particularly high demands on the capabilities of the middle management and executives of the lower level of management. The management strategies pursued in this connection may be classified as following:

The volume of the national-economic net yield after the deduction of all production costs (= national consumption fund) as well as the business proceeds available for the payment of wages and salaries were the basis for the implementation of the "socialist principle of work performance". The individual stage of qualification reached, the measurable individual worker performance of the degree of responsibility, own initiative, and the level of competence has yielded the criteria for the finally granted individual wages (salary). On entering into an employment contract the worker was put on a wage or salary grade according to the effective wage schedule. The classification must be checked annually and needs to be confirmed or changed in the framework of individual talks. (Employees were very rarely put on a lower wage or salary grade again). Such talks had to take place in the presence of shop stewards on principle. The classification was effected according to two wage components: First, a fixed sum was laid down, then a variable extra pay was fixed which depends on the work performance and was granted for a short time and needs to be confirmed tiem and again at relatively short intervals. In addition, the employees were granted cash bonuses, quarterly premiums, and premiums at the end of the year that annually amount to one or two monthly wages or salaries. All these stipulations were openly dealt with, discussed, and assessed by the work team.

Experience shows that it was not easy to translated these principles into practice in an ideal way because a strong "socialism-specific" trend towards the elimination of distinctions and for the equalizing was effective. But nevertheless, the motivation and readiness to do well was promoted or accepted through this, negative manifestations were limited and sanctioned.

To complete the picture it must be mentioned that it was a practice in the GDR to relatively extensively give sums or allowances to the working people although the latter will not find them in their pay packets. They amount to some 30 per cent of the average income on an national scale. (They consist of subsidies for rents, heating, electricity, basic needs products, subsidies for creches, kindergartens, allowances for the care of the school-children in their spare time or during their holidays, holiday places for the families, spa treatment, cultural events, and other things. But what was also subsidized is prices of building material and installations for owner-occupied homes, extensions and rebuilding of flats, building of bungalows (weekend garden houses) and summer houses. People willing to do some building may ask for loans, the interest rate was two per cent, the period of validity was 30 years).

Experts often put the fact up for discussion that these social allowances and subsidies are not differentiated and do not stimulate performance thus having to be done away with. But the political leadership had put forward their own opinion in opposition, namely that these means essentially promote the quality of life and convey the feeling of social security and thus − in the long term − could have a positive effect on the citizens' behavior. Finally, these experts were right.

2.3 The Impact of Collective Bargaining

Every year new agreements were concluded with the work teams/brigades. These agreements were called Wettbewerbsverpflichtungen (obligations in the framework of socialist emulation). Working results aspired to or technical developments were specified quantitatively and qualitatively. In most cases the same is true of planned personal developments (acquisition of qualifications and specialist knowledge) as well as cultural activities. The result of the realization of such agreements were periodically evaluated in discussions and annual "upholding events". "Working in a socialist way" means that what the worker makes stand out is excellent craftsmanship and quality work, it means that he actively supports the works interests, that he selflessly contributes to fulfilling his collective's tasks, submits draft innovations and commits himself to help implement technical innovations, discovers and exposes sources of losses, continues his education and lends other workers a hand with their qualification.

In the enterprises or − if they are too big − in single departments, the main items of such obligations of the work teams and the "reply obligations" of the management (planned social allowances and benefits, activities of further education, modernization of the work stations, elimination of work hazards, health care − e. g. extension of factory policlinics − expenditures on culture, leisure time and sporting activities, special assistance for young people and employed mothers, canteen meals and catering during the breaks, commuter service and many other things) were compiled to form the so-called "union agreement" or "enterprise collective agreement". Working out and checking this agreement was an essential part of trade union work. The union agreement was of relevance in view of industrial law, it was judged to be a legal fact. All these regulations sanctioning the relations between management, trade unions and work teams were meant to make the works behavior lucid to the individual and morally and legally involve him in the interests of the enterprise. This was to help achieve identification with the work and motivation for high performances, acceptance of the technical and social conditions of the production process and activities for the modernization of the latter, it was to arouse and increase sense or responsibility to reach the targets.

As already mentioned, the measures of qualification and the qualification behavior were an essential aspect of the interaction and interplay of the enterprise and the employees. The following things were striven for: a) the acquisition of a higher level of qualification, b) new specializations (e. g. now: handling of modern mainframes), c) greater disposability of the real abilities and skills. This was meant to contribute to better taking up the work station taking possession of — and that by showing greater occupational competence — or to contribute to creating favourable subjective conditions for necessary job transpositions or the radical reorganization of work stations. Most of the qualification measures were shopfloor related and carried out in the firm's time. The respective expenses of the enterprises were on the increase. Most of the large enterprises have an enterprise training centre initiating all qualification activities, coordinating and supervising them. Furthermore, there are intra-enterprise seats of learning everywhere, or respective departments of the personnel departments. Part of the qualification courses are to make up for backlogs (for trainees, for employees working outside their trades). But the enterprises' education strategy was orientated to future requirements — in part towards technological developments already in the offing, in part towards attaining higher levels of qualification, in part towards the safeguarding of planned careers of cadres.

All the outlined methods of the GDR-typical human resource management were aimed at creating an efficient, dynamically governing "social infrastructure" sensibly responding to the growing demands of the scientific-technological progress and, in general, to the conditions of the modern technological regime that are becoming more complex, achieving high technological acceptance but, at the same time, producing motivations end forms of work behaviour that are conducive to the development of personality and favourable in view of the vocational competence.

A direct feedback of the working result and the expenses for the "human resources sector" was not very much pronounced in the socialist countries and it is just for this fact that attempts were made to create a qualitative state in the staff and between the employees and the enterprise that has a self-regulating, "autogenerative" and dynamic effect on the everyday work behaviour and, particularly, on the interest taken in the process of technological innovation.

2.4 Age Structure

As in other European industrial countries, the age structure of the employees will shift in favour of the age-groups of the over fifties. Their share in the total number of employees will rise from 26.7 per cent to over 33 per cent in the next five years. This effect will be stronger as far as engineers, management personnel, and scientific personnel are concerned where the share of the over fifties will quickly reach or pass the mark of 50 per cent. In the result of the emigration which increased in the time since summer 1989 until 1st March 1990 to the volume of 2.4 per cent of the GDR-population, but perhaps twice the rate in the young-age-classes − 18 − 30 years old, the overbalance-proportionality of the older people in the structure of employers will further on rise.

This will get a number of effects off the ground that always and everywhere result from an advanced age of the employees. Some of these effects are positive, others are negative. The bad points are the greater proneness to diseases that must be expected and the minor ability to take stress, furthermore: a tendency towards conservative behaviors, towards a certain reservation about taking risks in the process of making relevant decisions at work, less flexibility, minor activity. What, presumably, may be put in the good book is the high degree of job and life experience, a steadfast motivation for work and occupation, a marked sense of responsibility, a tendency to precision, exactness, reliability. It is hardly possible to decide what will prevail, the positive or the negative aspects. It will be another kind of activity and work behaviour, another kind of creativeness.

2.5 Characterization of the GDR's Manpower Situation

Generally speaking, the manpower situation of the GDR may be characterized as follows:

1) Aggravating factors: decreasing volume of the resources due to demographic trends specially migration, continuation of the cutting back on the annually available labor force due to retraining and continued professional training, different social measures, increase in the number of

workers of older age-groups and decrease in the number of workers of younger age-groups, trends of an increase in the percentage of old employees in some occupational groups, low rate of release in connection with technological innovations.

2) Speeding-up factors: growing percentage of the groups with high quali-fications, rapid increase in the number of modernized work stations, particularly due to information-processing technologies, stabilization of the personnel of the enterprises, and increase in the percentage of em-ployees that have job experience and are strongly motivated.

A high rate of unemployment will be expected, specially for high skilled employers and for the olders of them. The matter is that the low level of productivity by which the industry and agriculture of GDR is characterized, guaranted a high rate of employment as long as the products were sell on the market of the easteuropean ("socialist") countries. But now, in confron-tation with the conditions of western markets the plants are unable to continue their strategy to compensate a low level of technology by occu-pation of mass of workers.

3. Qualification Structure

But taking into consideration the growing percentage of highly qualified employees (graduates from technical colleges and universities, postgraduate levels), we must not close our eyes to the fact that it is a special problem and a particularly difficult one in view of the shift of labor in the GDR to continue to quantitatively and qualitatively meet the population's demand and urge for high education and occupational qualifications steadily repro-duced and intensified through the state's education policy, to meet this demand even under the conditions of diminishing rates of employment. Why is this a particular problem? Because the qualification structure of the age-groups retiring in the next years differs from that one of the age-groups starting their professional life.

The qualification structure will change from the late '80s up to the year 2000 as follows (percentage compared with the total of employees).

The change in the qualification structure is given rise to by the fact that the general structure is approximated to the structure of education pursued since the early '70s (through the retiring of the older age-groups that included a smaller number of highly qualified employees).

	in the late '80s	in the year 2000
employees graduated from ...		
universities	7.5	10
technical colleges[1]	13.4	15
	20.9	25
qualification as a foreman/		
technician	3.9	5
employees with skilled		
worker's certificate	60.2	60
employees without skilled		
worker's certificate	14.9	10

To mention an example: 122,000 scientists, academically trained and technical-school engineers have started their professional life in the years 1949 − 1958 will retire in the years 1990 − 2000. They will be replaced by 307,000 young employees, graduates of the age-classes 1980 − 1990. Thus the average annual replacement rate is 2.5-fold. This is the average value of the entire decade. This ratio will decrease by the end of the '90s because outnumbering age-classes will advance to the age limit.

The number of academically trained employees is likely to further increase considerably whereas there will be a downward trend as for the qualification group of the skilled and partially trained skilled workers, which is due to the age-classes 1972 − 1977 having a low birth-rate.

So it might be possible to largely replace retiring skilled workers by graduates from technical colleges and universities, namely some 20 per cent per age-class.

What was said about industrial workers in this connection is also true of all branches of the national economy.

---

[1] Training at a technical college is approximated to university education. It is three-year vocational training according to the pattern of university studies (presupposing obtaining a skilled worker's certificate after attending a vocational school for 2 − 3 years subsequent to leaving the 10-class polytechnical secondary school), a type of training that in part is on a remarkable scientific level. At the same time it qualifies the students for university entrance. More than 90 per cent of the students are full-time students, correspondence courses (extramural studies) and evening classes are possible, attendance is free, the students receive grants. The graduates are mostly appointed to management posts of the lower or intermediate levels. Many technical-college graduates also work in the health service, in the sphere of public education, as social workers, in libraries, and as junior scholars in the field of research. The main type of graduate is the technical-school engineer.

At present the resources of academically trained employees amount to slightly more than 600,000 persons, and the present number of technical-school graduates is slightly over a million. These are 10.2 per cent of the residential population or 20.2 per cent of the gainfully employed (level as of the late '80s).

But 12 per cent of the young people are trained at institutions of higher education and 13 per cent of them attend technical colleges, which makes a total of 25 per cent. Expressed in terms of the residential population that would mean 2.4 million people at the end of the '90s. But such figures will not be reached for the time being because the high percentage of graduates from technical colleges and universities were assigned not sooner than at the end of the '60s and, consequently, the older age-groups have further on another qualification structure.

But these age-classes will terminate their professional life by the year 2010 so that — provided that the education policy is continued in the way as determined at the end of the '60s — the academically trained groups will clearly exceed the three-million mark (with a total figure of less than 8 million employees). The number of academically trained employees alone will be 0.8 million. This is a situation that makes effectively employing these workers very difficult.

One could say that it might be relatively easy to drastically reduce the percentage of graduates from universities and technical colleges per age-class immediately. But it is not as easy as one might think. This is likely to be easily understood in the FRG, a country where some 24 per cent of the age-groups strive for university education, and that in realizing an individual demand for scientific vocational training. This is just the core of the problem.

The basis of education and qualification is a double determination. They arise from a social requirement accruing from the economic dynamism, from the level of the productive forces that is an element of the scientific-technological revolution of our time, and they also arise from the individual demand of the working people reflecting, in a very complex way, the development of the productive forces abd their technical tangible world and converting them into a factor of the cultural-intellectual life of society. As for the present time and, above all, the time to come it will be necessary to state that what matters is not only the demand for and the thus resulting right to work but also a demand for and — increasingly — a right to highly qualified work, which characterizes industrial and highly civilized societies. What remains to be discussed and decided is the question whether the education and qualification dynamism will come to an over-qualification (or its increase) or whether it, on the contrary, is a companion piece of the scientific-technological dynamism that meets with a favourable concomitant circumstance in the form of its being socially ensured through the working people's own demands for education and qualification.

It is easy to recognize that the increase in high qualifications is not to be achieved to the debit of the share of foremen and skilled workers but through the reduction of the share of the unskilled or semi-skilled workers. Of course, this can be realized only on condition that the activities — in part still labor-intensive but less qualified — in the auxiliary processes in the sphere of production and the service sector are quickly retrenched. So it is a question of developments that preferably have to be realized at the lower end of the qualification spectrum in order to pass through the whole spectrum from that point.

Now, what is it that these activities to be eliminated have to be replaced with? It is a latest-style technology with a very small periphery of auxiliary processes but with an extending sphere of production-preparing activities in the fields of design and development, software initializing, disposition of material, material control, and it must be replaced with increasing production-accompanying activities such as maintenance of machinery and equipment, re-equipment and retooling, analysis and control of the manufacturing process, particularly its technical parameters, its technological workplace safety, its non-polluting character. What furthermore is necessary is rationalization measures as well as R & D service without interrupting production, increasing consideration of changes serving the humanization of the process of labour. And all that without laying claim to completeness.

It is still impossible to see the whole extent of the requirements as to qualifications above the skilled-worker level in the framework of such development as just described because today a lot of activities in the economy must do without subcritical shares of high-quality production-preparing and production-accompanying work since, as already mentioned, the technical peak growth bates are still surrounded by a too broad periphery of labour-intensive auxiliary processes. It must also be taken into account that there is a smooth transition of the labor-functional determination from the skilled-worker qualification to the qualifications of foremen and technical-school graduates. The work organizers in the GDR's enterprises, as sociological investigations revealed, tend to rate the qualification requirement one level higher in case of doubt. This is also supported by the fact that the income differences between these levels are not very high. This practice may be appreciated to a reasonable extent because it offers the chance to better exhaust the full scope of creative possibilities, high sense of responsibility, self-reliance and activity — which is a characteristic feature of most of these new-type activities. In numerous cases, sociological investigations have revealed that technological and organizational broadness, flexibility, higher self-responsibility, possibilities to command services, individual influence on the quantity and equality of the outcome of one's labor are essential elements of the anticipation in view of modern work stations. Another aspect is that, for the time being, the individual branches of the economy and industries have very different resources of personnel who are university graduates and are employed accordingly. Leaving the managerial bodies and administrative organs out of consideration, the following relation is effective: One leading group stands out clearly: electrical engineering/electronics with 6.6 per cent, metallurgy with 6.3 per cent, energy and fuels with 6.4 per cent, chemical/ pharmaceutical industries with 6.9 per cent. The following branches have the relatively smallest resources of manpower: agriculture and forestry: 2.2 per cent, textile industry: 2.3 per cent, light industry: 2.4 per cent, building materials: 3.2 per cent. If one, in future, should start from the assumption that all industrial and economic branches described here must reach the figures of the most science-intensive branches in order to meet the requirements of the scientific-technological advance it would be necessary for the total resources employed here to be increased by more than 50 per cent (400,000 instead of the present figure of 236,000). Of course, this is not very likely to happen, but this characterizes the large scope possible in the case of radical modernization. The increased resources of engineers in the GDR have been discussed much (viz. 1,860 in every 10,000 employees, estimated for all manufacturing branches and services excluding agriculture). They result from the enforced technical-school training in the 1960s and 1970s and the latter, in turn, was a response to the urgent necessity to technically train minor and intermediate managerial personnel in the production process. This qualification group was also preferably employed in panel organs as well as in the apparatus of state and in social organizations whereby their activities were more or less outside their professions. 50,000 of them work in R & D institutions, but this number represents less than 7 per cent. One can state that this enormous rate of technical-school qualification has had a very positive effect on many economic and political development processes in the GDR. What, last but not least, added to this was the thus realized career including skilled worker's training and/or other practical activities, which led many young and older people to responsible and productive functions (through the high share of extramural studies and evening classes) that would not have been worth considering for a school imparting knowledge of the A-levels or for universities. The present development is characterized by the reduction of the resources of graduates from technical colleges, which will gradually take place up to far into the next century, and then these resources will (or are expected to) be stabilized.

But it is different with the resources of academically trained engineers. Taking into account all producing spheres and services the rate is 400 in every 10,000. Of course, the industries' shares are higher, they reach up to 1,000 — depending on the branch of industry.

Twenty-five per cent of the workers out of this qualification group are employed in the field of R & D.

According to the present trends the resources of engineers will slowly continue to grow by the year 2010 or so and will stabilize then. An excess of cadres of this educational level is out of the question in many respects. The improving of the technological level in some industrial and economic branches alone would entail a relative lack rather than meeting the requirements. Another aspect arises out of the fact that it is somewhat naive to estimate the resources in such a way that the group of the over 50 year-olds up to the 65 year-olds is fully included. At least 15 per cent of the employees of the said group become unavailable due to death or early disability, and that in addition to the fact that the total mortality rate during the proportional professional life amounts to nearly 10 per cent up to the 50th year of the employees' life.

Furthermore, this age-group has reached a form of occupational creativity that is different from what is typical of young people of this educational level. Therefore it is not only necessary to physically reproduce the resources of personnel, it is also necessary to regenerate them with regard to the qualification structure, the behaviour, the occupational dynamism. This is also true of the almost 250,000 technical-school graduates that will reach this age-group in the course of the 1990s or will have been in this group for several years then.

The whole range of functions occupied by them affects the activity of the academically trained engineers who already have to compensate many unsatisfactory occupational activities in this respect.

At first sight there is an over-employment of highly qualified cadres in the GDR, but classifying the problems reveals that a clear-sighted strategy has been pursued that has created favourable conditions for the group of highly qualified employees thus, at the same time, creating good preconditions to successfully solve the problems of the further development that will be of importance in the 1990s.

This strategy has its roots in the 1960s. They are connected with a very common social assent to the effect that the technological development up to the end of the century will result in the fact that the engineer instead of the skilled worker will be the predominant type of industrial worker. What also played a major role was the tradition of the working-class movement since the 19th century, namely that education (in the form of vocational qualification, too) is not only a necessity but power and a kind of self-esteem, an intrinsic value, a characteristic feature of personality. What appeared to be absolutely absurd in this context was the idea of over-qualification as it was discussed as a real phenomenon in the mid-seventies (discussed by economists; the sociologists preferred speaking of the dangers of the dequalification).

4. Some Current Problems

Today, the development of living labor in the GDR, the qualification structure, and the dimensions of the development of cadres at the upper end of the qualification spectrum are problems that are investigated in detail and discussed heatedly or even controversially. What stands out clearly is a polarization advocated by economic experts as well as theorists. One trend is aimed at stabilizing the resources of skilled workers — if not increasing them — and to lay emphasis on providing the basic production processes with workers. Here it is evident that the difficulties arising from the release of labor find a theoretical expression. One aspect in this connection is the analytically proved over-staffin of the enterprises with engineers which, above all, is evidenced by the fact that in the GDR there are many more engineers per 10,000 employees than in the FRG or the USA.

Another conception arrives at the demand to further increase the resources of engineers and to guarantee a considerable growth of the resources of R & D cadres. Many economic experts also argue in favour of this because they directly see the increasing demand for engineers in connection with technological innovations. In this case it is also possible to give convincing theoretical reasons.

No doubt, what is increasingly important is the elaboration of a theoretical conception that is capable of integrating in an overlapping statement the various aspects of the development of the resources, their structural-organizational as well as qualitative components.

The bases of such conception in the elaboration of which the author is involved shall be outlined in the following: The qualification structure of the workers as required in the economy is a dynamic quantity. There is no monocausal structure/function mechanism that is directly determined by a well-defined technology level. Manpower resources are potentials, their efficiency is a probabilistic quantity depending on a multi-layered correlation of the involved social, technological, and economic components.

Thinkable are qualification structures at a high level of efficiency that are very technocratical and characterized by a dichotomous, polarized structure: A few very capable specialists with great disposition authorization (power!) control big masses of semi-skilled workers through a few mediators.

It seems to us that a very differentiated structure with strongly capillary features better does justice to the present-day type of technology. Small functional groups must be integrated that can manage the different lines of the science and technology transfer. What we have in mind apart from the fields of industrial R & D, the research at universities and out of universities with its different types of cooperation is technical schools of research, technology parks, small independent high-tech enterprises, departments for the in-house manufacture of equipment for rationalization purposes, for software developments, as well as for the scientific manufacture of devices that also produces more and more prototypes for high-tech elements. All these new structures are in the process of creation in the GDR, too, and they require the availability of highly qualified personnel.

The concept of the synergetic effect in potentials has been introduced in connection with physical theories of evolution, and we have adapted ourselves to replace a simplified understanding of merely linear dependencies by such effects that come into being through interaction.

The conception of understanding labor resources as potentials finally comes to deriving their efficiency from the synergetic concurrence of the individual structural elements. This concurrence has many aspects one of which is the availability of highly qualified workers that may be used to quickly form efficient partial potentials.

It is not in the least true that the use of high technologies results in the development of structures which then have to be filled with appropriately trained personnel according to a prescribed pattern but the order is vice versa: existing and flexibly employable potentials in the sphere of high qualification are used to create structures that are staged through high-tech developments and applied on an industrial scale. These potentials are not confined to aiming at and reaching a goal — as it was true of the classical Manhattan Project — but they are "evolution-controlled", they develop their goals themselves and optimize ways and means to achieve them. They function in an "autogenerative" way. To vary a great word: in the beginning there is the potential. The extensive development of the potentials (in view of personnel, technology, information, structure) yields an effect that is decisive in the end: the possibility to more efficiently stimulate the evolution of new technologeis and labour regimes (i. e. it is impossible to intentionally direct them to a prescribed goal). Potentials develop as a historical quantity, as the cumulation of scientific-technological resources comprising workers with a differentiated qualification spectrum as well as equipment and information resources. They are the base of a system science/research/technology/ production that has been developing for decades, a continuous basic element that, at the same time, contains all components of advancing developments.

Provided that there are exogenous peripheral conditions that are not limited, the endogenous components of such potentials are of such kind that their efficiency is unlimited on principle. Therefore there is no "real" over-qualification of manpower potentials as far as it is possible to classify the trained personnel into the functional correlation science/production. On the contrary, the problem is whether a society can afford the expenses of high qualifications or, to put it in other words, how much it can other sectors deprive of to be in a position of affording a somewhat oversized sector of education/qualification — and whether it is able to create conditions to realize these expenses on a profitable basis in the development of technology and industry.

We consider it to be a disfunction of science/production systems if the profit planning is the preferential target and if education, qualification, and scientific work are nothing but pertinent expense factors to be minimized. In our country we caution the respective decision-making bodies and enterprises against following bad examples and against loosing sight of the long-term losses in potency through possibilities to be successful at short sight.

The GDR — although small in size and, in addition, faced with quite a number of unfavourable peripheral conditions — has succeeded in holding some (but few) auspicious positions in the international scientific-technological revolution and has been able to create capable initial conditions for the accelerated technical advance. Last but not least, this results from the significant potential-forming processes in the late 1960s and 1970s whereby the expectations possibly were exaggerated but the processes were carried out in a way that showed the due understanding of basic correlations of science and technology. At the same time it pays if we do not consider the constitution of the human resources as a minor expense factor to be minimized but as an intrinsic value, as a self-evident social target. It is undisputed that education and qualification in the GDR for a long time were a component of the cultural quality of the society more important than many other social goals.

Part III
Human Resource Management in Asian Countries

Human Resource Management in China: Recent Trends

Wang Zhong-Ming

1. Introduction

China as a socialist country has three kinds of economies, i. e. state owned, collective and individual ones. Since 1979, China's economic and management reform programme has made rapid progress. Tens of thousands of entrepreneurs have thrust themselves forward, and 130 million work force now go about their tasks with a new sense of responsibility. With the development of the economic reform, human resource management is becoming a key aspect of management modernization in China.

As a background for the recent development of human resource management in China, four significant changes in Chinese management in general should be mentioned, which have had great impact upon the human resource management in China:

(1) The power of the Communist Party is detaching from the management and administration. This has greatly changed the political structure and the administrative system in enterprises and other organizations.
(2) There has been a tendency of decentralizing the management power, seperating the ownership from the management of enterprises. As a result, managers have more power to run their enterprises and employees have more saying on managing their organizations.
(3) The drafting and promulgation of China's Enterprise Law has changed the economic and management environment. In the meantime, the new "Law of Trade Unions" has been drafted, which gives trade unions new power to take a greater part in running the enterprises and other organizations. Therefore, many reform practice are no longer only experiments today, as they are written into the country's legal system.
(4) There has been a closer link between practitioners and researchers. More and more organizational and management researches have been carried out in the field settings, which provide with scientific evidence and theoretical guidance for the management reform.

All of those changes have created an open and new environment for the development of human resource management.

In recent years, there have been great developments in the following four areas of Chinese human resource management: (1) Management responsibility systems; (2) Labor system and wages/reward systems; (3) Vocational and management training; (4) Trade unions and Enterprise Law. In the following sections, those four areas of developments will be discussed.

2. The Development of Management Responsibility Systems

2.1 Three Phases of Responsibility System Reform

Recent Chinese enterprise reform has roughly proceeded in three phases. From 1979 to 1983, the transfer of self-government to enterprises marked the first stage. In this period, many enterprises got the right to retain their profits in proportion to those turned over to the State. They were evolved from subsidiaries of the government to real economic entities.

The second phase was from 1983 to 1986, characterized by a shift of focus to creating conditions for fair competition among enterprises. The enterprise responsibility systems were introduced in some large and medium-sized companies. In 1983, a programme of changing profits into taxes was imposed on most State-owned enterprises.

The third phase of responsibility system reform came in 1986, in which enterprises' ownership was changed as an initial step in restructuring them. By the end of June 1987, about 80 percent of China's enterprises had adopted the Director Responsibility System and their output value had risen by 13 percent and profits and taxes by 16 percent. At the same time, about 90 percent of large and medium-sized enterprises had implemented contract management responsibility systems, and 53 percent of the small State-owned companies had been handed over to collective ownership or leased to individuals.

2.2 Some Characteristics of Management Responsibility Systems

One of the important characteristics of those management responsibility system is that a competitive procedure is usually adopted in establishing the new system, which facilitates the utilization of competence and human resource potentials.

The most popular procedure for setting up the management responsibility system is the use of "competitive application". The procedure usually includes four stages:

(1) Preparation stage, forming assessment committees (people from the Bureau of the Industry, representatives of the staff and workers' congress, external consultants and some ordinary workers are members of this committee), evaluating the capital of the enterprise, calling for applications;
(2) Application stage, advertising applications, checking qualifications of the applicants, field investigation, drafting proposals of the management work plan;
(3) Evaluation and decision stage, evaluating the proposals, assessing previous performance of the applicants by both employees and the committee, oral defence meeting, and deciding on the director selected;
(4) Conclusion stage, self-organizing the management group, signing management contract, implementing the Director Responsibility System.

Since such a procedure is characterized by openness and democracy, more competent directors can often be selected and the new management responsibility system is more acceptable to employees (Fan Bonai 1988).

There are many types of management responsibility systems being implemented in enterprises all over China. A survey revealed that there were mainly 16 types of responsibility systems in the country (Yu Zhanming et al. 1987). This actually reflects the general practice of human resource management in China.

Among those types of management responsibility systems, the following ones are proved to be more effective:

(1) Director period-objective responsibility system

In this system, the director (or manager) signs a three-five year management contract which consists of five kinds of management objectives to be accomplished such as personnel competence, enterprise development, efficiency, workers' welfare, and reward/discipline goals. This system is suitable to some large and medium-sized enterprises.

(2) Director rolling-objective responsibility system

This system is similar to the first one except the management target (or objective) will be rolled or increased each year and assessed in terms of profits. It may be used in some previously ill-operated enterprises for which the period-objective is difficult to define.

(3) Enterprise shareholding responsibility system

With this system, the shareholders are responsible for the management of the enterprise and share the risk. The management decisions are made through the director responsibility system under the leadership of the board of directors.

(4) Leasing responsibility system

The representative of the capital owner of the enterprise publically recruit the leasing person to whom the management power will be given.

We are recently conducting field research in many enterprises to investigate and compare the patterns of human resource management under various kinds of management responsibility systems.

2.3 Shareholding System

In the last few years, the shareholding system has been gradually brought into small and medium-sized collectively-owned enterprises and already produced better-than-expected results. According to some preliminary statistics obtained by Business Weekly, about 6,000 enterprises in China have issued shares valued at a total of 2 billion yuan. The current Chinese shareholding system is quite different from the one adopted in Western countries. It involves State, enterprise and individual stock.

It was shown that the shareholding system may actually separate public ownership from the right of managing an enterprise and leave the enterprise completely free of unnecessary administrative interference. Many enterprises with the shareholding systems have set up committees to represent shareholders' interests and to exercise power over property and management. The shareholding system is therefore proposed as an important way to deepen the reform of State-owned enterprises.

2.4 Joint-ventures and Township Enterprises

It was said that in the recent ten years, more than 13,000 Chinese enterprises with foreign investment were approved. Of the 6,000 joint-venture enterprises that have been put into operation, 85 percent are doing well. Joint-ventures have introduced into Chinese enterprises not only advanced technology, but also effective management methods. In most of joint-ventures, managers and employees share both interests and risk, which facilitates the sense of responsibility and the creativity. Generally, managers have the full power to make personnel and wage decisions. All the employees are employed by contracts. Besides, the personnel system of the joint-venture enterprise is usually more flexible. However, the coordination between Chinese managers and their foreign counterparts and the adaptation of the two kinds of management styles are proved to be very crucial to the success of joint-ventures in China.

A new type of business, township enterprise, appeared ten years ago, are making great contributions to the economic reform and to Chinese society in general. Since 1978, township enterprises have provided jobs for more than 60 million surplus rural laborers, about half of the total of surplus rural laborers. Most of township enterprises have adopted payment reforms such as piece rates and wages that fluctuate with the enterprise's profitability. They are largely functioning as autonomous management units.

In recent years, private enterprise has become an independent category in China and seen as a supplement to the reformed public sector. They were playing an important role in expanding employment opportunities, particularly for the excess farm labor force. Shareholding is becoming a major approach to developing private enterprises. Many businesses have been set up through the joint efforts of State-owned, collective and private enterprises. Boards of directors are organized for joint management of those businesses. A lot of collectively-owned enterprises make use of private workshops.

2.5 Enterprise Merging

The desire for expansion of powerful enterprises is breaking down the barriers of ownership, government departments and regions in China. By the end of 1988, more than 1,500 enterprises have been merged in the country. With the development of the management reform, the State delegates more power to enterprises, which stimulates the strong enterprises to increase their profits by expansion in merging other ill-managed ones. This has been an effective method to solve the problem concerning the lack of vitality in some enterprises and yielded better economic results. Enterprise merging has not only changed the operational mechanism of the State capital, but also led to the more rational utilization of human and material resources.

3. Changes in Personnel, Labor and Wage Systems

3.1 Labor Contract System

The Chinese labor system has in recent years undergone great changes. Many State-owned enterprises have introduced the practice of "optimization through regrouping" in a bid to improve productivity. By the end of 1988, this practice has been implemented in more than 26,000 State-owned enterprises, which allows the enterprises more freedom and power over where they put their employees to work within the organization.

In the meantime, the labor contract system has been introduced in enterprises throughout China. The system is widely seen as a solution to the problem of the "three guarantees as firm as iron", i. e. guaranteed job assignment, guaranteed pay irrespective of performance and guaranteed tenure in leading positions (Xin Xinming 1988). By the end of July 1988, more than 7.6 million workers, about 8 percent of the total in China, were employed under the labor contract system which allows enterprises and workers to choose each other. In Bejing, about 550 enterprises involving around 600,000 workers have implemented this new system. For example, about 1,600 workers in the Beijing Micro Electric Motor Plant recently signed labor contracts with the plant's director on the basis of the practice of "optimization through regrouping". However, the present labor contract system in State-owned enterprises does not permit the firing of workers and it allows redundant workers to take other jobs in the enterprises.

The specific forms of labor contract system vary with different enterprises depending upon their current productivity, personnel composites, type of trade and regional employment situations. Among the labor contract systems, the following four kinds of systems are most common practices:

(1) Directly-transfered contract system

   All the personnel in the previous labor system are directly transfered into a labor contract system.

(2) Selective contract system

   Only those employees who pass the performance appraisal are qualified to work under the new labor contract system. The rest of employees will be either dismissed or re-trained for other jobs.

(3) Laborer regrouping contract system

First-line supervisors who are either recruited by the director of the enterprise or elected by employees will select workers to form their work groups on the voluntary base.

(4) Post contract system

Employees sign their post contracts directly with supervisors, defining their responsibilities and interests. Supervisors sign their post contracts with directors or managers of the enterprise concerning their work objectives.

Solving the problem of surplus labor force is an urgent task in human resource management under the new system. Some enterprises have begun to re-channel surplus workers, resulting from the implementation of the labor contract system, into attached service trades or send them to labor markets to hunt for new jobs. Many enterprises settle the problem by developing new products, tertiary industry, diversified production, labor export, giving long holidays to female workers with small children, and even early retirement. However, the key to solving the problem lies in reforming the current labor management system and bringing competition into enterprises.

3.2 Labor Market

The recent development of labor market in China has undergone three phases:

(1) Implementation of employment service

From 1979–1984, China faced the second peak of employment since 1949. Many cities then set up employment service and implemented a policy of multi-channel employment, i. e. employment through labor departments, voluntary grouping or self-employment.

(2) Establishment of labor market

As the reform of labour system deepens, from 1984 to 1986, some labor markets were established mainly for skilled workers. Enterprises and laborers have had freedom to choose each other.

(3) Rapid development of labor market

In the late 1986, a nationwide programme of labor system reform was promulgated for enterprises, including public recruitment, comprehensive assessment and selection by merits. Since then, a large number of labor markets have been developed in 67 large and medium-sized cities in China, dealing with purplus labor force and helping skilled workers learn about job opportunities. Many employment centres give information about pay, pensions, contract positions and openings.

A recent forum on job exchanges held in Guangdong province. In Jinan, capital of Shangdong province, about 12,500 people have found new jobs through regular and irregular labor exchanges in the city. Some city governments are working on unemployment insurance plans to guarantee basic living standards for the unemployed. However, because of the insufficiencies of the social welfare system, most surplus manpower has to remain attached to the enterprises.

3.3 Industrial Workforce and Personnel Systems

In recent years, there have been great changes in industrial workforce in China. A survey of 8,285 large and medium-sized enterprises by the State Statistical Bureau in 1988 revealed that 94.9 percent of cadres (managers, supervisors, etc.) were young or middle-aged, 51.9 percent had a university or college education, 16.5 percent studied at a secondardy vocational school, and 10.1 percent at a senior middle school. Overall, 54.4 percent of the cadres had technical qualifications, of which 38 percent were high or medium grade.

Of the 22.05 million workers and stalls surveyed, 1.11 million were scientists and technicians (5.1 percent), young workers made up 65 percent of the workforce, and middle-aged workers 34.1 percent. Those with middle school education amounted to 67 percent. Those changes indicate a rapid improvement in the composite of Chinese workforce after the "Cultural Revolution".

Most of cadres in Chinese enterprises are now either elected or selected through some open and democratic procedures. Since 1984, there have been a nationwide practice of leader assessment. In many enterprises, candidates for leading positions were assessed by their subordinates, co-workers and supervisors and then selected as directors or managers. Leader assessment was also used in regular performance appraisal. The methods of leader assessment include multi-level evaluation by subordinates and colleagues, management case analysis, and assessment centre using simulated management tasks. In some leader assessment studies carried out in Zhejiang province, job analysis was made in about 60 enterprises with more than 2,800 respondents, which provided useful information and indicators for performance appraisal and management training (Xu Liancang and Wang Zhongming 1989).

Recently, China is preparing for the full-scale adoption of a civil service system which will be introduced on a nationwide basis. The provisional regulations on civil servants have been revised 15 times since 1984. The draft makes specific provision for classification of civil service posts, employment, rewards and punishments, promotions and demotions, training, salary and welfare benefits.

3.4 Wage systems

The reform of Chinese wage system is somewhat behind the development of other management systems. At present, the most popular wage systems in China are the rank fixed wage for enterprise employees and the structured wage system based on positions for employees at universities and government organizations. In recent years, although the economic conditions have changed, there remains equalitarianism in the wage management systems.

Since 1978, various kinds of reward or bonus systems have been implemented as a supplement to the current fixed wage system. The reward systems are often incorporated into the job responsibility systems, linking the reward with work responsibility. As a reaction to the previous "iron bowl" system, the piece rate bonus system had close relation with individual performance, it did discourage collective responsibility and group work which are emphasized in China. Thus, some research was carried out to compare the individualistic system with a group responsibility bonus system in Chinese enterprises (Wang Zhong-Ming 1986, 1988 a). It was shown that in the economic reform, group responsibility is very important for effective management and high morale. A kind of multi-responsibility bonus system has then been proposed and implemented, linking bonus with both individual and collective work responsibilities (or performance). Some enterprises have adopted a type of multi-bonus system which offers different kinds of bonus for employees at different ages and with various psychological needs (Chen Li 1987).

Since 1984, an "unlimited" bonus policy has been implemented with a bonus tax regulation. By 1987, more than 3,000 large and medium-sized enterprises with about 1.3 million employees have adopted a kind of wage/bonus system which has a very clear link between the total amount of wage and bonus in the enterprise and its economic efficiency.

4. Vocational and Management Training

4.1 Vocational Training

Vocational training is a very important approach to human resource management and has been one of urgent tasks for Chinese enterprises and other organizations partly because of the ten-year interruption of education by the "cultural revolution", and partly due to the rapid economic development and technological innovations in the country. Since 1984, a nationwide programme of vocational re-training has been implemented in all State-owned and collective enterprises. By 1985, more than 30 million young workers have attended training courses of secondary education and/or elementary technical education, and more than 5 million skilled workers have passed either intermediate or advanced technical training, more than 2 million first-line supervisors joined training courses for supervisory positions. Besides, about 240,000 workers have obtained certicates from middle technical schools, and more than 360,000 were attending training programs by the long-distance education. By the end of 1984, more than 28,000 vocational schools were established within enterprises throughout the country. All of those developments in vocational training have greatly raised the level of competence of our workforce.

4.2 Management Training

In addition to the nationwide general vocational training, management training has made significant progresses. During the period of 1979–1985, more than 8 million managers and supervisors passed some sorts of management training courses. Since 1984, a nationwide programme of management training has been carried out by the Chinese State Economic Commission. Drectors and managers from various industries were required to join and pass the training before they could carry on their management jobs. By 1988, eight national management training courses have been organized involving more than 176,000 directors and managers, 98 percent of them from large and medium-sized enterprises. And about 115 management and business schools or colleges have been run in China.

The State Economic Commission has, since 1980, collaborated with organizations from USA, United Kingdom, West Germany, EEC, Canada and Japan respectively in a number of management educational programmes, and trained more than 5,000 advanced management personnel, 280 MBA students who were managers before the training and about 300 teachers for management training. Some of the training programmes have been incorporated into technical schools in large enterprises and proved to be effective and practical. For instance, a West German on-job educational system, sponsored by the Hanns-Seidel Foundation, was introduced into the technical school at China's No. 2 Automobile Factory in Hubei province in 1985 and has received good results. The students graduated from the new system in the school demonstrated, soon after they went to work, their management skills and technical know-how were more advanced and practical than those of their predecessors from the conventional technical training system. Therefore, the international collaboration in training offers the enterprise a chance to make up for its shortage of employees with technical and management skills, positive attitudes and discipline.

One important aspect of management training is the learning of organizational psychology. In recent years, numerous short training courses of organizational psychology have been run all over China. Among the participants are directors, managers, supervisors and Party secretaries from various industries as well as teachers who would then teach organizational psychology at other schools or universities. For example, the Psychology Department at Hangzhou University has, since 1981, run 17 short training courses of organizational psychology for managers and directors from such industries as mechanical engineering, electronics, textile, petroleum and telecommunications. Those training courses have had very positive results since they offer not only general principles of organizational psychology, but also problem-solving methods through case analyses and field surveys of the management practice. Similar training courses have been conducted in Beijing, Shanghai, Dalian and many other cities in China. Now, organizational psychology training is becoming one of the most important tasks in Chinese management education.

5. Trade Unions and Enterprise Law

5.1 Trade Union and its Role in Economic Reform

China's trade unions have, in recent years, played a more and more active role in the economic reform and modernizations. Trade unions were in the past involved more in things like workers' welfare rather than management of the whole enterprise. It is now proposed that in the primary stage of socialism in China, trade unions should safeguard the legal interests and democratic rights of the masses, encouraging participations in reform and in the running of enterprises, organizations and State and social affairs under the leadership of the Chinese Communist Party.

Recently, on the basis of a trade unions law adopted in 1950, the new "Law of Trade Unions" has been drafted by the All-China Federation of Trade Unions. Accordingly, trade unions will participate in the making of laws related to the interests of workers, such as laws covering minimum wages, working hours, employment protection, social welfare, and unemployment benefits. They also have the right to negotiate or hold talks as equals with the government representing the workers when issues concerning enterprise development are discussed. For example, in Shaanxi province, the provincial trade union leader was now holding regular conferences with the governor to help solve major labour problems. In Liaoning and Hebei provinces, trade unions were setting up committees to stop the unfair distribution of wages and bonuses.

With the progress of implementing management responsibility systems, manager's authority and position has been strengthened and, in the meantime, the sense of masters of enterprises and the initiative have been emphasized among the employees. Trade unions in many enterprises have participated in the making of Enterprise Law and Regulations for Management Responsibility Systems. They have actively organized workers to take part in democratic management, participating in responsibility contracts, planning for enterprise objectives, monitoring the implementation of labour contracts and safeguarding workers' interests and rights. Trade unions have also been involved in efforts to solve the problem of surplus labor fource (Chen Binquan 1988).

In addition to what people conventionally expect a union, most of China's trade unions stress a sense of business and seek to help the management. They are concerned about the success of the enterprises or organizations as well as the workers' livelihood. In recent years, many joint-ventures have started in China and the trade unions faced the question of how a workers' union should function under a management joined by socialist China and capitalist investors from the West. After recent practice in reform, many trade unions in joint-ventures have succeeded in helping workers adapt to the new management style and in working with management. The human resource management in joint-venture enterprises has also been a hot topic in organizational psychology research. Since 1987, we have been working in some joint-ventures on the industrial democracy and participation in decision-making, which has received interesting findings and evidence for improving human resource management in those enterprises (Wang Zhong-Ming 1988 c).

5.2 Enterprise Law

China didn't have an enterprise law at the beginning of its economic reform. It was throughout the past decade of economic reform that the law was drafted. In April 1988, the Law of the People's Republic of China on Industrial Enterprise Owned by the Whole People was adopted at the First Session of the Seventh National People's Congress. According to the Enterprise Law, the enterprise in China is a socialist commodity production and operation unit which shall, in accordance with law, make its own managerial decisions, take full responsibility for its own profits and loses, practice independent accounting and implement the principle of distribution according to work (Article 2). It shall, through the staff and workers' congress and other forms, practice democratic management (Article 10). The enterprise shall ensure that the staff and workers enjoy the status of the masters and their lawful rights and interests shall be protected. The Law also defines rights and obligations of the enterprise in human resource management. Among other things, the enterprise shall have the rights to determine forms of wages and methods of bonus distribution, to employ or dismiss its staff members and workers in accordance with the provisions of the State Council, to decide on its organizational structure and the number of its personnel and to reject the exaction of its manpower. The enterprise shall improve labor conditions, strengthen various kinds of education so as to raise the quality of its staff and workers, and support and reward them in carrying on enterprise activities.

The Enterprise Law points out that the staff and workers' congress shall be the basic form for the practice of democratic management in the enterprise and the organ for the staff and workers to exercise their powers of democratic management. And the working organ of the staff and workers' congress shall be the trade union committee of the enterprise, responsible for the daily work of the congress and supporting the factory director in exercising his or her functions and powers. Therefore, the new Enterprise Law indicates the direction of China's continuing industrial reform. It provides a lawful general framework for the development of Chinese human resource management.

6. Conclusion

It is clear that great progresses have been made in many aspects of human resource management in recent economic reform in China. With the development and implementation of the Enterprise Law and other related laws,

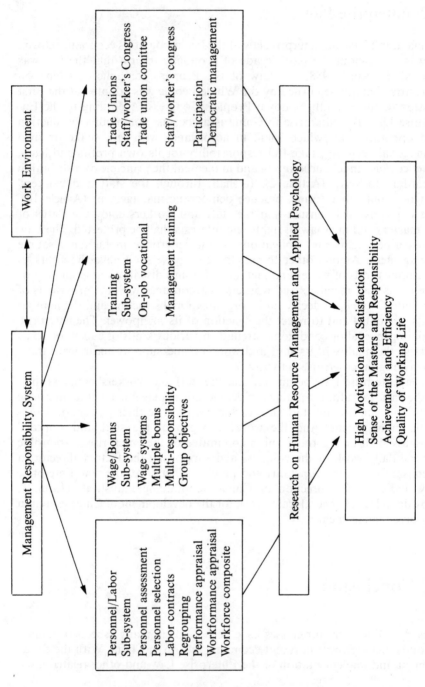

Figure 1: A System Model of Human Resource Management

the practice of human resource management have become more legalized. Along with researches on human resource management as well as personnel and organizational psychology, a system model of Chinese human resource management has been proposed (Chen Li 1988, Wang Zhong-Ming 1988 b, Xin Xinming 1988, Zhang Yanning 1988). That is to use a system approach to human resource management, taking together into account subsystems of labor, wage and bonus, management responsibility, training, trade unions, and staff/workers' Congress. Emphasis has been put on the coordination and cooperation among those subsystems. None of reforms of any subsystem of human management resource would be really effective without coordination or adjustment in other subsystems. Figure 1 presents the model.

As an effort for the further development of human resource management in China, some comprehensive reform will be carried out in a guided and orderly way with various subsystems of human resource management supplementine and promoting each other. Government administration will be further separated from the enterprise management so that enterprises meeting certain conditions may operate on their own. Besides, the contract responsibility system will be further improved, the shareholding system will be continuously experimented with public ownership remaining predominant and new enterprise groups will be developed on a trial basis. Enterprises' decision-making power will be further expanded. The past decade has witnessed tremendous achievements in human resource management in China. It is expected that the new development of human resource management will continuously promote China's economic and social progress and greatly improve the livelihood of the people.

References

Chen Binquan (1988): The role of trade unions in Chinese enterprise reform, *Modern Enterprise Herald*, No. 5.

Chen Li (1987): *Some recent studies in organizational psychology at Psychological Department of Hangzhou University,* Paper presented at the Sixth Conference of the Chinese Psychological Society, 19–22, Sept., Hangzhou.

Chen Li (1988): Macro-ergonomics in Chinese industrial modernizations, *Chinese Journal of Applied Psychology*, Vol. 3, No. 1.

Enterprise Management (1988): *News on results of vocational training in China*, No. 3.

Fan Bonai (1988): *A study on director responsibility system by competitive application,* Unpublished BA thesis, Hangzhou University.

Lian He (1988): The drafting of the new Enterprise Law, *Modern Enterprise Herald*, No. 4 (Chinese).

State Restructuring Commission (1988): A review of ten-year enterprise reform in China, *Enterprise Management*, No. 12 (Chinese).

Wang Zhong-Ming (1986): Worker's attribution and its effects on performance under different responsibility systems, *Chinese Journal of Applied Psychology*, Vol. 1, No. 2.

Wang Zhong-Ming (1988 a): The effects of responsibility system reform and group attributional training on performance: A quasi-experiment in Chinese factory, *Chinese Journal of Applied Psychology*, Vol. 3, No. 3.

Wang Zhong-Ming (1988 b): *Work and Personnel Psychology*, Zhejiang Educational Press.

Wang Zhong-Ming (1988 c): *Decision making and competence utilization of Chinese managers*, Paper presented at the Symposium on Decision Making of the 24th International Congress of Psychology, August 28 – Sept. 2, Sydney, Australia.

Xin Xinming (1988): The practice of reforms in labour system in China, *Modern Enterprise Herald*, No. 1 (Chinese).

Xu Liancang and Wang Zhongming (1989): New development in organizational psychology in China, *International Journal of Applied Psychology*, (in press).

Yu Zhanming, et al. (1987): Sixteen forms of contract responsibility systems, *Economics Daily*, August 3.

Zhao Dong wan (1987): On reforms of labour and wage systems in China, *Chinese Labour Science*, No. 9.

Zhang Xiaojian (1988): The development of labour market in China, *Modern Enterprise Herald*, No. 10 (Chinese).

Zhang Yanning (1988): Experience and effects of management contract systems, *Enterprise Management*, No. 3 (Chinese).

Zhang Yanning (1989): Tasks of enterprise reform in 1989, *Enterprise Management*, No. 1.

Human Resource Management in Japan

Yoshiaki Takahashi

1. Introduction

The term "Human Resource Management or Development" has been gradually popularized and used in the world of Japanese scholars and businessmen under the influence of the American management theory. But, this term has not become popular enough for it to be used for the title of Japanese text books of "Personnel or Labour Management". Human resource management generally consists of two large parts; the knowledge and principle of industrial psychology, and personnel management. The problems of industrial psychology have, even if not enough, been treated in Japanese text books with the title of "Personnel management". The reason why this terminology has until today not been so popular is that the Japanese economy, as widely known, has grown through the exportation of articles manufactured from imported raw material since the early stage of industrialization at the end of 19th century. Therefore, Japanese employers have recognized the importance of manpower or human resources more strongly than employers in the early development countries. Nowadays not so many scholars feel the necessity of using this terminology.

The subject matter of personnel management or human resource management is wide and broad, and includes: 1) employment and selection system, 2) Promotion, 3) Personnel transfer, 4) dismissal, 5) job analysis and job description, 6) evaluation of employees' ability, 7) training and development of human power, 8) job evaluation, 9) wage and salary, 10) safety and sanity, 11) employer-employee relation or trade union, and so on. These subject matters of personnel management are common in the enterprise of every country. However, concrete contents of measures or implemented systems and functions are different from enterprise to enterprise and from country to country, because the management style of one enterprise or one country in one era might be influenced by the behavior of management and employee (labor union), and by the economic and social background in the era. Before we begin to describe the character of Japanese human resource management compared with foreign countries, we should discuss the analytical method of this subject.

2. The Analytical Method of HRM in International Comparisons

One Japanese business historian, Nakagawa, K. has pointed out three fundamental factors which determine the management style of a country, namely cultural structure, economic process, and internal and external organisation of the enterprise (Nakagawa 1981). The "cultural structure" means the behavior style, and the life goal or value system of the individual person in a particular era and country. "Homo Economics", on which traditional economics has been based, is a model of the individual in one particular area and country, which can not be adapted for the explanation of individual human behavior in any area and any country (Nakagawa 1981).

A. H. Cole, J. A. Schumpeter and T. C. Cochran asserted, according to Nakagawa, that the analysis of capital and technology alone was not enough to make clear the concrete contents of the economic development of a country, but that it was necessary to analyse the adaptability of its human behavior style to economic development (Cole 1956, Nakagawa 1981). It seems that these scholars were not satisified with the assumptions of "Homo Economics".

The behavior style or value system of the individual person in a particular era and country may be conditioned by the dominant religion, law, education system and so on, of which cultural structure of the country is composed on the one hand, and well as by the economic process and the internal and external organisation of enterprise on the other hand. The speed of the change of the behavior style or value system of the individual person must be more gradual than the two other fundamental factors.

The second factor, the "economic process" means economic factors which condition the decision making of the entrepreneur or manager. In order to make clear the economic process concretely in the context of decision making by the entrepreneur or manager of the country, it is not sufficient to analyse this process only under the aspect of economic process or stage, as the "industrial Revolution" or "industrialization" of a country. Its contents were very different between the early development countries of Europe and

USA and the late developed countries, such as Japan etc. Gerschenkron's model explains these different phenomena fairly well.

Gerschenkrons' model consists of the following four propositions:

1) The later the industrialization of a country is, the faster its speed. This is because the late developer can introduce the newest production techniques from the starting point of its industrialization which were developed by early developers over long time: and also because the late developer can occasionally borrow capital from early developers where accumulation has been promoted.
2) The industrialization of the late developed countries must be promoted on a large scale from the starting point. If the later development cannot introduce the newest techniques at the same level and on the same scale as the early developer, the late developer can not compete on equal terms in the product market, because of higher prices of its products.
3) The industrialization of the late developed country must be guided by a certain strong institution at the national level. The existence of such an enterprise or national bank, which was seen in the phase of Japanese industrialization in the MEIJI era, is an example of such a fact.
4) "Laissez-fareism", "individualism", and "rationalism", which were the ideas of the early developer, cannot be applied to the late developer. Instead of these ideas the latter need "nationalism" or a "semi-religious" idea (Gerschenkron 1951, Nakagawa 1981, Takahashi 1987a).

Even if Gerschenkron's propositions may be adaptable to some extent in order to explain the process of Japan's industrialization, it is doubtful whether this model can aptly explain the process of industrialization in other late or hardly developed countries. In addition to these explanations, we can point out the matter, of course, that trade unions have developed lately in the late developed countries. In the present age, we can easily find examples of economic process conditioning the behavior of employees or labor unions: employees will demand a high wage in the phase of high economic growth, but they will not in phases of economic recession etc. Any way, we cannot deny that the economic process is a factor that conditions the decision making of managers and the behavior of employees.

The third factor, the internal and external organization of the enterprise, is a relatively, independent factor in determining management style. For that reason we find that organizational behavior in some enterprises fits into the cultural structure and the economic process while in other enterprises it does not fit despite of the same situation. Therefore, whether organizational behavior fits or not, depends upon the performance of the manager and the employees of the enterprise, based on its manpower development.

However, we must not overlook the fact that enterprises receive the influence of the cultural structure and the economic process. This is because the members of an enterprise are individual persons whose behavior patterns or value systems are conditioned by the cultural structure of their time and their country, and because the decisions of the managers are normally made after considering the behavior of competitiors, along with the industrial tendency of the domestic and foreign economic situation.

These three factors, namely the cultural structure, the economic process, and the internal and external organisation of the enterprise, are relatively independent of each other. But, each has some effect on the other factors. Therefore, we can find the case that the first factor has a strong effect on the other factors in a particular a rea, or the other case that the second or third factor has a strong influence on the others in another particular a rea. Therefore, we must analyse the mutual influence of the three factors not only from a historical perspective but also from international comparisons. The cultural structure has been studied in the field of sociology (inclusive of the study of politics, law, education, religion, etc.), the economic process in economics, and the organization of the enterprise in organization theory and management research (Takahashi 1987). For that reason, we must use an interdisciplinary approach in order to discuss any international comparison of human resource management.

3. General Characteristics of the Japanese Employment System — Japanese HRM before the Second World War

It was said in a report of the Organisation for Economic Cooperation and Development in 1973 that, "Japanese employment system is characterized by three principal elements"; life time commitment (employment), seniority wage system, and enterprise unionism. But, that statement was supplemented in 1977 as follows; "the three pillars of the system" "cannot be understood without also taking account of the peculiarly Japanese social pattern of 'vertical' relationship and the consensual nature of managerial decision-making" (OECD 1973: 98, OECD 1977: 10). This assertion is generally right in the characterization of the Japanese employment system, although it is doubtful whether the behavior patterns of Japanese people are to be defined by 'vertical relationship' instead of 'groupism' or not. But this system has changed under the influence of the economic process, the cultural

structure, and internal and external organisations of the enterprise. Therefore, we will review, at first, the generation and diffusion process of this
system from a historical perspective.

The life time employment and the seniority wage system were introduced
drawing the change process from indirect to direct employment, especially
for workers on the shop floor level, after the First World War. From the
beginning of Japanese industrialization until the end of the War, the labor
market was fluid and the length of service of skilled workers were generally
short since they were transfered frequently from one company to another
by their OYAKATA (boss), their employer. With the expansion of large
companies, based on the mechanization of plants and modernization of
manufacturing process, the large companies in those day began to make
efforts to develop their management techniques or management policies so
that they might win in the competition with other companies both within
and outside their country. The most important policy measure was to stop
the mobility of skilled workers, and to let them continue to work in the
same enterprise for long terms. In order to realize this objective, enterprises
undertook the following measures:

1) Changing the hiring system from an indirect to a direct system
2) Establishing welfare benefit systems in the company
3) Introducing the seniority wage system, and
4) Establishing an education and training system within the enterprise.

3.1 The Change in the Hiring System from the Indirect to the Direct System

Until the end of the World War I., it was very popular for large Japanese
companies to implement an indirect hiring system, the so called internal
sub-contract system, whereby the manager hired only the boss of individual
workers on the shop floor and instead of paying the workers, payed the
total wage to him. As the boss moved normally to another company with
the skilled workers under his control after finishing his contract, enterprises
needed to hire directly both the boss and skilled workers to stop the indirect
hiring. With the implementation of the system of hiring employees directly,
large Japanese enterprises began to distinguish the hiring authorities into
three types in accordance with the management levels such as; a foreman
of production department had the authority to hire the workers of the shop
floor whose academic career were old elementary school graduation; a
manager of the factory or office department had the authority to hire
technicians or clerks whose accademic career were old junior hig schoolor
technical and commercial school graduation; and the president of the head-

quarter had the authority to hire the candidates of manager or engineers whose accademic career were old university or special senior high school graduation (Shirai 1982: 111).

In addition to that, enterprises began to distinguish also the hiring system into two types such as: periodical and non-periodical or occassional hiring. And regular employees were hired in periodical form and irregular, temporary or part time employees in non-periodical form. The wage systems were different among the employees hiring in each case. Only about the third of all employees, it is said, could become regular in large Japanese enterprise of those days, because the labor supply was much higher than the demand, and workers had just begun to organize their unions and their power was not yet strong. Therefore, the regular workers who were periodically hired, did not want to retire. Since then, the system of periodical hiring at spring has settled in Japanese companies and prevailes today.

3.2 The Establishment of a Welfare Benefits System by Enterprises

The welfare benefit systems established in those days gave the regular employees a strong motivation to continue to work in the same companies a long time. These systems consisted of a type of insurance that paid employees for job-related injuries and illness, the congratulatory money for marriage and childbirth, company housing and so forth, by which typical Japanese paternalism (business familyism) was gradually brought up in enterprises. Naturally, the irregular workers, such as temporary and part time workers, could not share the fringe benefits from the enterprise and were treated only as buffer in the case of recession. Only the regular employees, who were about one third of all employees in large companies could share the benefits of lifetime employment, and other temporary and part time workers and the employees of small-medium size enterprises had to move from company to company to look for higher wages. This phenomenon which is called "dual structure of economy" exists until now and has determined the economic process in Japan.

3.3 The Introduction of a Seniority Wage System

The introduction of a seniority wage system had played the same role to let the regular employee remain in the same company. Since the wage increase and promotion of employees on each grade level were decided on the basis of the length of their service years, if employees of a company moved to another, their wage level went down because of the shorter service years in the new company.

As stated earlier, the hiring authority at each management level was different and was related to the employees status and wage payment forms. Until the end of World War I the status of employees were clearly distinguished between white and blue collar workers and each status consisted of 4−5 ranks, which determined wage pay forms, such as: daily, weekly and monthly wage pay (Ohmi 1981: 207, Shirai 1982: 111). Any way, the introduction of the seniority wage system was promoted in Japan in those days to establish and diffuse the life time employment system at micro-level on the one hand, and to enlarge the internal labour market instead of external labour market at macro-level on the other hand.

3.4 The Establishment of an Education and Training System in Enterprises

Under the situation of the internal labor market, enterprises must have the conditions where employees could be transferred between jobs and jobs within plant and enterprise. In order to create such conditions, managers of large Japanese enterprises at that time, although the number of such enterprises was limited, endeavoured to establish an education and training system in their companies. The contents of education and training were mainly of three types, such as the course for the graduates of the old elementary schools where the education and training of job-related and general diciplines included the philosophy of the company man; the course for the graduates of the old junior high school or technical and commercial school where technical education and practice were implemented for two or three years; and the course for the candidates of foremen where not only special techniques but also knowledge of general techniques and shop management were taught for 3 to 6 years (Yoshikawa 1982: 276).

With the establishment of the education and training system, enterprises wanted to hire those applicants as regular employees who had the potential for performing multi-functions and wanted to develop them through by the On-the-Job or Off-the-Job Training. Since then in Japanese enterprises, there has been no philosophy to hire an applicant for a certain job like in most Western countries. The regular employees except that individuals with special skills are transferred periodically (per 3−7 years) from job to job within the same department and the same enterprise. Personnel evaluation will be implemented by each upper authority from a long aspect, and the promotion of employees will be decided on the criteria of their academic career, service years, job performance, potential ability and so on. Transfer between jobs has become an essential requirement for the equirement for the employees to be promoted to a high position. The terminology "Promotion through job rotation" has become very popular in Japanese society.

In conclusion, we can say that the development of education and training systems in large Japanese enterprises was an important step to introduce the system of transfering employees within departments and enterprises, and consequently to perpetualize the life time employment system as the backbone of Japanese management.

4. The Management Organization of Japanese Enterprises before and after the Second World War

Before and just after World War II, there was no demarcation between line and staff functions, nor between the jobs of individual employees in Japanese companies. Jobs of group units were demarcated from each other and organized vertically. Only line departments, production and sales departments were regarded as important. There was no delegation of decision making, and the final decisions were mostly made by top managers or the president of the company. This centralized decision making style in Japanese companies is called 'RINGI System'. It originated in the management method of the government office and national enterprises in the beginning stage of industrialization in the MEIJI Era 1968 – 1900. The rules of RINGI system are as follows:

1) The business plan or proposal about important problems which required a budget must be sent from the lower to the higher positioned staff and be finally decided by the president.
2) The business plan or proposal must be sent from the connected lower group-head by the connected section head to the connected upper department head.
3) If the connected group or section head or department head cannot consent to the plan, it must be sent back to the original lower section and modified or planed newly, and be sent to the upper level again.

The RINGI system had several serious weak points:

a) The authority to make a final decision rests on the president; it will not be delegated to another position; the extent of job and individual responsibility is unclear.

b) Since the final decision is not made by the president until plans are sent from the lower group to the higher department, the final decision is usually late.

This system, however, has positive aspects, too, namely, that the implementation of plans decided finally by the president is very smooth, because the problems to implement those plans are understood by every group, section and department (Ono 1979).

In order to modify or modernize this old management system, Japanese management tried to introduce American management system at the beginning of the 50s. The scope and content of the individual job (authority and responsibility) of managers and workers were clearly defined in the American system, which could not fit to the Japanese management culture of RINGI system and so on. Japanese managers came to know that it was impossible to define the content or scope of an administrative job objectively, even if authority was formally assigned to it as far as possible, and that it was unrealistic to expect such change within the context of Japanese organisational and personnel practice such as seniority wage system and group-decision making system (Noda 1975: 138).

Clarification of the job and its authority in particular was contrary to the traditional RINGI system. For this reason, the American system could not be introduced directly, and had to be modified with the modernization of the RINGI system. That is, the content and scope of a job was clarified by groups, by sections and by departments, where the authority to decide was delegated from the upper to the respective head in accordance with the degree of importance of a problem. In addition, staff function was demarcated from the line, and the concepts of service, control and general staff functions were also introduced and established gradually in the process of modernizing or modifying the RINGI system. Therefore, RINGI system before and after the introduction of American management system was different. But, group consensual decision making has been maintained and implemented within group, section and department (Takahashi 1985: 51 – 54).

Why has the group decision making through consensus been popular in Japan? We can point out two reasons. The first is related to the characteristic of the Japanese people who do not like to inherently insist on their own opinion clearly, and are very anxious to find mutual agreement from different opinions. Such characteristic can be called 'groupism'. The second reason is related to the system of life time employment and seniority wage payment, which support group decision making. Since the employees normally continue to work in the same company until retirement, they have the tendency to avoid opposite opinions about any management decision which might develop into personal antagonism between individual employees. Therefore, almost all people in a Japanese company make an effort to solve management problems through consensus finding. And since wage increases are not directly linked with job performance, rather connected with the length of service, academic career and so on, group-work or team-work can be functionalized easily, although in the long run competition for promotion among employees with the same number of service years and same academic career is very strong.

5. Japanese HRM after the Second World War

5.1 Establishment of Enterprise Unions

Here we will mention Japanese trade unions, which influence human resource management. The defeat of Japan in the Second World War changed the society remarkably. Just after the war, female suffrage was given for the first time under the situation of American army of occupation. A trade union law was enacted and three basic rights (to organize, to bargain collectively and to strike) were ensured, all of which had been prohibited during the war. Consequently, labor movement was able to have a strong influence on the Japanese society. The proportion of union membership of all employees increased drastically and reached 55.8 percent in 1949 (after this time it decreased gradually, falling to 27 percent at present). However until now the influence of Japanese labor unions on their society has not been as strong as those of Western countries, because the unions have been organized in the companies. Why was the enterprise union organized in Japan? There are many opinions about the question, some of which will be introduced here.

Just after the Second World War, the Japanese labor movement was agressively developed and its first objective was to safeguard the workers' standard of living in the face of the stringent economic conditions caused by the inflation during this period. Since the employers and managers sabotaged normal production activities because of the confusion caused by the defeat in the war, the labor movement was oriented towards having white-collar and blue-collar workers cojointly controlling production for the sake of their own standards of living. The concrete demands of the workers were to remove the traditional status (grade) system, to get job security, to reform management organization, to set up a participation system, to recognize the labor union, to conduct labor agreements, to democratize management, and to expand workers' rights. During the early development of union, organizations' laborers decided to launch a joint effort of white and blue collar workers, who were to be organized in one union at the enterprise or plant level. This is the reason why Japanese trade unions are organized at the company level (Yoshikawa 1982: 393).

But it must not be overlooked that employers exerted considerable effort to bring up this style of enterprise union. H. Hazama writes on this point as follows:

It was the biggest objective for the employers just after the Second World War to restore the balance of power in favor of the employers over the workers. This objective meant that employers had to recover their dominant position in relation to the workers and thus they regained their original rights. For this purpose, managers took three measures. The first one was to make the labor relation vertical, thus weakening the horizontal solidarity of workers per district or per industry, and strengthening labor relations per enterprise. The second one was to make a cooperative employer-labor relation to reestablish order at the work by the removal of those union members who propagated radical thoughts and were agressive toward the management. The third one was to establish the right of management by setting up a new employer-labor relation system in every company (Hazama 1981: 256).

As the consequent of these measures from the employer's side, the style of Japanese trade unions has been fixed as an enterprise union.

The structure of enterprise unions limits the effectiveness of labor union activity. The level of union organization such as headquarter, chapter and group are parallel to components such as head office, plant, department and section or work place in the management organisation of enterprise. Each level of the unions is in constant interface with its' corresponding management level. This fragmentation of labor union and influence of management discourages a healthy level of negotiation in collective bargaining or labour-management joint consultation on specific issues.

Another problem is concerned with the regulation of membership eligibility. Article 2 of the Labor Union Law in Japan stipulates that all regular employees may organize into unions regardless of their job, hierarchical level below section head and qualifications, provided that they are not in charge of labor management. This fact means nothing less than that the policy of management filters easily into the minds of union members. The ambiguous position of the lower management gives credence to the idea that their activity as labour union member is questionable. The manager or supervisour at the work-shop level has double roles as a union member and lower management. For example, the sub-sectional head stands opposite to his subordinates as a member of the ordinary management organisation, while acting as a member of the union in joint consultation and collective bargaining system. In practice, there are many cases in the large Japanese companies where supervisors are elected as representatives for the union organisation at work place level. It is, therefore, easier for the Japanese manager to have influence on labor unions in the individual enterprises than for their Western counterparts (Takahashi 1987b).

5.2 Complete Establishment and Revision of the Life Time Employment

The life time employment and seniority systems were disturbed during the Second World War and at the period of inflation after the war. During the war time, the age structure of employees in the enterprises changed on account of conscription of male employees to the military forces, and wage increases based on age (not service years) of employees and a system of payment of added allowance pays in accordance with the age of the employees were implemented to safeguard of minimum living standard during the period of inflation. However, employers and managers began to recover their original activities under the regulation to labor movement by the General Headquarter of American Occupation, and revived the life time employment and seniority wage systems. But, these systems were revived mainly in large Japanese companies during the end of the 1940s and the beginning of the 1950s.

However, life time employment and seniority wage systems before and after the Second World War and in the inflation period were not the same. The first difference is that the power of the labor union against dismisal strengthened job security much more. The second one is that the enterprises began to allow employees to be hired throughout the year (not fixed periodically at spring), especially among the temporary workers as regular employees, and to give them job security, although the conditions of such employees were not perfectly equal to those of the employees hired periodically. The third one is that the wage difference between different status (white and blue collar workers) disappeared by the labor union demand. However, the difference among employees through school career has been maintained (Okamoto 1976: 118).

Especially, the proportion of irregular workers to the regular decreased when Japan entered into the period of high economic growth caused by shortage of labor supply. Therefore, almost all employees in large Japanese companies could be under the benefit of the life time employment in the 1950s. However, life time employment was compelled to be changed with the gradual modification of the seniority wage and promotion system after the high economic growth. The situation of present life time employment system and modified seniority wage system is shown in table 1 and figure1,

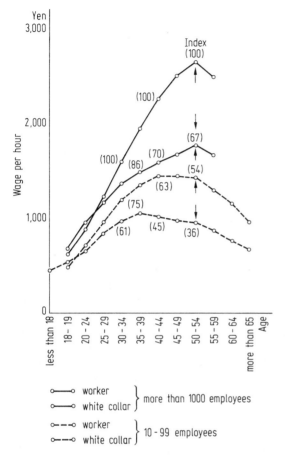

worker
white collar } more than 1000 employees

worker
white collar } 10 - 99 employees

Note: Number (100), in brackets, means the index of wage cost of white collar and technician workers in the companys which employs more than 1,000 persons, and other numbers in brackets, of the companys which employ less than 100 persons, means the proportion to 1.

Figure 1: The Present Situation of Wage Increase Through the Service Years for Example of Workers in Japanese Manufacturing Enterprises in 1978.

according to statistics of 1978. The main reasons of such change or modification are as follows:

a) Revision of the seniority wage system by introduction of the Japanese style of job-qualification system
b) Changing the structure of labor demand and supply.

Table 1: The Percentage of Life Long (more than 20 Years) Employees Aged 45 –
          49, who are Employed in Japanese Companies of Various Sizes

Size of Enterprise	Proportion
more than 1,000 employees	64%
10 – 99	19.3%
All sizes	38.6%

Source: Ministry of Labor, Elementary Statistics of Wage Structure. 1978.

5.3 Revision of the Seniority Wage System by the Introduction of the Japanese Style of Job-Qualification System

As mentioned earlier, in the process of the introduction of the American management system, Japanese employers failed to introduce a wage system based on job evaluation on account of difficulty in demacating individual jobs in Japanese management culture. So Japanese employers tried to mix the Japanese seniority wage system and American wage system linked with job, and established a new job-qualification system, which was built on a mixture of Japanese traditional qualification system depending mainly upon the evaluation of school career and service years, and the American system of employees' performance evaluation (job analysis, job evaluation and so on).

The job-qualification system is defined as follows:

a) Job-qualification has been built on two factors: job ranking (for example, to the special positions such as section, deputy and department head) and formal grading (for example, to the SHUJIHO, SHUJI, SANJIHO and so on) of employees, which are considered for payment and promotion.

b) The classification of qualifications does not depend on the job for which the employees are responsible, but depends on the ability of employees to do the job, the school career and service years of employees, and other personal factors. On the contrary, the classification of a job is done only on job rank (special position).

c) The classification of qualifications is not designed for the necessity of one technique which disposes of a management problem. However, the wage increase and the promotion of the employees, and their education and training methods are decided on the basis of this classification of qualifications (Yoshikawa 1982: 151).

The aim of introducing this job — qualification system was two-fold. The first one is, since positions at the upper level such as department head (BUCHOU) and section head (KACHOU) became relatively few compared to the number of employees processing to such posts, the company had to establish this system not only to relieve the dissatisfaction of the employees who could not be promoted to in spite of having ability and experience for such positions, but also to provide promotion opportunities in qualification rather than promotion to these positions. Secondly, companies established this system to weaken the weightage of factors like service years and school career as evaluation of qualification as well as to strengthen the factor of the employees' ability to perform jobs.

The system of performance evaluation for promotion in position and/or in qualification is as follows:

a) Considering evaluation at the general job level of the beginner class and middle class: the service years, the attitude to work, and the ability of employees to perform are evaluated.
b) Considering evaluation of the general job level of the upper class: ability to perform the job, and the actual performance are mainly evaluated and, futhermore, service years are partially evaluated.
c) Considering evaluation of managers: the power to perform the job and actual performance are evaluated, but service years are not taken into consideration (Yoshikawa 1982: 171).

Thus, it can be said that the seniority wage system was modified in the introduction process of job-qualification system since the middle stage of high economic growth.

5.4 Changing the Structure of Labor Demand and Supply

An important characteristic of the Japanese employment system consisted of the fact that the wage form and promotion style were different among the employees with different school career. This system could be maintained functionally, only when the enterprises could hire the new graduates from junior and senior high school, and university in the proportion which the enterprises wanted. The proportion of graduates each school hired in the enterprises was harmonized until the beginning of the high economic growth, because every enterprise could hire many younger workers with low school careers who were plentifully supplied from the agricultural to the industrial district. But, the Japanese labor market changed after about 1965 gradually from over-supply to over-demand especially for the young labor force, since the birth-rate had begun to decrease, and the number of young people who wanted to go on to the higher academic school or university increased.

Table 2: The Changing of the Academic Structure of the New Graduates (%)

Year	No. of the graduates from junior high sch.	No. of the graduates from senior sch.	No. of graduates from university	total
1965	44.4%	44.8%	10.7%	100%
1970	21.6%	58.1%	20.3%	100%
1975	11.8%	59.1%	29.1%	100%
1980	8.4%	61.1%	30.5%	100%
1985	3.7%	41.1%	55.2%	100%
1987	3.0%	35.9%	61.0%	100%

Sources: The Ministry of Education. The fundamental research of schools.

In this situation of a shortage of younger workers, the younger employees with low academic careers began to move from enterprise to enterprise in order to gain higher wages. It occured in one company that about 20 percent of all employees newly hired from junior and senior high school left in the first year, 15 – 16 percent in the second year and 12 – 13 percent in the third year, and about 50 percent in all left. Furthermore, the increase of young people who wanted to get higher academic careers added to the shortage of younger workers. Table 2 shows the changing structure of the number of the new graduates. The percentage of new graduates from junior high school who were the main labor source on the shop floor, has decreased gradually from 44.4% in 1965 to 3.0% in 1987. Conversely, the percentage of new graduates from university who were candidates for executive positions, has increased gradually from 10.7% in 1965 to 61% in 1987. This situation means that enterprises have not been able to use cheap labor and thus have been compelled to change the personnel management policy. Managers have begun to evaluate more the factor of job performance than the factor of length of service or school careers.

6. The Problems of Current Japanese HRM

At present, human resource management in Japanese enterprises has began to change, due to social, economic and technological changes in society. The contents of these changes are the increasing of number of employees in the service sector, the trend towards multinational enterprises, and the aging of people. These factors have progressed more in connection with the terminological innovation of microelectronics which has developed since the end of Japanese high economic growth at the time of the Second Oil Shock in 1975. These social, economic and technological factors have caused the following problems for Japanese HRM.

6.1 The Strengthening Evaluation of Ability Over Length of Service of Employees

According to the survey conducted in 629 companies by the Ministry of Labor, 86.6 percent of all surveyed companies mentioned as the most important aim of personnel and labor management in the future, "the enrichment of education and training systems". 78.9 percent of the companies mentioned "strengthen the evaluation of ability over the length of service years of employees" (The Ministry of Labor 1987: 85). Concerning the former Japanese promotion practice of employees with the same length of service years and school career being promoted at the same time, 27.8 percent of 629 companies answered "we will evaluate the different abilities of employees and not be concerned about the promotion of employees at the same time". However, 36.0 percent answered "we will take the promotion measure of employees at the same time only five years after they enter the company". Concerning the wage system, 83.9 percent of all companies answered "we will decide the wage increase and promotion of our employees based upon their ability or job performance (The Ministry of Labor 1987: 25. 29).

6.2 The Diffusion of the Career Development Programm (CDP)

At the beginning of high economic growth, Japanese managers and employers' organizations made an effort to establish a new education and training system along with modifying the American system. The main content of the new system was that their own education and training system was settled by hierarchy, job and qualification in the company in which OJT (On-the-Job-Training) was generally used. In addition, Japanese companies have begun to use CDP for individual employees. CDP means the education and training program in long term of individual employees inclusive of their ability, relocation, promotion to the position and qualification and so on, which is used for the total career development of employees. The number of companies which have CDP has increased gradually and about one third of the surveyed large companies used such a program in 1984 (The Ministry of Labor 1988: 48).

6.3 Greater Use of Part Time Workers and the Restriction of the Number of Regular Employees

According to a survey on hiring policy, 51 percent of 629 companies responded "the greater use of part time workers" and 38.5 percent "the decreasing of labor costs by the restriction of the number of regular employees". The average service years of part time workers lengthened from 2.9 years in 1976 to 4.0 years in 1986. The tasks of part time workers are not simple and monotonous jobs but also special and complicated jobs, on which the pay depends. Therefore, there are two or three ranks of payment for part time workers (Ministry of Labor 1988: 47). The number of part time workers whose tasks are equal to that of the regular employees, has increased.

6.4 The Increasing of the Relocation of Employees Within Establishments and Between Establishments

Another survey on relocation of employees conducted by the Ministry of Labor in 1986 shows that 41.4 percent of all surveyed companies responded "the relocation of employees within the establishment increased", 10.4 percent "it decreased" and 48.5 percent of those responded "no change". Concerning with the reocation between establishments, 46.0 percent of the surveyed companies responded "it increased", 10.3 percent of the companies "it decreased" and 43.7 percent was "no change" (Ministry of Labor 1988: 51 − 51, the same 1987). The introduction of microelectronics into the production process and office has reduced labor force at the work place, thereby increasing the relocation of the spared workers within and between establishments increased (Takahashi 1988: 433).

6.5 The Increasing of the Number of the Regular Employees who are Lent or Transfered to the Daughter and Related Companies

Recently, the number of the regular employees who are lent from the mother company to the daughter or related companies has gradually increased. Such a lending of employees is called SHUKKOU in Japanese terminology. the transfer is called TENSEKI. The employees in the situation of SHUKKOU and TENSEKI must accept a lower wage at the daughter company than at the mother company. According to the former survey by the Ministry of Labor in 1987, the share of lent employees to all employees of the mother company was 5.9 percent, and the percentage of the employees over 45 years old to all lent employees was 30.4 percent (the Ministry of Labor 1988: 52, the same 1957). Thus, a strict selection between employees has been implemented based on their ability in the mother company, and the same percentage of employees of high age group compelled to be lent or transfered to the daughter or related companies. The mother company is able to influence the policy of the daughter and related companies through financing, sending officers, transactions and so on.

6.6 The Development of the Employment and the Wide Personnel Management within Enterprise Groups

Large Japanese companies have organized enterprise groups horizontally and vertically based on the stock holding, financing and personnel exchange to one another. In the case of the vertical relationship between the mother and the daughter or related company, the upper company normally influences the subordinate company from one-side. Such a grouping of vertical relations between the companies is called KEIRETSUKA in Japanese terminology.

According to a survey conducted by the National Institute of Employment and Vocational Research in 1985, the 148 mother companies that responded (the average number of employees of a company: 8,302 persons) controlled 3318 vertically grouped companies (the average number of employees of a company: 230.2 persons). Therefore, a mother company subordinates an average of 22.4 daughter or related companies. Since the end of the high economic growth in 1975, such vertically grouped companies increased. The same survey shows that the share of mother companies which responded "it increased in five years" reached 73.6 percent (National Institute of Employment and Vocational Research 1985: 5—7). The desire to found subordinate companies or to have such a link with the companies, are for the policy of diversification, for the seperation of non-productive department or establishment as well as for the lending and transference of employees especially in the higher age bracket.

The importance of lending and transfering employees within an enterprise group is shown in another survey conducted on 709 companies by the National Institute of E.V.R. (see table 3). The average number of the regular employees in 709 companies was 1,897.7 persons. The mother companies subordinated average 4 daughter companies at home and 9.8 company abroad. The average number of daughter companies was 439.8 persons at home and 70.8 persons abroad. The share of the number of employees in

Table 3: The Situation of the Employment Within Enterprise Groups (Average)
(the Number of the Surveyed Comparies: 709)

	(I) The surveyed year April 1983		(II) The surveyed year November of 1986	Proportion (II)/(I)
1) Number of regular employees (persons)	1848.0		1897.7	102.7
2) Number of daughter companies	3.9	3.3	4.9	
a) domestic	0.6		4.0	
b) abroad			0.9	
3) Number of employees of daughter companies (persons)	438.1		510.6	116.7
a) domestic	388.5		439.8	113.2
b) abroad	49.6		70.8	142.7
4) Number of the lent employees to the mother (persons)	97.6		110.0	112.7
a) daughter (domestic)	47.1		56.3	119.5
b) related companies	47.3		49.3	103.6
c) daughter (abroad)	3.2		4.4	137.5
5) Number of the transfered employees to the daughter (persons)	3.7		6.9	186.5
	1.7		3.0	176.5
a) daughter (domestic)	2.0		3.9	195.5
b) related companies				
6) Proportion of the employees of the daughter to the regular employees of the mother (%)	23.7		26.9	
a) domestic	21.0		23.2	
b) abroad	2.7		3.7	
7) Proportion of the lent employees to the regular of the mother (%)	5.3		5.8	
a) daughter (domestic)	2.5		3.0	
b) related companies	2.6		2.6	
c) daughter (abroad)	0.2		0.2	

the domestic daughter companies reached 23.2 percent of all employees of the mother companies. On an average 56.3 percent were lent from the mother company to the domestic daughter, 49.3 persons to the related, and 4.4 persons to foreign daughter companies. The relation of lent employees to all employees of the mother company was 5.8 persons. The average number of the transferred employees was 6.9 persons of which 3.0 persons went to the domestic daughter, while the others went to related companies. The number of lent and transfered employees increased from 1983 to 1986 (National Institute of E.V.R. 1987: 58 – 59).

Against this background, large Japanese companies have begun to take the wide personnel management policy beyond one company within an enterprise group. They have tried to take some measures for personnel management within the enterprise group, such as: the education and training of employees from daughter and related companies by the mother company, the evaluation of the performance of lent and transfered employees in the mother company, the arranging of the wage level between the mother company and the daughter or related companies and so on (National Institute of E.V.R. 1987: 7 – 89).

References

Cole, A. H. (1956): *Business Enterprise in its' Social Setting*, Cambridge, Mass.: Harvard University.

Gerschenkron, A. (1951): Economic Backwardness in Historical Perspective, in: B. F. Hoselitz (ed.), *The Progress of Underdeveloped Areas*, Chicago: University of Chicago Press: 3 – 29.

Graham, H. T. (1974): *Human Resource Management*, London: Macdonald & Evans.

Hazama, H. (1981): *The Employers' Organisation and Industrial Relation in Japan* (in Japanese), Tokyo: The Japan Institute of Labour Press.

Ministry of Labor (1987a): *The Change and Prospect of Japanese Employment Practice* (in Japanese), Tokyo: Oukurashou Press.

Ministry of Labor (1987b): *The Research of Employment* (in Japanese), Tokyo: Oukurashou Press.

Ministry of Labor (1988): *The Maintaining Management Power and Personnel and Labor Management in Future* (in Japanese), Tokyo: Roudou Hourei Kyoukai Press.

Nakagawa, K. (1981): *Japanese Style Management* (in Japanese), Tokyo: Japan Broadcast Association Press.

National Institute of Employment and Vocational Research (1986): *The Research Report of the Lending and Transference of Employees to the subordinate grouped Companies*, Tokyo.

National Institute of Employment and Vocational Research (1987): *The Research Report of the wide Personnel Management and Adjustment of Employment* (in Japanese), Tokyo.

Noda, K. (1975): Big Business Organisation, in: E. F. Vogel (ed.), *Modern Japanese Organisation and Decision Making*, Tokyo: University of California: 115–145.

Ohmi, N. (1982): The Industrial Relation in the Japanese Style Management (in Japanese), in: M. Tsuda (ed.), *Japanese Style Management at Present Age*, Tokyo: Yuhikaku Press: 195–226.

Okamoto, Y. (1976): *The Management Organisation at Present Age* (in Japanese), Tokyo: Japan Economic News Paper Press.

Ono, T. (1979): *The Organisational Strategy of Japanese Enterprise* (in Japanese), Tokyo: Management Press.

Shirai, T. (1982): *Japanese Labour Management at Present Age* (in Japanese), Tokyo: Toyou Keizai Shinpousha.

Takahashi, Y. (1985): Merkmale des Japanischen Managements unter besonderer Berücksichtigung des Personalmanagements, in: S. J. Park, U. Jürgen und H. P. Merz (eds.), *Transfer des Japanischen Management Systems*, Berlin: Express Edition: 39–60.

Takahashi, Y. (1987a): The Theoretical Problems of the Transferability of Management, in: M. Trevor (ed.), *The Internationalization of Japanese Business*, Frankfurt am Main: Campus Verlag: 156–176.

Takahashi, Y. (1987b): The Structure of the Enterprise Union and the Present Situation of Labour Participation in Japan, in: W. Dorow (ed.), *The Business Corporation in the Democratic Society*, Berlin: Walter de Gruyter: 307–326.

Takahashi, Y. (1988): The Impact of Increased Utilisation of Microelectronics on Employment, Production Process, and Job Organisation — The Japanese Viewpoint, in: G. Dlugos, W. Dorow and K. Weiermair (eds.), *Management Under Differing Labour Market and Employment Systems*, Berlin: Walter de Gruyter: 427–442.

Yoshikawa, E. (1982): *Japanese Personnel and Labour Management* (in Japanese), Tokyo: Yuhikaku Press.

Part IV
Human Resource Management and Multinational Companies

Strategic Human Resource Management: A Global Perspective[1]

Nancy J. Adler and Faribarz Ghadar

For all practical purposes, all business today is global. Those individual businesses, firms, industries, and whole societies that clearly understand the new rules of doing business in a world economy will prosper; those that do not will perish.

Ian Mitroff, 1987: ix

1. Introduction

New approaches to managing research and development (R & D), production, marketing, and finance incorporating today's global realities are occurring rapidly, an equivalent evolution in conceptualizing and managing international human resource systems appears absent. According to Evans (1987):

A review of research since the late 1960s shows that our understanding of the human resources strategies of multinational firms has advanced little since the pioneering studies of Perlmutter into the meaning of multinationalism that led to his Ethnocentric-Polycentric-Regiocentric-Geocentric typology [see Heenan & Perlmutter, 1979].

What is compelling about such apparently unchanging human resource practices is that the 1980s have made it mandatory for corporations to use global strategies if they are to succeed in the 1990s.[2]

---

[1] The issues are discussed in the Canadian context in a paper entitled "Globalization and Human Resource Management", originally presented at the founding conference of the Ontario Centre for International Business on "International Business Research for the Twenty-first Century: Canada's New Research Agenda", University of Toronto, Canada, 9 September 1988, and published in Alan M. Rugman (ed.), *Research in Global Strategic Management: A Canadian Perspective*, Volume 1. Greenwich, Connecticut: JAI Press, 1989 (in press).

[2] See among others, Doz 1985; Doz, Bartlett, & Prahalad 1981; Doz & Prahalad

As a context for addressing human resource management issues, this chapter will begin by reviewing four primary stages of operation of multinational enterprises. Within that context, we will then ask two fundamental questions.

First, how does national culture effect the firm and, thereby, its management of people? One of the central questions facing international human resource professionals in the influence, or lack thereof, of culture on the management of people worldwide. Yet, discussions concerning the influence of culture on strategic efficacy remain time-lagged, disconnected from other corporate realities. We continue to ask *if* culture impacts organizational functioning rather than the more relevant *when*, or under what conditions, does it do so. Perhaps we would give more attention to the second question if we placed our inquiry within the context of the evolving strategies and structures of global firms, rather than confining it to the more static assumptions that have governed international personnel decisions for years. In this first question, we thus investigate the consequences of culture at each phase in the multinational firm's strategic relationship with its external environment.

Second, what does each phase's strategy imply for effectively managing people? What are the implications for traditional human resource management decisions as well as for those decisions that will only make sense when taken from within a future perspective? Issues needing to be addressed include the cultural homogeneity of top executive teams, the purpose and process of expatriation, the firm's recognition and use of cultural diversity, and the overall management of geographic dispersion. Based on this third question, we will suggest some more appropriate approaches to managing people within today's and tomorrow's multinational enterprises (MNEs).

This chapter focuses on global strategy from the perspective of people and culture. It uses a decription of North American multinationals as a base, starting with the product life cycle in international trade and investment and proceeding to a commonly accepted three-phase model[3] decribing the evolution of multinational enterprises (MNEs) from World War II to the present. Then, going beyond the third phase, it outlines some of the possible characteristics of future phase four MNEs. Within this framework of the evolving multinational firm, the chapter suggests some new and more powerful approaches to managing human resource systems and the cultural

---

1987; Dunning 1985; Gluckk, Kaufman, & Walleck 1980; Grub, Ghadar, & Khambata 1986; Hammel & Prahalad 1985; Hout, Porter, & Rudden 1982; Leavitt 1983; Porter 1980, 1985, & 1986; Porter & Millar 1985; Prahalad & Doz 1981; and Watson 1982.

[3] While originally espoused by Vernon in 1966, this argument has been picked up by many commentators; also see (Vernon 1971 & 1981), Ghadar (1977, 1985 & 1986), among others.

diversity engendered in global operations. It suggests that firms can compete successfully in the global economy, but that the majority of them can no longer do so without fundamental change.

2. A Model

One way that has been used to understand the evolution of multinational enterprises is through the products and services they produce. The changes that a product (or service) undergoes in the course of its life cycle have several important implications for the firm's relationship with the external environment as well as its internal functioning. At each stage, the product's characteristics dictate the environment in which it can be produced, and, to a certain extent, the environment dictates the possible products. In North America, post World War II economic conditions played a determining role in the way businesses approached the development, manufacturing, and marketing of products. Vernon first described these forces in 1966, just as international markets were beginning to change. He astutely observed that one could divide the international product life cycle for trade and investment into three principal phases: high tech, growth and internationalization, and maturity. Although equally applicable to products and services, the model used product characteristics to describe each phase. As shown in the expanded framework in Table 1, these form the basis of a three-phase development model for multinational enterprises.

2.1 Phase One: A Product Orientation

The salient characteristics of Phase One's high tech products and services is that they are new and unique. Hence, they depend on research and development (R & D); that is, on the application of advances in science and engineering to product development. By definition, Phase One products have never been produced successfully before. Moreover, at most, only a handful of firms are capable of developing and manufacturing any specific product. High tech products are purchased by a highly specialized and limited market. Not surprisingly, given their uniqueness and the few firms capable of producing them, Phase One products generally command a high price relative to direct costs.

2.2 Phase Two: A Market Orientation

The entrance of competition marks the beginning of Phase Two, growth and internationalization. All firms embarking on this phase must now focus on expanding their markets and production. Frequently, they expand internationally. Firms based in countries with smaller domestic markets (such as Sweden) generally begin such expansions earlier than those operating in countries with larger domestic markets (such as the United States). Initially, the firm supplies new foreign markets through exports from the home country. Gradually, production shifts to those countries with the largest domestic markets, with firms erecting foreign plants and assembly lines to supply local demand. As these foreign markets grow, more is produced locally and exports from the original home country begin to diminish.

Thus, as products reach Phase Two, market penetration and control replace research and development as the most important functions. Because the product technology has been perfected in Phase One, R & D as a percentage of sales decreases. The firm's activity need no longer center on developing the product, but rather on refining the means of production. Consequently, the focus shifts from product engineering to process engineering, although the firm still may address specialized engineering problems associated with design modifications to suit the product for international markets. With other firms continuing to enter the market as producers, competition increases and drives down both price and the production of price to cost.

2.3 Phase Three: A Price Orientation

Products enter Phase Three, originally labelled "maturity", when standardization of the production process makes further reductions in production costs impossible. The product has become completely standardized. The technology inherent in both the product itself and the production process have become widely available; hence, R & D drops off completely. Moreover, the market, while large, is completely saturated with competitors. The potential for growth in either market or market share therefore becomes severely limited. Due to the competition, price often falls to a bare minimum above cost.

Given these conditions, Phase Three firms can gain a competitive advantage only by managing factor costs; that is, by shifting production to those countries in which the elements of production are least expensive. Market considerations no longer determine location, but rather production costs. Because product development occurs in countries with a high standard of living and relatively high labor costs, by Phase Three, home country production usually ceases to be competitive and therefore declines markedly. As a result, the home country market now is supplied primarily by production imported from offshore plants.

2.4 The Accelerated Product Life Cycle

In the years immediately following the Second World War, products generally took between fifteen and twenty years to move through the international product life cycle described above. During these years, products progressed gradually through the three phases from high tech development to maturity. Their evolution seemed inevitable (see Stopford and Wells 1972, among others).

While the international product life cycle provided a fairly reliable guide to business strategy throughout the twenty-year period following World War II, by the 1970s, its acceleration made the need for new strategies and models, and thus for new kinds of multinational enterprises, imminent. By the 1980s, instead of taking fifteen to twenty years for a product to move through the cycle from development to maturity, it generally took three to five years. For some products, it now takes considerably less than six months. While the changes in strategy, structure, production, and marketing appear evident, what has been less clear is how these changes effect human resource management systems.

2.5 The Future: A Possible Phase Four

Many scholars are attempting to describe the future of society and of corporations within that society (e. g. Naisbitt 1982). One particularly insightful management scholar, Stan Davis, in his most recent book *Future Perfect* (1987) tells us that we are headed for an era of mass customization, with products being designed to meet individual needs but assembled from components sourced worldwide. Firms will need to understand and respond to individual clients' needs by delivering top-quality products and services at the least cost. Successful firms will be responsive; that is, they will listen to clients, accurately identify trends, and respond quickly. In many ways, firms will compete in Phases One, Two and Three simultaneously.

To succeed in such a Phase Four environment, firms must become simultaneously more highly differentiated and more integrated or coordinated. Structurally, successful firms will have passed far beyond the international divisions and foreign subsidiaries of Phase Two as well as the global lines

Table 1: International Corporate Evolution

	Phase I Domestic	Phase II International	Phase III Multinational	Phase IV Global
Competitive Strategy	Domestic	Multidomestic	Multinational	Global
Importance of World Business	Marginal	Important	Extremely Important	Dominant
Primary Orientation	Product or Service	Market	Price	Strategy
Product/ Service	New, unique	More Standardized	Completely Standardise (Commodity)	Mass-Customized
	Product Engineering Emphasized	Process Engineering Emphasized	Engineering Not Emphasized	Product & Process Engineering
Technology	Proprietary	Shared	Widely Shared	Instantly & Extensively Shared
R & D/Sales	High (10 – 14%)	Decreasing	Very Low	High
Profit Margin	High	Decreasing	Very Low	High
Competitors	None	Few	Many	Significant (Few or Many)
Market	Small, Domestic	Large, Multidomestic	Larger, Multinational	Largest, Global
Production Location	Domestic	Domestic & Primary Markets	Multinational, least cost	Global, least cost
Exports	None	Growing, high potential	Large & saturated	Imports & Exports
Structure	Functional Divisions	Functional with International Division	Multinational Lines of Business	Global Alliance, Heterarchy
	Centralized	Decentralized	Centralized	Centralized & Decentralized

of business offering mature, standardized products of Phase Three to global heterarchies[4] (Hedlund 1986) that weave together complex networks of joint ventures, wholly-owned subsidiaries, and organizational and project defined

---

[4] Heterarchies, as used by Gunnar Hedlund (1986), describe non-hierarchically organized systems; e. g., holographic coding where entire systems are represented or "known" within each component of the system.

alliances (Galbraith & Kazajian 1986). Managers in this type of environment will use multifocal approaches combining Phase Two's demands for increased local responsiveness with Phase Three's opportunities for global integration (Doz & Prahalad 1986). To maintain responsiveness, successful firms will develop global corporate cultures that recognize cultural diversity and its impact on the organization (Adler & Jelinek 1986), thus allowing them to integrate culture specific strategic choices within a global vision of the firm (Laurent 1986). Appropriate approaches to human resource management in these types of cooperative ventures will have to be redefined (Lorange 1986), if not reinvented altogether.

3. The Consequences of Culture

How important are cultural differences to organizational effectiveness? To what extent must firms differentiate their products and operations by country and region, versus maintaining global products and integrated, undifferentiated worldwide operations? Integration versus differentiation; the dilemma is certainly not new. Some observers of corporate behavior say cultural differences are not at all important. Others claim them to be extremely important. Those adherents of the cultural convergence perspective argue that organizational characteristics across nations are free, or becoming free, from the particularities of specific cultures. This position suggests that as an outcome of "common industrial logic" — most notably of technological origin — institutional frameworks, patterns and structures of organizations, and management practices across countries are converging (Adler & Doktor 1986: 300–301)[5]. By contrast, others argue that organizations are culture-bound, rather than culture-free, and remaining so. They conclude that there is no one-best-way to manage across all cultures, but rather many equally effective ways exist, with the most effective depending, among other contingencies, on the cultures involved (Adler & Doktor 1986: 301)[6].

Perhaps this dilemma has not been resolved because we have been asking the wrong question. Using the four phase model described above as a guide,

---

[5] Among the most notable proponents of this position are Kerr et al. 1952; Hickson et al. 1974 & 1979; Form 1979; Negandhi 1979 & 1985; Child 1981; Child & Tayeb 1983; and Leavitt 1983 among many others.

[6] Proponents of the culture specific perspective include Laurent 1983; Lincoln, Hanada & Olson 1981; Hofstede 1980; Bass et al. 1979; England 1975; Heller & Wilpert 1979; and Haire, Giselli & Porter 1966 among many others.

Table 2: Corporate Cross-Cultural Evolution

	Phase I Domestic	Phase II International	Phase III Multinational	Phase IV Global
Primary Orientation	Product/ Service	Market	Price	Strategy
Strategy	Domestic	Multidomestic	Multinational	Global
Perspective	Ethnocentric	Polycentric or Regiocentric	Multinational	Global/ Multicentric
Cultural Sensitivity	Unimportant	Very Important	Somewhat Important	Critically Important
With whom	No one	Clients	Employees	Employees & Clients
Level	No one	Workers & Clients	Managers	Executives
Strategic Assumption	"One-way" or "One-best-way"	"Many-best- ways" Equifinality	"One-least- cost-way"	"Many-best- ways" simultaneously

we can ask *when* culture has an impact on organizational functioning rather than *if* it does or does not. As shown in Table 2, the importance of cultural differences depends on the phase or phases of the life cycle in which the firm operates. Phase One firms can appropriately operate from an ethnocentric perspective, and ignore most cultural differences they encounter. These firms have one unique product that they offer primarily to their own domestic market. The Phase One product's uniqueness and the absence of competitors negate the firm's need to demonstrate sensitivity to cultural differences. If the firm exports the product at all, it does so without altering it for foreign consumption. Cultural differences are absorbed by the foreign buyers, rather than by the home country's product design, manufacturing, or marketing teams. In some ways, the implicit message Phase One firms send to foreigners is "We will *allow* you to buy our product" and, of course, the more explicit assumption is that the foreigners will want to do so.

By Phase Two, competition brings the need to market and to produce abroad. Consequently, sensitivity to cultural differences becomes critical to implementing an effective corporate strategy. As Phase One's product orientation shifts to Phase Two's marketing orientation, the firm must address each foreign market separately. Whereas the unique technology of Phase One products fits well with adopting an integrated, ethnocentric, one-best-way approach, the competitive pressures of Phase Two fit better with an equifinality approach; that is, with assuming that many-good-ways to manage exist, with the best being contingent on the particular cultures involved. Successful Phase Two firms can no longer expect foreigners to absorb cross-cultural mismatches between buyers and sellers, but rather must modify their own style to fit with that of their foreign clients and colleagues. While managing cultural differences becomes important in designing and marketing culturally appropriate products, it becomes critical in producing them in foreign factories.

As firms enter Phase Three, the environment again changes and with it the demands for cultural sensitivity. By Phase Three, many firms produce the same, almost undifferentiated product. Firms compete almost exclusively on price. This price competition reduces the importance of many cross-cultural differences along with most advantages the firm could have gained by sensitivity to them. The appropriate Phase Three assumption for product design, production, and marketing can neither remain one-best-way nor even many-best-ways, but rather must become one-least-cost-way. With primary markets having become global, there is little market segmentation based on culture or other national considerations. Firms gain competitive advantage almost exclusively through process engineering, sourcing critical factors on a worldwide basis, and benefiting from the resultant economies of scale. During Phase Three, price competition reduces culture's influence significantly.

By Phase Four, top-quality, least-possible-cost products and services emerge as the minimally acceptable standard. Competitive advantage comes from sophisticated global strategies based on mass customization. Firms draw product ideas, as well as the factors and locations of production, from worldwide sources. However, firms tailor final products and their relationship to clients to very discrete market niches. One of the critical components on which Phase Four firms segment the market again becomes culture. Successful firms understand their potential clients' needs, quickly translate them into products and services, produce those products and services on a least-possible-cost basis, and deliver them back to the client in a culturally appropriate and timely fashion. By Phase Four, the product, market, and price orientations of prior phases almost completely disappear, having been replaced by a strategic orientation combining responsive design and delivery with quick, least-possible-cost production. Firms continually scan the globe, often including geographically dispersed and culturally diverse alliance partners. Since a strategic orientation requires firms to develop global R & D, production, and marketing networks, it forces them to manage cultural diversity within the organization as well as between the organization and its supplier, client, and alliance networks. Attention to cultural differences becomes critical for managing both the firm's organizational culture and its network of relationships outside of the firm (see Figure 1).

Does culture impact the organization? The question has no single answer. The impact of culture varies with the type of environment and the firm's

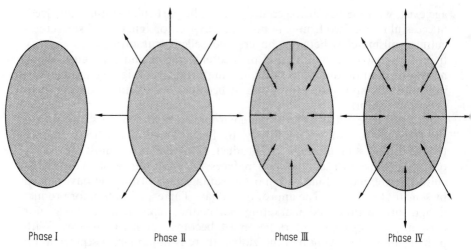

Phase I   Phase II   Phase III   Phase IV

Figure 1: Location of Cross-Cultural Interaction

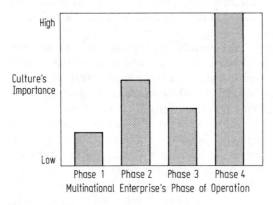

Figure 2: The Importance of Culture

overall strategy. In Phase One, culture has a minimal impact; in Phase Two, a maximal impact; in Phase Three, again a reduced, moderate impact; and in Phase Four, again a pronounced impact. Similarly, the location of the impact varies with the firm's environment and strategy. In Phase One, cultural diversity effects neither the organizational culture nor the relationship with clients. By Phase Two, cultural differences strongly effect relationships with the external environment, especially with potential buyers and foreign workers. By Phase Three, there is less recognition of cultural differences outside of the firm, but a growing awareness of culture diversity within the firm. And by Phase Four, the firm must manage cultural diversity both within the firm and between the firm and its external environment. This progression from culture's lack of importance, to its critical importance with respect to the firm's external environment, and then with respect to its organizational culture underlies the efficacy of various international human resource management strategies (see Figure 2).

4. International Human Resource Management

International human resource management (HRM) involves the worldwide management of people (see Tung 1984 and Miller et al. 1986, among others). Traditionally, it has focused on the selection, training and development, performance appraisal, and rewarding of international personnel. The effectiveness of particular HRM approaches and practices depends directly on the firm's environment and strategy. As summarized in Table 3, who the firm considers an international employee, who it selects for international assignments, how it trains them, what criteria it uses to assess their international performance, and what impact international experience has on employees' careers, should all fit the external environment in which the firm operates and its strategic intent. The central issue for MNEs is not to identify the best international HRM policy per se, but rather to find the *best fit* between the firm's external environment, its overall strategy, and its HRM policy and implementation. Unfortunately, many firms continue to use Phase One and Two approaches to managing human resources, while operating in Phase Three and Four environments. The following section describes which approaches to managing people best fit with each phase in the firm's development.

Phase One. In Phase One, the firm products a unique product and sells it primarily to its own domestic market. Given this domestic focus and the absence of competition, the firm's needs for internationally sophisticated people are minimal. The firm generally sends few employees on international business trips and none on expatriate assignments. Neither cross-cultural management nor language training is essential because potential buyers have few options other than the particular firm for purchasing Phase One products. This monopoly situation forces potential buyers (rather than the seller) to absorb the cross-cultural mismatches. Foreign buyers must speak the language of the home organization and accept business practise appropriate to the home environment. Moreover, foreign buyers must alter products

Table 3: Globalization and Human Resource Management

	Phase I Domestic	Phase II International	Phase III Multinational	Phase IV Global
Primary Orientation	Product/ Service	Market	Price	Strategy
Strategy	Domestic	Multidomestic	Multinational	Global
Worldwide Strategy	Allow foreign clients to buy product/service	Increase market internationally, Transfer technology abroad	Source, produce & market internationally	Gain global, strategic, competitive advantage
Staffing				
Expatriates	None − (Few)	Many	Some	Many
Why sent	Junket	To sell, control, or transfer technology	Control	Coordination & Integration
Who sent	−	"OK" performers, Sales people	Very good performers	Hi-potential managers & top executives
Purpose	Reward	Project "To get job done"	Project & Career Development	Career & Organizational Development
Career Impact	Negative	Bad for domestic career	Important for Global Career	Essential for executive suite
Professional Re-entry	Somewhat Difficult	Extremely Difficult	Less Difficult	Professionally easy
Training & Development (Language & Cross-cultural Management)	None	Limited One week)	Longer	Continuous throughout career
For Whom	No One	Expatriates	Expatriates	Managers
Performance Appraisal	Corporate Bottom Line	Subsidiary Bottom Line	Corporate Bottom Line	Global Strategic Positioning
Motivation Assumption	Money Motivates	Money & Adventure	Challenge & Opportunity	Challenge, Opportunity, Advancement
Rewarding	Extra money to compensate for foreign hardships		Less generous, global packages	
Career "Fast Track"	Domestic	Domestic	Token International	Global
Executive Passport	Home country	Home country	Home country, Token foreigners	Multinational
Necessary Skills	Technical & Managerial	Plus cultural adaption	Plus recognizing cultural differences	Plus cross- cultural interaction, influence & synergy

and services, once purchased, to fit their needs. Not surprisingly, the majority of firms operating under Phase One assumptions provide no cross-cultural or predeparture training. As one manager aptly describes this Phase One perspective:

Managing a company is a scientific art. The executive accomplishing the task in New York can surely perform as adequately in Hongkong (Baker & Ivancevich 1971: 40) as reported in Mendenhall, Dunbar, & Oddou 1987).

Based on Phase One assumptions, firms select the very few candidates for international work almost exclusively on product- or project-specific technical competence (see Mendenhall, Dunbar, & Oddou 1987).

In the past, understandably ethnocentric assumptions underlying Phase One strategies have led to numerous linguistic and human resource blunders (see Ricks 1983). While foreigner buyers rarely appreciate being forced to accommodate to the seller's language and culture. Phase One firms get away with such ethnocentric behavior because they are "the only game in town"!

Since domestic sales dominate Phase One profits, firms generally do not assign their best people to the few international positions. In selecting people for international travel, the firm's primary consideration is "getting the job done". Neither international career development for the employee nor international organizational development for the firm is considered important because international is not important. Consequently, in evaluating employees, most Phase One firms ignore international experience or, worse yet, treat it as hindering potential career advancement. As one manager of a Phase One firm said, "It is best to get your international experience standing next to the globe in the president's office."

Phase Two. Unlike Phase One, Phase Two firms face competition and respond by expanding from domestic to international operations, including actively marketing internationally and beginning to assemble and to produce overseas. Phase Two firms are polycentric. They are organized — and thus differentiated — into distinct national markets and operations, and only minimally integrated beyond the regional level. To maintain home country dominance, Phase Two firms often have overseas personnel reporting to an international division. Since executive decisions are generally made at a level above the international division, international is rarely considered either central or of primary importance.

Phase Two firms frequently select and send home country sales representatives to market products overseas, technical experts to transfer technology to overseas production sites, and managing directors and financial officers to control overseas operations. Since most R & D, and thus most innovation, still takes place at home, firms view foreign operations primarily as sites for replicating that which has already been done at home. Therefore, while not selecting marginal performers, Phase Two firms rarely send their very best people abroad.

Selection criteria for Phase Two should emphasize cross-cultural adaptability and sensitivity. However, in reality, many firms often continue to use Phase One's primary criterion — technical competence — supplimented by a willingness to go. As Torbiorn (1982: 51) bemoans:

The mass of possible selection criteria proposed in the literature is rarely likely to be matched by a wide range of available candidates and the man chosen is often simply the man who happens to be there.

This approach would be inconceivable if international activities were truely considered central. Consistent with this view of international is the lower stature and influence generally granted Phase Two's international personnel managers[7].

Unlike the prior phase, cross-cultural sensitivity and language skills become extremely important for Phase Two managers' effectiveness. Given the competition, firms create a comparative advantage by producing culturally appropriate products, using culturally appropriate management techniques, and marketing in culturally appropriate ways. To effectively implement these culturally appropriate strategies, international managers themselves need to develop cross-cultural skills. To this end, a number of techniques have been developed to reduce cultural shock and enhance both cross-cultural adaptation and effectiveness[8].

Unfortunately however, while numerous techniques exist, many firms — and, in particular, North American firms — generally have not recognized the importance of cross-cultural training to international effectiveness. Schwind (1985) claims that "a majority of companies involved in international trade do not provide any preparatory training for managers and employees destined to work abroad." Consistent with Schwind's observation, Mendenhall and Oddou (1986: 77) note that "there is a marked deficiency on the part of U.S. firms in offering comprehensive cross-cultural training to their imployees who are assigned overseas." Tung (1981) corroborates others' observations with empirical evidence[9], reporting in 1982 that only 32% of U.S. companies conducted formal international training programs, as compared with 57% of Japanese companies and 69% of

---

[7] For a discussion of Phase Two selection practices see, among others, Baker & Ivancevich 1971; Miller 1973; Hawes & Kealey 1981; Tung 1981; Church 1982; Torbiorn 1982; Abe & Wiseman 1983; Oddou & Mendenhall 1984; Mendenhall & Oddou 1985; and Zeira & Banai 1985.

[8] For a discussion of cross-cultural training approaches and techniques, see, among others, Hall 1959; Oberg 1960; Smalley 1963; Byrnes 1966; Guthrie 1967; Higbee 1969; Torbiorn 1982; Ratiu 1983; and Oddou & Mendenhall 1984; Mendenhall & Oddou 1985).

[9] For similar observations, see Korn/Ferry International 1981; Runzheimer 1984; Dunbar & Ehrlich 1986; and Mendenhall, Dunbar, & Oddou 1986).

European companies. Ronen (1986) has noted that the 32% reported in Tung's 1982 study is the same figure as reported in earlier research by Baker and Ivancevich (1971): "this figure has remained virtually unchanged over the last two decades even though large numbers of overseas managers have indicated that proper predeparture preparation is absolutely necessary to improve overseas performance" (Ronen 1986: 548). This low and unchanging level of expatriate training in U.S. companies again exposes Phase One assumptions ill-fitted to the Phase Two (Three and Four) environment.

Moreover, this low and unchanging level of training also probably explains Americans' high expatriate failure rates — 25—40% (Mendenhall & Oddou 1985) — when compared with Europeans' and Japanese' (see Tung 1982). What it does not explain is the acceptance of such high rates, especially when Tung (1982) has found a correlation of −.63 between expatriate failure rates and the rigor of the selection and training procedure used. One again, the problem appears to be that firms operating in a Phase Two environment continue to make Phase One assumptions as an unquestioned convenience in their human resource planning. Needless to say, the consequences of this mismatch between environmental realities and HRM assumptions are quite serious.

While the firm sends expatriates from the home country to fill positions designed for integration and control (those of managing director, financial officer, and sometimes technical expert), it often includes host nationals in marketing and personnel positions. The selection of host nationals for positions in their own countries gives some recognition to the importance of cultural understanding and language fluency, even if this recognition is not extended to most home country employees. Kobrin (1984: 43) found that over half the U.S. firms surveyed had significantly decreased their expatriates over the past decade. Similarly, Berenbeim (1983: v) found that 80% of U.S. firms had local nationals heading the majority of country operations.

Phase Two firms generally evaluate expatriates performance based on that of the foreign operation. Yet, even the best evaluations rarely lead to significant career advancement. Most returnees from overseas assignments find re-entry extremely difficult. While abroad, the firm frequently views them as out-of-sight and out-of-mind. As returnees, it sees them as out-of-date and unimportant. To returnees' disappointment, their colleagues often evaluate them as somewhat inconsequential to the domestic mainstream (see Schein's (1971) discussion linking centrality in the organization to career (advancement). The home organization generally neither values nor uses their understanding of overseas operations or the external international environment (see Edstrom & Galbraith 1977). For ambitious managers who want to make it to the top of Phase Two firms (especially in North American companies), going abroad is generally a bad career strategy (For a discussion of re-entry, see, among others, Howard 1973; Adler 1980 & 1981; and Harvey 1982).

Similarly, host nationals rarely, if ever, make it to the top of Phase Two firms. In most cases, an invisible ceiling stops them at the level of the country managing director. To get beyond the invisible ceiling, one must hold a passport of the home country. The almost complete absence of non-Americans on the boards of directors of American firms (and the similar absence of non-Japanese on Japanese boards) underscores the strength of the invisible ceiling.

Phase Three. By Phase Three, the competitive environment again changes. Price, rather than either product or market, allows Phase Three firms to survive in the now global markets. Geographical dispersion often increases and with it the firm's need to integrate. This geographical dispersion not only includes divisions within the firm, but also worldwide supplier, manufacturer, and distributor networks external to the enterprise. Phase Three firms accomplish integration primarily through centralizing and standardizing as many aspects of their products, processes, and structure as possible.

Given the critical role that multinational production and operations play in corporate survival, Phase Three firms attempt to select their best, rather than their marginal, employees for international positions. Specifically, rather than limiting selection to home country employees, they choose managers for international positions from throughout their worldwide organization. Integrating this diversity of employees, however, is not easy. One of the explicit purposes of international assignments, beyond getting-the-job-done, therefore now becomes firmwide integration. The firm uses international positions to develop an integrated, global organization through the international career development of high potential manages and thus the creation of a global cadre of executives. Similar to the role global lines of business play in integrating Phase Three products and markets worldwide, the international cadre of executives takes on the central role of integrating the firm through its top managers[10].

Whereas Phase Three makes international experience essential to firmwide management and career advancement, the importance of cross-cultural sensitivity and language skills diminishes somewhat. Rather than using cultural diversity, Phase Three firms often either assume or create similarity when attempting to integrate the global firm. For example, they frequently assume that consumers' tastes are essentially similar worldwide, thus allowing the firm to create generic products and services and to benefit from substantial economies of scope and scale (see Leavitt 1983, for an excellent

---

[10] See Edstrom and Galbraith (1977) for a discussion of the use of international transfer as an organizational development strategy.

exposition of this position). Similarly, Phase Three firms recognize that price substantially determines both market and market share, hence negating their need to differentiate products and services for individual or culture-specific tastes. Likewise, internal to the organization, Phase Three firms generally adopt the mother tongue of the home organization or English as a common language.

Moreover, organization culture is assumed to dominate national culture. Under the rubric of organization culture, firms generally require foreign nationals to accommodate to parent company — and implicitly parent culture — styles of interacting. The underlying assumption is that cultural differences either can be ignored because the organizational culture has molded nationals of all countries into similar employees — professionals who are "beyond passport" — or must be minimized because they cause problems (see Adler 1983). The first assumption becomes apparent in the lack of recognition for varying cultural styles of conducting business; that is, in the firm's cultural-blindness. The second assumption becomes apparent in such behaviors as the decision to use English exclusively, or the selection of host nationals who exhibit attitudes and behaviors typical of the parent company's culture. Many American companies traditionally have recruited host nationals from U.S. college campuses to insure that new hires would have an excellent command of English and an adequate socialization into American ways of doing business. In this way, American firms have been able to hire Americanized foreigners rather than those more typical of their home country and culture.

As shown in Figure 1, Phase Three differs fundamentally from prior phases in that the primary location of cross-cultural interaction moves inside the organization. Phase One firms encountered little cross-cultural interaction because both their employees and their clients are from the same domestic environment. Phase Two firms encounter cultural differences when interacting with their external environment, primarily as home company nationals attempt to market abroad and to manage foreign workers. By contrast, Phase Three firms, having hired people from around the world and integrated them into the overall organization, encounter cultural differences within the firm's internal organizational culture. The human resource management system should reflect the location of the cultural diversity. Unfortunately however, as has been described, Phase Three firms often attempt to assume away the culture differences by choosing to believe that organizational culture overrides differences in national perspective and behavior. Research, however, has shown this assumption of similarity to be incorrect. Organizational culture neither dominates nor erases national culture, but rather, in the case of multinational corporations, appears to accentuate it[11].

---

[11] See Hofstede (1980) for a study of the cultural diversity within IBM's corporate

Re-entry in this environment poses less of a problem than in prior phases. Because firms value international experience, they often select top people to send overseas, recognize their international accomplishments, and bring them back to significant positions. Rather than hurting the expatriate's career, international assignments often become essential to career success.

Phase Four. In Phase Four, which combines aspects of Phases One, Two, and Three, firms face severe competition on a global scale. Successful strategies involve producing least-cost, top-quality products that, while differentiated for individual tastes, are produced globally and marketed globally. The increased severity of global competition forces multinationals to reexamine their traditional [Phase One, Two, and Three] approaches to human resource management (see Pucik 1984).

The Phase Four environment requires firms to assign their best people to international positions, because, by this time, the overwhelming dominance of the domestic market has become a relic of the past. Key employees must be multilingual and culturally sensitive to identify the needs of culturally differentiated market segments and to respond quickly and appropriately to each. Moreover, top-quality, least-cost production necessitates worlwide operations, with location dictated by strategic, political, and economic constraints, along with the supply of inputs and market access. Hence, people from all over the world constantly must communicate and work with each other; in the vernacular, they must "think globally" to become global managers (see Murray & Murray 1986). Boundaries between expatriate and local personnel become obsolete (Doz & Prahalad 1986). Neither cultural forms of control emphasizing more homogeneous selection, socialization and training nor more bureaucratic forms of control can independently address the needs for integration and differentiation (see Jaeger 1983 and Baliga & Jaeger 1984). The first emphasizes integration through eliminating differences while the second emphasizes integration by controlling differences. The former is more appropriate to Phase Three's highly centralized organization while the later fits best with Phase Two's emphasis on decentralization. Because neither simultaneously emphasize integration and differentiation, neither fits particularly well in Phase Four.

Effectively managing such a culturally diverse organizational culture becomes an essential Phase Four skill. As Doz and Prahalad (1986) note, multinational corporations must find new ways to manage the dichotomy of cultural diversity and global integration, of national responsiveness and centralized coordination and control. One of the firm's major competitive weapons is its ability to use global human resources along both dimensions; that is, to enhance national responsiveness and global integration.

---

culture and Laurent (1983) for a study of cultural differences within a number of major American corporations.

By Phase Four, as shown in Figure 1, cross-cultural interaction takes place both within the firm and between the firm and its external environment. Consequently, understanding and managing cultural differences becomes essential both internally and externally. The firm's home country culture can no longer dominate its organization culture. Ignoring or minimizing cultural diversity has become a luxury of the past, as the firm must now continually recognise and manage it. Beyond recognition, successful Phase Four firms develop skills at identifying those situations in which cultural diversity can be used as an asset and those in which it must be regarded as a liability. Managers can then choose to accentuate and use differences, or attempt to minimize them, according to the particular situation. In no case does the firm ignore the differences (see Adler 1983).

Cultural diversity, by increasing differentiation, makes integration more difficult. However, if managed appropriately, cultural differences become a key Phase Four resource. For example, when they need differentiation, firms that recognize cultural diversity can use the differences to gain multiple perspectives, develop wider ranges of options and approaches, heighten creativity and problem solving skills, and thereby increase flexibility in addressing culturally distinct client and colleague systems. Simultaneously however, these same firms must be able to create similarity from the diversity when they need integration. This consciously created universality, Phase Four's form of organization culture, goes beyond cultural differences to heighten coordination and control[12]. Unlike firms in the prior phases, global Phase Four firms never assume similarity nor rely on naturally occurring universality to heighten integration: they create similarity — "universals".

For Phase Four managers, the salient question is not *if* there is cultural diversity, but rather *how* to manage it. They constantly use cultural diversity to balance three organizational tensions. First, they minimize the impacts of cultural diversity when integration is needed. Second, they use cultural diversity to differentiate products and services when culturally distinct markets or workforces must be addressed. And third, they use cultural diversity as a primary source of new ideas when innovation is needed. Thus, cultural diversity clearly takes on a role of primary importance in Phase Four. To achieve the appropriate balance, managers must become acutely sensitive to cultural nuances and highly skilled at managing culturally diverse environments.

Balancing cultural integration and differentiation influences all aspects of the human resource management system. For example, when firms promote managers from the local culture to positions of significant power in their own country, they are using cultural diversity to increase differentiation. By

---

[12] For a discussion of cultural synergy, see Adler 1986, Chapter 4.

contrast, when they design multinational career paths for high potential managers and bring them together to create new approaches to managing innovation, production, finance, and marketing, they are using the diversity to create cultural synergy, Phase Four's powerful form of integration.

Phase Four firms no longer have an international division, rather, similar to Phase Three, they are international. They select their best people for global assignments and responsibility. They continually train them in the skills necessary for national responsiveness and culturally synergistic integration. Promotions go to those managers who skillfully assess and balance the needs for differentiation and integration; those who are continually learning and therefore capable of continually making new choices. Re-entry problems diminish significantly given the centrality of global operations and the need for highly trained, experienced, and sophisticated international managers. Given this global perspective, international human resource management is no longer marginal, but becomes central to firmwide success. Without a human resource system well integrated into the firm's global strategy, the Phase Four firm cannot succeed. With anything other than a global perspective, the human resource system will cause the Phase Four firm to fail.

5. Implications: Future Trends

As has happened over the past two decades, the world has again changed. Today firms face a global economy. "Fully 70% of ... [U.S.A.] industries, up from 25% only a dozen years ago, are under full-scale attack by foreign competitors" (Peters 1986: 11). Some firms have changed, while most will have to change significantly to compete successfully in the 1990s and the twenty-first century. Unfortunately, whereas most other functional areas have already begun to respond, many firms' human resource systems have failed to adapt sufficiently to this changing environment. In all too many firms, human resource systems are managed as if they were in Phase One, Two, or Three — the domestic, international, or multinational worlds that were — not the global world that is nor in the multiphase world that will be.

Already today, and certainly in the future, firms must understand cultural differences to successfully implement global R & D, global marketing, global production, and global financial strategies. Cultural awareness has become essential not only within global firms', but also for coordinating and integrating activities among alliance partners of often differing national origins.

If executives do not recognize and manage cultural diversity appropriately, their firms will not survive.

To compete globally, people involved in all aspects of the firm must not only think globally, they must realize that competition, and perhaps more importantly, collaboration is now on an equal footing. For most multinational enterprises, significant comparative advantage based on technology, production, or market share has rapidly become a vestige of the past.

The research agenda is clear. Management scholars need to study human resource management in context. They must study international HRM within the context of changing economic and business conditions. Similarly, they must study international HRM within the context of the industry and the firm's other functional areas and operations. Studying HRM out-of-context is not only no longer helpful, it has become misleading. Similarly, management scholars need to use multiple levels of analysis when studying international HRM: the external social, political, cultural, and economic environment; the industry, the firm, the subunit, the group, and the individual. Research in contextual isolation is misleading: it fails to advance understanding.

References

Abe, H. and R. L. Wiseman (1983): A cross-cultural confirmation of the dimension of intercultural effectiveness, *International Journal of Intercultural Relations*, 7 (1): 53–68.

Adler, N. J. (1986): *International Dimensions of Organizational Behavior*, Boston: Kent Publishing.

Adler, N. J. (1983): Organizational development in a multicultural environment, *Journal of Applied Behavioral Science*, 349–365.

Adler, N. J. (1981): Managing cross-cultural transitions, *Group and Organization Studies*, 6 (3): 341–356.

Adler, N. J. (1980): *Managing International Transitions*, Montreal: Alcan.

Adler, N. J., R. Doktor and S. G. Redding (1986): From the Atlantic to Pacific century: Cross-cultural management reviewed, *Journal of Management*, 12 (2): 295–318.

Adler, N. J. and M. Jelinek (1986): Is 'organization culture' bound?, *Human Resource Management*, 25 (1): 73–90.

Baker, J. C. and J. M. Ivancevich (1971): The assignment of American executives abroad: Systematic, haphazard, or chaotic?, *California Management Review*, 13 (3): 33–44.

Baliga, B. R. and A. M. Jaeger (1984): Multinational corporations: Control systems and delegation issues, *Journal of International Business Studies*, 15 (2): 25–40.

Bartlett, C. (1983): How multinational organizations evolve, *Journal of Business Strategy*, 4 (1): 10–32.

Bass, B. M., C. Burger, R. Doktor and B. V. Barrett (1979): *Assessment of Managers*, New York: Free Press.

Berenbeim, R. E. (1983): *Managing the International Company: Building a Global Perspective*, New York: The Conference Board.

Byrnes, F. C. (1966): Role shock: An occupational hazard of American technical assistants Abroad, *The Annals*, 368: 95−108.

Child, J. (1981): Culture, contingency and capitalism in the cross-national study of organizations, in: L. L. Cummings and B. M. Staw (eds.), *Research in Organizational Behavior*, Vol. 3. Greenwich, Conn.: JAI Press: 303−356.

Child, J. and M. Tayeb (1982−83): Theoretical perspectives in cross-national organizational research, *International Studies of Management and Organization*, 12 (4): 23−70.

Church, A. T. (1982): Sojourn adjustment, *Psychological Bulletin*, 91 (3): 540−571.

Davidson, W. H. and P. Haspeslagh: Shaping a global product organization, *Harvard Business Review*, 60 (4): 125−132.

Davis, S. (1987): *Future Perfect*, Readding, Mass.: Addison-Wesley.

Doz, Y. L. (1985): *Strategic Management in Multinational Companies*, Oxford: Pergamon Press.

Doz, Y. L., C. A. Bartlett and C. K. Prahalad (1981): Global competitive pressures vs. host country demands: Managing the tensions in MNCs, *California Management Review*, 23 (3): 63−74.

Doz, Y. L. and C. K. Prahalad (1986): Controlled variety: A challenge for human resource management in the MNC, *Human Resource Management*, 25 (1): 55−72.

Doz, Y. L. and C. K. Prahalad (1987): *Multinational Companies' Missions: Balancing National Responsiveness and Global Integration*, New York: The Free Press.

Dunbar, E. and M. Ehrlich (1986): *International Human Resource Practices, Selecting, Training, and Managing the International Staff: A Survey Report*, The Project on International Human Resources, New York: Columbia University-Teachers College.

Dunning, J. (1985): *Multinational Enterprises, Economic Structures and International Competitiveness*, New York: John Wiley & Sons.

Edstrom, A. and J. R. Galbraith (1977): Transfer of managers as a coordination and control strategy in multinational organizations, *Administrative Science Quarterly*, 22 (2): 248−268.

England, G. W. (1975): *The Manager and His Values: An International Perspective from the USA, Japan, Korea, India and Australia*, Cambridge: Ballinger.

Evans, P. A. L. (1987): Strategies for human resource management in complex MNCs: A European perspective, in: V. Pucik's Academy of Management Proposal *Emerging Human Resource Management Strategies in Multinational Firms: A Tricontinental Perspective*: 9−11.

Evans, P. A. L. (1986): The strategic outcomes of human resource management, *Human Resource Management*, 25 (1): 149−168.

Form, W. (1979): Comparative industrial sociology and the convergence hypothesis, *Annual Review of Sociology*, 5: 1−25.

Galbraith, J. R. and R. K. Kazajian (1986): Organizing to implement strategies of diversity and globalization: The role of matrix designs, *Humans Resource Management*, 25 (1): 37−54.

Ghadar, F. (1985): Political risk and the erosion of control: The case of the oil industry, in: T. Brewer (ed.), *Political Risks in International Business: New Directions for Research, Management, and Public Policy*, New York: Praeger.

Ghadar, F. (1986): Strategic considerations in the financing of international investment, in: P. Grub, F. Ghadar, and D. Khambata (eds.), *The Multinational Enterprise in Transition*, revised edition, Princeton, N.J.: The Darwin Press.

Ghadar, F. (1977): *The Evolution of OPEC Strategy*, Lexington, Mass.: Lexington Books.

Grub, P., F. Ghadar and D. Khambata (eds.) (1986): *The Multinational Enterprise in Transition*, third edition, Princeton, N.J.: The Darwin Press.

Gluck, F. W., S. P. Kaufman and A. S. Walleck (1980): Strategic management for competitive advantage, *Harvard Business Review*, 58 (4): 154 – 161.

Guthrie, G. M. (1967): Cultural preparation for the Philippines, in: R. B. Textor (ed.), *Cultural Frontiers of the Peace Corps*, Cambridge, Mass.: MIT Press.

Haire, M., E. G. Ghiselli and L. W. Porter (1966): *Managerial Thinking: An International Study*, New York: Wiley.

Hall, E. T. (1959): *The Silent Language*, New York: Doubleday.

Hammel, G. and C. K. Prahalad (1985): Do you really have a global strategy?, *Harvard Business Review*, 63 (4): 139 – 148.

Harvey, M. G. (1982): The other side of foreign assignments: Dealing with the repatriation dilemma, *Columbia Journal of World Business*, 17 (1): 53 – 59.

Hawes, F. and D. J. Kealey (1981): An empirical study of Canadian technical assistance, *International Journal of Intercultural Relations*, 5 (3): 239 – 258.

Hedlund, G. (1986): The hypermodern MNC – a heterarchy?, *Human Resource Management*, 25 (1): 9 – 36.

Heenan, D. A. and H. V. Perlmutter (1979): *Multinational Organizational Development: A Social Architectural Approach*, Reading, Mass.: Addison-Wesley.

Heller, R. A. and B. Wilpert (1979): Managerial decision making: An international comparison, in: G. W. England, A. R. Negandhi, and B. Wilpert (eds.), *Functioning Organizations in Cross Cultural Perspective*, Kent, Ohio: Kent State University Press.

Hickson, D. J., C. R. Hinnings, C. J. M. McMillan and J. P. Schwitter (1974): The culture-free context of organization structure: A tri-national comparison, *Sociology*, 8 (1): 59 – 80.

Hickson, D. J., C. J. McMillar, K. Azumi and D. Horvath (1979): Grounds for comparative organization theory: quicksands or hard core? in: C. J. Lammers and D. J. Hickson (eds.), *Organizations Alike and Unlike*, London, Routledge & Kegan, Paul: 25 – 41.

Higbee, H. (1969): Role shock – a new concept, *International Educational and Cultural Exchange*, 4 (4): 71 – 81.

Hofstede, G. (1980): *Culture's Consequences: International Differences in Work-Related Values*, Beverly Hills, Calif.: Sage.

Hout, T., M. E. Porter and E. Rudden (1982): How global companies win out, *Harvard Business Review*, 60 (5): 98 – 108.

Howard, C. G. (1973): The expatriate manager and the role of the NNC, *Personnel Journal*, 48 (1): 25 – 29.

Jaeger, A. M. (1983): The transfer of organizational culture overseas: An approach to control in the multinational corporation, *Journal of International Business Studies*, 14 (2): 91 – 114.

Jaeger, A. M. and B. R. Baliga (1985): Control systems and strategic adaptation: Lessons from the Japanese experience, *Strategic Management Journal*, 6 (2): 115– 134.

Kerr, C. J., T. Dunlop, R. Harbison and C. A. Myers (1952): *Industrialism and Industrial Man*, Cambridge, Mass.: Harvard University Press.

Kobrin, S. J. (1988): Expatriate reduction and strategic control in American multinational corporations, *Human Resource Management*, (in press).

Korn/Ferry International (1981): A study of the repatriation of the American international executive, New York.

Laurent, A. (1986): The cross-cultural puzzle of international human resource management, *Human Resource Management*, 25 (1): 91–102.

Laurent, A. (1983): The cultural diversity of Western management conceptions, *International Studies of Management and Organization*, 8 (1–2): 75–96.

Leavitt, T. (1983): The globalization of markets, *Harvard Business Review*, 61 (3): 92–102.

Lincoln, J. R., M. Hanada and J. Olson (1981): Cultural orientations and individual reactions to organizations: A study of employees of Japanese-owned firms, *Administrative Science Quarterly*, 26 (1): 93–115.

Lorange, P. (1986): Human resource management in multinational cooperative ventures, *Human Resource Management*, 25 (1): 133–148.

Mendenhall, M. E., E. Dunbar and G. R. Oddou (1986): *The state of the art of overseas relocation programs in U.S. multinationals*, Academy of International Business Meetings, London, England.

Mendenhall, M. E., E. Dunbar and G. R. Oddou (1987): Expatriate selection, training and career-pathing: A review and critique, *Human Resource Management*, 26 (3): 331–345.

Mendenhall, M. E. and G. R. Oddou (1986): Acculturaltion profiles of expatriate managers: Implications for cross-cultural training programs, *Columbia Journal of World Business*, 21 (4): 73–79.

Mendenhall, M. E. and G. R. Oddou (1985): The dimensions of expatriate acculturation: A review, *Academy of Management Review*, 10 (1): 389–47.

Miller, E. L. (1973): The international selection decision: A study of some dimensions of managerial behavior in the selection decision process, *Academiy of Management Journal*, 16 (2): 239–252.

Miller, E. L., S. Beechler, B. Bhatt and R. Nath (1986): The relationship between the global strategic planning process and the human resource management function, *Human Resource Planning*, 9 (1): 9–23.

Mitroff, Ian I. (1987): *Business Not As Usual*, San Francisco: Jossey-Bass Publishers.

Murray, F. T. and A. H. Murray (1986): Global managers for global businesses, *Sloan Management Review*, 27 (2): 75–80.

Naisbitt, J. (1982): *Megatrends*, New York: Warner Books.

Negandhi, A. R. (1979): Convergence in organizational practices: An empirical study of industrial enterprise in developing countries, in: C. J. Lammers and D. J. Hickson, *Organizations Alike and Unlike*, London: Routledge & Kegan Paul: 323–345.

Negandhi, A. R. (1985): Management in the third world, in: P. Joynt & M. Warner, *Managing in Different Cultures*, Oslo, Norwegen: Universitetsforlaget: 69–97.

Oberg, K. (1960): Culture shock: Adjustment to new cultural environments, *Practical Anthropology*, 7: 177–182.

Oddou, G. and M. Mendenhall (1984): Person perception in cross-cultural settings: A review of cross-cultural and related literature, *International Journal of Intercultural Relations*, 8 (1): 77–96.

Peters, T. (1986): Competition and compassion, *California Management Review*, 28 (4): 11–26.

Porter, M. E. (1980): *Competitive Strategy: Techniques for Analyzing Industries and Competitors*, New York: Free Press.

Porter, M. E. (1985): *Competitive Advantage*, New York: Free Press.

Porter, M. E. (ed.) (1986): *Competition in Global Industries*, Boston: Harvard University Press.

Porter, M. E. and V. E. Millar (1985): How information gives you competitive advantage, *Harvard Business Review*, 63 (4): 149–169.

Prahalad, C. K. and Y. L. Doz (1981): An approach to strategic control in MNCs, *Sloan Management Review*, 22 (4): 5–13.

Pucik, V. and J. H. Katz (1986): Information, control, and human resource management in multinational firms, *Human Resource Management*, 25 (1): 103–132.

Pucik, V. (1984): The international management of human resources, in: C. Fombrun, N. Tichy, M. A. Devanna (eds.), *Strategic Human Resource Management*, New York: John Wiley.

Pucik, V. (1985): Strategic human resource management in a multinational firm, in: H. V. Wortzel and L. H. Wortzel (eds.), *Strategic Management of Multinational Corporations: The Essentials*, New York: John Wiley & Sons: 424–435.

Ratiu, I. (1983): Thinking internationally: A comparison of how international executives learn, *International Studies of Management and Organization*, 13 (1–2): 139–150.

Ricks, D. A. (1983): *Big Business Blunders: Mistakes in Multinational Marketing*, Homewood, Ill.: Dow Jones-Irwin.

Ronen, S. (1986): *Comparative and Multinational Management*, New York: John Wiley.

Runzheimer Executive Report (1984): *1984 Expatriation/Repatriation Survey*, Number 31, Rochester, Wisconsin.

Schein, E. H. (1971): The individual, the organization, and the career: A conceptual scheme, *Journal of Applied Behavioral Science*, 7 (4): 401–426.

Smalley, W. A. (1963): Culture shock, language shock, and the shock of self-discovery, *Practical Anthropology*, 10: 49–56.

Stopford, John M. and John H. Dunning (1982): *U.S. Competitiveness in the World Economy*, Boston: Harvard Business School Press.

Stopford, John M. and John H. Dunning (1983): *The World Directory of Multinational Enterprise*, London: Macmillan.

Stopford, J. and L. T. Wells (1972): *Managing the Multinational Enterprises: Organization of the Firm and Ownership of the Subsidiaries*, New York: Basic Books.

Torbiorn, I. (1982): *Living Abroad: Personal Adjustment and Personnel Policy in Overseas Settings*, New York: John Wiley.

Tung, R. (1981): Selection and training of personnel for overseas assignments, *Columbia Journal of World Business*, 16 (1): 68–78.

Tung, R. (1982): Selection and training procedures of U.S., European and Japanese multinationals, *California Management Review*, 25 (1): 57–71.

Tung, R. (1984): Strategic management of resources in the multinational enterprise, *Human Resource Management*, 23 (2): 129–144.

Vernon, R. (1966): International investment and international trade in the product cycle, *Quarterly Journal of Economics*, 80 (2): 190–207.

Vernon, R. (1981): Sovereignty at bay ten years after, *International Organization*, 35 (5): 517–529.

Vernon, R. (1971): *Sovereignty at Bay: The Multinational Spread of U.S. Enterprises*, New York: Basic Books.

Watson, C. M. (1982): Counter-competition abroad to protect home markets, *Harvard Business Review*, 60 (1): 40–42.

Zeira, Y. and M. Banai (1985): Selection of expatriate managers in MNCs: The host-environment point of view, *International Studies of Management and Organization*, 15 (1): 33–51.

Human Resource Management in Multinational and Internationally Operating Companies

Eberhard Dülfer

1. Some Basic Notions

1.1 'Human Resource Management'

During the last few days we have been told a lot about human resource management. It became evident, that not all the speakers are interpreting the term in the same way. Everybody agrees that human resource management is an important partial function in the framework of entrepreneurial activities. However, different opinions exist with respect to what has to be attributed to this functional area and which authorities or persons within the enterprise have to take care of this function. At the same time we find a lot of *different approaches* to our subject in the scientific literature. The methodologically different approaches are varying between the pure productivity-oriented input-factor-approach of Erich Gutenberg on the one hand, and an emphasized behavioural approach on the other which is interpreting the enterprise as a coalition of persons involved (see Gutenberg 1971: 285–292; Marr and Stitzel 1979: 58 pp.). From this point of view human resource management is a subject of entrepreneurial leadership, mainly from the point of view of the legitimated top managers in their task to motivate the other members of the coalition 'enterprise' to a well-determind cooperative behavior in the framework of labor-divided processes.

In a second dimension a differentiation is made with regard to leadership and style of management in the variation between pure autocratic/technocratic management on the one hand and a strongly participative co-operative style of directing on the other (see the clearly graphic representation by Tannenbaum and Schmidt 1958: 96).

Finally, there are further different definitions concerning different stocks of problems, as expressed by the German terms 'Personalwirtschaft', 'Personalwesen', 'Personalpolitik'[1].

As to my reflections, I presume that all these different approaches and the resulting modells of leadership[2] including the empirical research results in different environments are well-known to this audience, so that I can refer to details without any problems.

1.2 Internationally Operating Companies

In accordance with the sponsor of this meeting, my contribution should deal with the supplementary particular problems which occur in the area of human resource management — whatever this term may mean — in multinational and internationally operating companies.

Even these terms — which are formulated by the programme — need a short comment. There are rather sophisticated contributions in the English-speaking, as well as the German-speaking, scientific literature of the 60ies and the early 70ies on the definition of internationally operating companies. Terms suck as 'international company', 'transnational company', 'multinational company', 'world enterprise' and maybe others have been suggested. However, it became clear that all these differentiations did not bring about any advantage. Thus, it seems better to distinguish only between those companies which are exclusively operating in the national context or supply to exporters (indirect exportation), and those who develop border-crossing activities. My topic deals with the second group which I will simply call "internationally operating companies" (see Macharzina 1981).

1.3 Systems of International Business

In respect of the requirements of the staff members in such an enterprise, there are considerable differences depending on the intensity of the border-crossing activity (e. g. with respect to the transfer of capital and/or know-how (see Meissner and Gerber 1980; Berekoven 1979: 38 pp.; Kulhavy 1975).

---

[1] See for 'Personalwirtschaft': Kupsch and Marr 1985; see for 'Personalwesen': Wistinghausen 1975; see for 'Personalpolitik': v. Eckardstein and Schnellinger 1987.

[2] The Normative Model of Leadership Styles (Vroom/Yetton 1973), in: Staehle 1987: 583—589; The Path-Goal-Theory (Evans/House 1970/71), in: Wunderer and Grunewald 1980: 136 pp.

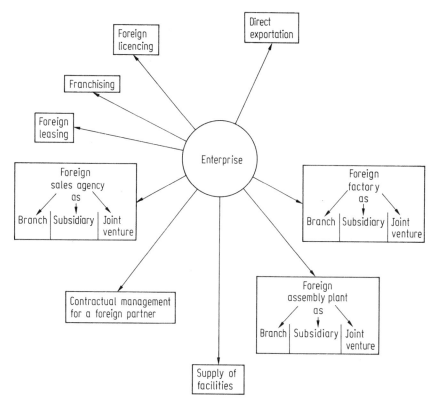

Figure 1: Alternatives of Internationalization
Source: E. Dülfer

This difference in intensity should be classified according to the usual types of business. Each kind of business, e. g. the direct exportation, international licencing or the opening of a production branch abroad, demands a lot of organizational and functional elements. Therefore, I speak of '*business systems*'. Normaly, the following business systems can be distinguished (see Dülfer 1985: 497) (*fig. 1*):

Regarding the available time it is not possible to analyse the problems of Human Resource Management in detail for every business system. I have to simplify and identify only two classes of business systems: Those in which the foreign activities are exclusively executed by the home company (e. g. direct exportation, licencing) maybe with single staff members in the field ("*functional internationalization*"), and those business systems in which an organizational unit (e. g. a production branch) is being established abroad ("*institutional internationalization*"). It will become apparent that there are considerable differences between both categories with respect to the personell requirements. They have to be differentiated further according to the "phases of internationalization" (see Steinmann et al. 1979: 3) and the potential sequence of business systems ("paths of Internationalization").

1.4 "Degree of Strangeness" of Host-Countries

A further differentiation has to be made with respect to the host-countries where to foreign business has to be run. In this regard there are countries whose legal and socio-cultural structure is similar or very similar to the home country and others which have remarkable, sometimes even imcomprehensible distinctions. In view of these facts I speak of a higher or lower "*degree of strangeness*" of the host-country as an operation field of business. This concerns the lack of information about the influences of environmental factors (see Dülfer 1981: 444 p.). It can always be observed in internationally operating companies that particularly staff members at headquarters responsible for foreign activities suppose that certain differences between the intended host-countries and the own home country exist but that these do not have any relevance on business transactions. More detailed studies prove that the reality is completely different. A considerable difference exists in case of language barriers (see Bauer 1989), even if this can be overcome by means of the internationally spread common English. However, the language aspect will be dealt with later on. But even in countries of the same language (e. g. Federal Republic of Germany/Austria/German Democratic Republic/Switzerland), relevant business terms can be different or at least have different meanings and the practical handling of the operations indicated by these terms can produce totally different results due to a different mentality of the actors.

It concerns in the most simple case phenomena which are a variation of facts well-known in the home country. There is a higher degree of strangeness if behavior and basic assumptions exist, which can be imagined on the basis of the own cultural experience, but which do not exist in the home country. In that case a bigger readjustment is necessary. Serious problems arise if foreign business encounters behaviour and meanings of reason-effect relationships which are completely different from the own experience and therefore unexpected, sometimes even unimaginable. These experiences were mainly made in developing countries.

From the point of view of the theory of decison-making, the latter means that not only the probability of expected results of potential decision-making alternatives are unknown, but also their quality (uncertainty of second degree) (see Albach 1976).

The combination of both aspects produce the following matrix of requirements:

	Case 1: Functional border crossing into well-known environment	Case 3: Functional border crossing into strange environment	Requirement level II
Requirement level I	Case 2: Institutional border crossing into well-known environment	Case 4: Institutional border crossing into strange environment	Requirement level III

Figure 2: Requirement Levels of Internationalization
Source: E. Dülfer

2. Environmental Influences to be Considered in International Business

2.1 Unification or Fragmentation?

During the last days a lot of influencing factors have been reported and analysed from the national point of view, factors which are being felt relevant in the different countries by their own fellow-citizens. The question is whether this insider's view is sufficient. In our case we are able to identify the danger of a certain cultural blindness. This means that even after a very precise analysis many facts and relations will be assumed as a matter of course, whereas they are well worth mentioning from the foreigner's point of view. As far as possible, legal, political as well as socio-cultural environmental influences at the level of international management must be treated differently from those at the level of national management.

In a purely pragmatic analysis the idea might occur that information on the relevant environmental influences of a new host-country could be obtained from appropriate geographical encyclopaedias or country surveys.

This may be helpful in some cases but it brings about the same effect as that of a snapshot. It is not taken into consideration that all countries, which are affiliated to the world economy, are subject to a permanent process of change, which is due to the highly increased worldwide process of communication and to the increased efficiency of the mass media. There are two fundamental approaches to the question towards which direction this process of change is heading. The one party presents the hypothesis of "international unification" (see Fayerweather 1969: 275) originally formulated by Fayerweather. The other party I'm more inclining to, is showing a strong tendency towards unification too but it puts more emphasis on the differences in development as a kind of "international fragmentation". It is after all more important, for correct decision-making in international business, to recognize and to observe at a very early stage the differences than to state the similarities. The consideration of differences requires more informational and training effort than the relapse into the own customary behaviour which is possible at any time.

2.2 Relevant Environmental Influences

On the basis of these reflections it is necessary to obtain an idea of relevant types of environmental influences and their interdependencies in international business. On the basis of long-term research in this field I formulated the 'strata model' of environment consideration (see Dülfer 1980) as shown in *fig. 3*. It is based on the hypothesis that the environmental consideration has to be made in two dimensions: For the first dimension we can refer to the inter-organization-approach on the basis of the statements of Dürkheim. He states that the environment of a social system is represented by the total of those social units which are in interaction with it (see Dürkheim 1933). In the case of the company, we can apply the well-known term "Task Environment" because the interaction is governed by the type of task.

We obtain an idea of the structure of external relationships of the company and the character of their interaction partners through the analysis of task environment (*fig. 3*). This can vary totally from country to country. The market and the competition structures are always relevant. Furthermore, in most industrialized countries the public is an important adressee for itself with regard to the necessary image building while in other countries e. g. religious authorities may play a more important role.

This explanation of the structure of task environment does not yet give any information on the behavior which has to be expected from the interacting partners and which as a consequence should be recommended for the own action. This requires a deeper-going analysis of the behavior

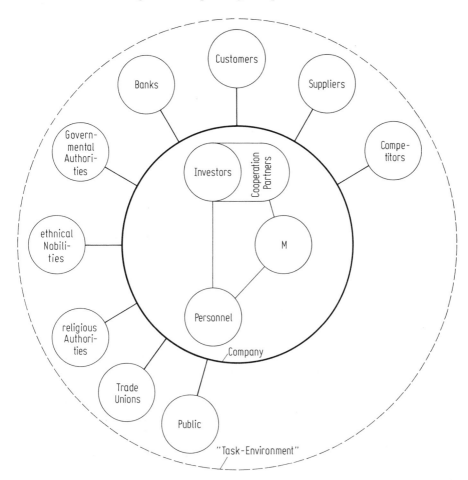

Figure 3: Task-Environment

influencing factors constructing the "*Global Environment*" which are included in the different strata of the model in the following way:

We can start from the hypothesis that all real facts in every cultural area consist of there existing natural elements. Therefore, the "*Natural Conditions*" of the environment are the lowest strata of the model. In the course of cultural evolution people used these natural conditions, studied them and made findings on the reason-effect-relationships. At a given time they reached a specific degree of "*Ability to recognize Reality*", which is the basis of the presently dominating *technology* and the resulting technical state.

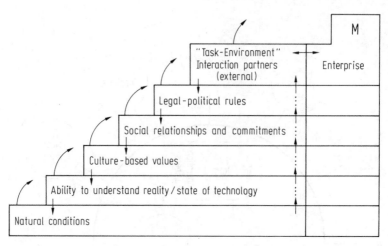

Figure 4: Strata-model of Environment Consideration

Examples from European history confirm that *"culture-based values"* are being developed on grounds of these basic assumptions and findings. They are changing according to the progress of the ability to recognize reality. Let us bear in mind the normative effects of 'Kopernikus' Cosmic World Model. Therefore, the "culgure-based values" form the next strata; these are on the other hand the basis of the actually given *"Social Relationships and Commitments"* of the individuals and groups. A legal conscience can only develop in the framework of such social structures with their corresponding norms. This is the basis for legal cementation of social behaviour into written *legal prescriptions*. Sometimes they are completed by *political imperatives* which have not yet legal character but are effective in a similar way, e. g. in the case of centralized national economies.

2.3 Process of Learning and Decision-Making of Staff Members Abroad

Thus, a staff member at a headquarter of an internationally operating company or a staff member as manager or expert in service abroad has to undergo a *process of learning* in which he perceives all these components of the different kinds of influences (strata) deviating from the home country experiences, and he has to internalize them. In doing so, he must begin, of course, with that category which implies, if overlooked, the most severe consequences. For this reason the sequence of influence strata is in reverse order form his point of view. He starts by identifying relevant communication partners (*"Task Environment"*), i. e. the "economic" structure. Secondly, the behavior influencing factors have to be taken into account, beginning with the "legal and political norms" potentially implying regative sanctions.

The decision-maker starts with his stock of experiences made in the home country in attacking the problems of his task achievement. Therefore, he sees a determinded quantity of decision-making alternatives.

This quantity will be successively reduced or enlarged. As a consequence, every strata works like a filter of the decision-making reflections. For this

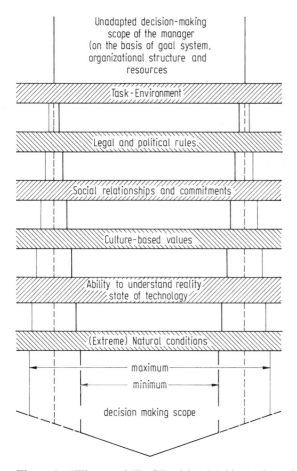

Figure 5: "Filter model" of Decision-Making Adapted to the Environment
Source: E. Dülfer

reason the resulting model can be called *"Filter-Model"* of environment considerations (see Dülfer 1980).

Finally, as a result a quantity of decision-making alternatives is formed which has been expanded in many respects and reduced in others and which is now much better adapted to the given environment in the guest-country (*fig. 5*).

It is the task of the *Human Resource Development* to prepare the foreign managers for this learn-process and to supply the necessary country-oriented information. Systems like BERI-Index or Country-Rating are usually used in this context, but do not suffice alone.

2.4 Early Recognitions in International Business

The preceding reflections enlighten the consequences of the strata model for the operational decision-making of the single foreign manager or staff member. However, a second aspect has to be mentioned with regard to the strategic planning of the company: It has been mentioned above that the socio-cultural and economic structure in all countries is in a permanent process of development.

The comments on each strata of the model made clear that the higher strata are always influenced by the lower strata in the long run while in the short run the opposed influence can also be stated. The culture-based values for instance may be influenced by the organizational changes of the social relationships; and the social structures themselves can be modified by legal regulations given by the legislator.

If we look at the interdependencies (indicated by the arrows) in the strata model we recognize the possibility to use it as an *early-warning-system*. The modifications perceived within a single strata (e. g. the culture-based values) permit the conclusion that respective effects in the next higher strata (e. g. the social relationships and later on the legal structures) will occur after a certain lapse of time (Example: Iran). It is a *further challenge* to the foreign manager to perceive such relationships.

3. Task of Human Resource Management in Internationally Operating Firms

3.1 Task Complexes with Respect of Goal Groups

I began with the systematization of the potential environmental influences which the foreign staff member faces in internationally operating companies in detail, because it will be evident, only in this way, which requirements result for the human resource management. Its task with regard to the *staff members delegated* by the headquarter to guest-countries is:

— to select them for the job in individual guest-countries applying the criterion whether they will be able to master the expected environmental influences;
— to supply them with the special information needed with regard to these influences and to stimulate them for auto-didactic studies;
— to give them recommendations for appropriate reactions, particularly for the needed degree of adaptation;
— to motivate them to carry out a uniform business policy valid for the entire company.

Further, human resource management has to deal with the *autochthonous staff members* in the different guest-countries, particularly:

— to integrate them into the company structure as a whole;
— to acquaint them with the headquarter, its entrepreneurial guidelines, and goals and the competent top managers;
— to assure an appropriate language communication for them;
— to give them the feeling of belonging to the company;
— to motivate them to perform conscientiously for the benefit of the entire company (beyond monetary incentives).

The first complex of tasks is always relevant in internationally operating companies, particularly in the case of only functional internationalization. In the case of institutional internationalization it is in the foreground if (according to the tri-partition by Perlmutter) (see Perlmutter 1965) an '*ethnocentric*' entrepreneurial policy is applied.

In every case, a second complex of tasks will be added in case of institutional internationalization: On the basis of an *ethnocentric* entrepreneurial policy it concerns mainly the executive staff members in foreign branches. On the basis of '*polycentric*' policy-making where normally guest-country-born managers are being employed to a larger extent, this second complex of task concerns mainly these middle-managers. In this case the integration of business policies of the different foreign branches into the company's policy-making as a whole is particularly necessary and important.

A third complex of problems for human resource management results in the case of an internationally operating company in which staff members from the home country and from different host-countries collaborate in a cooperative way at all organizational levels. This can be called correctly *"multi-national company"*. Here communication can easily be disturbed by (see Dülfer 1983):

- different patterns of thinking due to the differing language systems;
- different attitudes to labor and way of life;
- different opinion on appropriate behavior in leadership; diverse understanding of roles and style of leadership;
- lacking conformity between the firm-internal functional importance of the manager's position and his firm-external social status;
- clientele-building by individual managers within the firm;
- distribution of manager's positions according to national or race-ethnic proportions, independent from professional qualifications;
- obstacles in the firm-external social-familiar communication among the managers and their families together with the tendency to project group- or nationality-oriented clichés on the communication partner.

To overcome these difficulties a *third complex of tasks* is needed:

- to homogenize the behavior of managers and experts from numerous countries within the working groups and decision-making bodies concerned;
- to assure an effective language communication using well-defined working languages;
- to develop a consciousness for the company and its international and intercultural personell, based on the grounds of written guidelines and unwritten group-born-norms of behavior.

This case of a multi-national enterprise pursuing a *"geocentric"*, i. e. global business policy, makes understandable that "corporate culture" has a special importance for internationally operating companies.

3.2 The Importance of Corporate Culture for Internationally Operating Companies

During the last years a lot has been told and written on the topic of *"corporate culture"* (here taken as a synonym for "Organizational Culture") (see Heinen et al. 1987; Dülfer 1988). These contributions represent partly definitions not further reaching than earlier concepts like "Firm Climate", "Corporate Image" or "Corporate Identity". Some American publications (especially by Pascale/Athos, Peters/Waterman and Deal/Kennedy) (see Ouchi 1981, Deal and Kennedy 1982, Pascale and Athos 1981, Peters and Waterman 1982) declaring human resource management as the main task of entrepreneurial policy in contrast to the earlier pure capital- or invest-ment-oriented thinking, increased the confusion of concepts. They empha-sized too strongly the aspect of leadership and motivation in the direction of a corporate identity. Many American enterprises originally determined by the tayloristic concept of labor-divided task performance recognized the modified socio-cultural conditions in work behavior in the United States only when facing Japanese competition. From this situation Ouchi deduces his *type 'Z'* and Peters/Waterman the priority of 'soft-instruments' (staff; skills; shared values; style) in the *7S-Model* (see Peters and Waterman 1982).

Completely different conditions in this respect were prevailing in the Federal Republic of Germany, because here the old tension between "Cap-ital" and "Labor" recalls a long history of development. Because of this background personal questions of corporate structure found very concrete and even legally enforced solutions during the two great public discussions about co-determination on the one hand and humanization of work on the other.

Much of what has been newly discovered and recommended in the United States under the key word "Corporate Culture" has become since long time, daily routine in German enterprises. For this reason the simplified recom-mendation to manage the corporate culture exclusively with respect to style and relationship of leadership is not very relevant for us. Further, we can only be surprised about the naive suggestions by Deal/Kennedy for empha-sizing on 'champions' or even 'heroes'. This does not mean, of course, that charismatic leadership would not be possible any more in the Federal Republic; on the contrary: there are numerous examples for such relation-ships, particularly in the field of middle-scale and middle class undertakings. Nevertheless, we have to state — in agreement with Harvard Professor Edgar Schein (see Schein 1985: 314 pp.) — that corporate culture cannot simply be "managed". The top management is able to give orientations, depending on the degree of authority it has. But the corporate culture will always be characterized by all participants and therefore it will lead its own life which presents at all levels certain role expectations for the newcomer and requires a particular responsibility towards the corporate culture.

This importance is expressed by the definition of Jacques:

The culture of the factory is its customary and traditional way of thinking and of doing things, which is shared to a greater or lesser degree by all its members, and which new members must learn, and at least partially accept, in order to be accepted into service in the firm (Jacques 1951: 251).

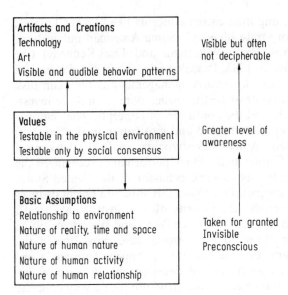

Figure 6: Levels of Culture and Their Interaction

Edgar Schein has demonstrated this opinion by his three-tiered structure-scheme quoted by most of the authors (*fig. 6*).

It is easy to understand that the elements of the highest strata can be influenced by the top management. Furthermore, the 'values' can be partly influenced too, to a certain extent. The 'basic assumptions' however are inputs of all the participants. This may explain why even in the process of selection of newcomers the following criterion is applied: "Who is suitable for us?", including heterogenous structures with corresponding '*sub-cultures*' as well.

3.3 The Problem of Competence for Human Resource Management

The phenomenon of corporate culture with its empirically confirmed influences of values and of basic assumptions on the performance of production processes makes clear, that human resource management consists principally of *two components*:

— on the one hand the (professionally determined) input of human labor in the framework of planned processes;

— on the other hand the construction of interpersonal relationships as industrial relations or management relations in a way which permanently assures the needed motivational basis for the vocational cooperation. In doing so, the managers can apply legitimate power, referent power or expert power in order to make the pure disciplinary authority (reward/ coercive power) (see French and Raven 1959) motivationally effective.

It is a very old practical experience and alleged by the scientific theory, too, that all this must interplay in the management relationship. It is therefore remarkable that very recently a modified point of view has been presented by different experts of human resource management:

They point out that in very large HighTech or HighChem corporations with a high degree of division of labor, a falling apart of the two components of leadership can be observed. In these cases the middle and top management functions are very often entrusted to persons who have been selected according to their professional-academic qualification, e. g. as engineers, chemists, physicists, informatiker. These managers rely on performing their leaders' job bona fide on the official position as a superior. They rely exclusively on reward and coercive power as a mean to gain authority. As a consequence, an obvious lack of motivational effect in the interpersonal relationship can be observed. The human problems of collaboration are neglected; no assistance is given for their solution by the superiors; an emotional assistance in task performance is lacking. The superiors are not presenting the needed magnetism, not to speak of charismatic leadership. Due to these facts representatives of this concept conclude that the obvious lack has to be filled up by the division of personnel and its staff members. The hierarchical management relationship should be supplemented by a kind of service supplied by the personal division (see, for example, Ackermann 1989, Reichhart 1989).

This concept is doubtlessly very debatable, but the real phenomenon is confirmed by science and practice. A reason for this fact is obviously that managers coming into their position because of their natural scientific/ technical studies did not undergo any training with regard to personnel policy and leaders' behavior. This is a typical lack of universities' study programmes.

Whatever the opinion will be about these problems — *one* consequence certainly has to be drawn: Such a personal division of leadership cannot be accepted in international management. Even there specialists may be appointed as consultants for special aspects according to a two-dimensional organizational structure. But it seems to be essential that the professional competence as well as the motivational management relation must be integrated in personal union into the framework of the hierarchy. Particularly the foreign manager, who in a production branch is for instance "number one" and who represents the 'umbilical cord' to the home headquarter must be introduced by the corporate and accepted by his staff members as the highest-ranking top manager. This does not only concern the professional directing but also the performance of a role which in many non-European cultures is seen analogous the patriarchical (in some countries matriarchical) family structure and in which the needed motivational effect can only be accomplished by a one-dimensional management relationship.

This aspect must be taken into consideration also in constructing the organizational structure, i. e. that in case of the foundation of a production branch in a special legal form an organizational structure must be chosen which clearly identifies 'number one", e. g. as Président du Conseil, Chairman of the Board or Chief Executive Officer. In the foreign branch he is accordingly the born authority for human resource management, but he can be assisted in some special aspects by corresponding staff members.

4. Requirements of Professional and Personality-based Qualifications

4.1 Professional-Managerial Requirements

The preceding reflections lead to the conclusion that foreign managers — to a certain extent this applies also to specialists abroad — must have a definite management qualification beside the purely professional capacity. For this the following *qualities* are needed:

- The ability and the readiness to perform certain preformulated tasks together with a bigger or smaller team of staff members on the basis of their own ideas and in taking over the resulting responsibility;
- the ability to reflect problems in an appropriate way but then to take a precise decision in favour of a specific solution and to perform this without any cognitive dissonance;
- being able to find new solutions in face of unexpected changes of situation and to improvise by changing the usual procedures if necessary;
- to impart confidence on the own ability to solve problems to the staff members in difficult or even dangerous situations and to motivate them to cooperate despite their own doubts.

The qualification requirements of foreign managers as the most important group of foreign staff members in internationally operating companies which are here only partially described, explain the consequences which have to be drawn with respect to the selection and development of personnel. These mentioned abilities cannot be stated in detail in the framework of the usual job advertisement, e. g. in selection discussions or the usual assessment programmes. Therefore, it is always risky to hire managers from outside the firm or such positions abroad, unless one knows their previous job performance in other firms. The firm-internal development and training of suitable persons is therefore the better way. But even this is the bottle-neck in medium-scale or middle class companies which have only recently entered into international business. Many failures are due to the wrong selection of personnel.

In large-scale companies it is possible to bring candidates early enough "on the way" through programmes of career planning and supplementary training in order to develop them fully for such a position. Possibly this will take years, but then they will be well prepared. This is a manifold field for the area of personal development in the framework of human resource management.

However, a successful job performance requires in addition very specific personal characteristics which cannot be imparted in a short time through training measures. These must also be applied as supplementary selection criteria. In case of long-term programmes of personnel promotion they must become effective early enough, maybe with the help of short-term jobs abroad with respective assessment by managers on the spot.

The characteristics mentioned are those which concern the physical and psychological condition of the candidate and his predisposition for the needed behaviour in strange environments.

4.2 Condition Requirements

The *physical burdens* due to the frequently changing surroundings and the different influences of climate (temperature, humidity, radiation) and the change of local times with its divergence to the individual biological rhythm require a physical stability above average. It concerns in the first place the functions of heart and blood circulation, the stability of the vegetative nerve system and a stable digestive system. Furthermore, the candidate should not suffer from allergic reactions. This complex also includes a sufficient suitability for vaccination. Before the worldwide elimination of small pox a prophylactic vaccination was indispensable in case of jobs in tropical countries. It could only be performed if the first vaccination took place in the childhood. Very often this fact was told to the candidate for the foreign job only by the vaccination doctor, i. e. immediately before the begin of the mission. It is important in this context that not only the objective suitability for vaccination is required, but also the subjective willingness of the candidate.

Very often it is neglected to consider that foreign missions especially in strange cultures and under extreme prevailing natural conditions also include considerable *psychological burdens*. These can be mastered more easily if the persons concerned collaborate and live with experienced colleagues from the home country. Then he has the possibility to solve and to minimize his problems and fears through talks with other persons who have made the same experience. *"Tutors"* can be helpful in this context. The situation is different if he has to master the actual or perceived burdens in isolation in a strange environment and without a discussion partner from home. The permanent confrontation with unaccustomed and also physically burdening conditions of life, the occurence of unknown and frightening physical reactions (skin diseases etc.) and the impossibility to discuss all this in the strange language of the guest-country can lead to a state of panic which in project terms is called *"cultural shock"*.

Apart from the individual characteristics the *family situation* also plays a role in the above-mentioned psychological burdens of a stay in strange cultural areas and/or under unaccustomed climatic conditions. The burdens can be suffered easier by married staff members abroad accompanied by their partner than by unmarried persons. On the other hand, the adaption to the strange social environment particularly the language of the guest-country is handicapped through the permanent communication with the spouse. But if the married staff member is delegated for a longer period abroad and separated from his wife the mentioned psychological burdens are mostly felt stronger than by an unmarried staff member.

But even in case of delegating married staff members together with their partner, additional problems can arise if the physical condition, e. g. of the wife does not correspond to the requirements given on the spot, or if the wife is not able to master the psychological burdens of living in a strange cultural environment to the same extent. This can also be caused by the fact that these burdens are more difficult for the wife than for the staff member himself, e. g. because of the special social norms prevailing in Islamic countries for women in public (see Kumar and Steinmann 1982: 213 pp.). We know examples that foreign staff members had to be called back from Arabic countries because of this reason.

In case of a longer stay abroad the *situation of the children* has to be taken into consideration, too. Especially when they are in the age for secondary school, problems arise often by the fact that either there is no secondary school, (e. g. if the parents are working in a development project in rural areas), or that the child can go to secondary school in the guest-country only by learning an unknown language (e. g. Arabic or Bahasia-Indonesian). The then resulting necessity to return the children back to the home country and to give them to a boarding school means a considerable burden for the foreign staff member which most find difficult to accept.

The problems of re-integration after finishing the stay abroad are also part of the individual and family condition requirements. However, they will be dealt with later on.

4.3 Communication Requirements

Even if the foreign staff member is able to bear the physical and psychological burdens of life in an unaccustomed climate in a strange cultural environment with a strange language, it does not yet mean that he automatically develops a behaviour which enables him to fulfill his professional task according to corporate policy in an optimal way. For these, further *characteristics and skills* are needed which are determined by the prevailing communication requirements in a strange environment.

The observation of foreign collaborators in the field makes clear that some people are totally missing the *ability to perceive the important elements of a strange environment*. They lack the understanding of the system relationships of the strange environment, the reasons for the specialities perceived. They are therefore not able to accept these specialities. The ability to perceive strange environments also supposes that the respective person is not a profiled egocentric, further, that he has interest in his environment and develops a certain curiosity for his surroundings. These characteristics are preconditions for a corresponding ability to learn with respect to strange conditions of life and to the needed willingness for adaptation.

It is remarkable, that even those persons who have the ability to perceive strange environments are, in spite of that, often not ready to accept the resulting deviating behavior of the communication partners. This behavior will be interpreted as a lack of personality of the communication partner. If the partner e. g. does not react to his own welcome ceremony, he is seen as a rude, aggressive human being. If the partner has a different attitude to work and to time division, he is lazy and indolent. If the partner does not write in the official working language of the firm, because he does it only in Arabic or Persian or because he is a member of an older generation who could not go to school (being illiterate), he will be assessed as stupid, less qualified and without any knowledge. Such a judgment in spite of the fact, that he possibly has a particular position in his social environment, e. g. as the oldest man of the village or mayor.

This confirms that a further quality is needed, namely the *deliberate tolerance against strange behavior*. It must be evident in the own behavior, too. For this, certain rules must be observed. The most important one is the principle never to be astonished, to take the most unusual phenomena as a matter of fact. This principle which is more an external one must be supplemented by the internal principle to accept the communication partner totally in spite of the differences perceived, and to give him the esteem he can expect because of his social position.

A further step of fruitful communication in strange cultures will be achieved if the foreign staff member is *able to adapt himself* to a certain extent *to the communication behavior of his partner*. This does not mean that he copies Lawrence of Arabia, changing himself into an individual of the strange culture. These intentions are mostly false and seem ridiculous or even insulting for the communication partner. The first step of adaption means simply that the staff member suppresses such actions which are not usual or even taboo in the other culture. Examples are shaking hands, patting the shoulders or welcoming the female companions of the communication partner in the same way as himself. This kind of *passive adaptation* also includes the omission of own habits.

Further, an *active adaptation* can take place to a limited extent, e. g. in the way that the staff member adapts himself to the welcome rites in East Asia, e. g. to the Indian or Japanese way of greetings. The expression used in welcoming, the application of titles, or the way how to give shorter or longer speeches at special occasions belong to the active adaptation too. The procedure of introducing someone and the way of taking a seat should be mentioned, too.

5. Re-Integration Problems

Special problems of human resource management arise when the staff member has to be re-integrated into the hierarchy of the home headquarter. This measure is particularly necessary in a middle-term rhythm for managers, because the unity of entrepreneurial policy may not be endangered by too much local adaptation. Difficult re-entry problems (see Welge and Kenter 1983: 175) result for both, the staff members as well as from the point of the company.

5.1 Re-Integration Problems of the Staff Members

The re-entry problems from the view of the delegates concern mainly the professional position and the work content. The foreign manager, especially as 'Number one' of the branch has the position of a quasi-entrepreneur in the guest-country. This the more if the informational linkages to the head-quarter are loose. He was used to formulate the whole entrepreneurial policy for the branch and to run it. However, after the re-entry he will be integrated into the greater division of labour in the home firm and subordinated directly to a superior, may be with a higher renumeration and corresponding position in the hierarchy. In spite of this it means a diminition of vocational position and firm-internal status.

The result is easily a lack of contentment with the task overtaken because his specialization has a lesser impact on the total policy of the firm than from his universal activity abroad.

These demotivating vocational restrictions are increased by the fact that the staff member abroad often belongs to the national prominence of the guest-country; without any problems he can talk with ministers about investments and similar problems. After the re-entry he must enter again into the usual rhythm of life and the social role of a normal higher employee without driver, cook and servants in charge of the firm. This aspect is very relevant for the wife of the staff member too, who was executing social tasks abroad in a similar way as in the Diplomatic Service having several servants, and who now has to change her role into that of a normal housewife in a suburb. The frustations resulting from these vocational and private combinations are dealt with in the scientific literature under the term 'Contra-Cultural-Shock' (see Welge and Kenter 1983: 177 pp.).

5.2 Problems of Re-Integration in the View of the Company

Problems of re-integration arise from the standpoint of the company, too.

It is normally not possible to reserve the former position of the delegates during their stay abroad. On the other hand, the number of management positions needed in the framework of goal-oriented organizational structure cannot be increased unlimitedly. Thus, an appropriate position is very often not at the disposal of the re-comers. A prolongation of the stay abroad leads easily to an overstressed adaptation ('going native') while 'waiting positions' are felt as a side-track. The frustrations mentioned produce a decrease of performance of the re-comers and endanger the firm's climate because of envy of staff members in the headquarters.

Before this background human resource management has to try to di-minish the problems of re-integration through a *long-term planning* of personnel and career.

In this context a *suitable assessment* of the activity abroad plays an important role as a basis for further missions and for remunerations. The performance assessment of foreign managers should be oriented not only on operational business variables, like turnover, product innovations and so on, but should also take into consideration the way of building of business relationships, the success in local adaptation and the ability to motivate staff members abroad.

This point makes clear again that the execution of human resource management in an internationally operating company can never be performed in the home headquarter only, but also requries a personal contact of the responsible top managers of the headquarter with the foreign managers and staff members in the guest-countries. This may sometimes be discredited as a 'supervisory tourism', but is an indispensable component in the leadership relation.

References

Ackermann, K. F. (1989): Europa 92 — Herausforderung für das Personalmanagement, *Talk at the Workshop 1989 of the Scientific Commission "Internationales Management" on the 02. March*, Wolfsberg (CH).

Albach, H. (1976): Ungewißheit und Unsicherheit, in: E. Grochla and W. Wittman (eds.), *HWB*, 4. ed., vol. 3, Stuttgart: col. 4036—4041.

Bauer, E. (1989): Übersetzungsprobleme und Übersetzungsmethoden bei einer multinationalen Marketingforschung, *Jahrbuch der Absatz- und Verbraucherforschung*: S. 174—205.

Berekoven, L. (1979): *Internationales Marketing*, Wiesbaden.

Deal, T. E. and A. A. Kennedy (1982): *Corporate Cultures. Rites and Rituals of Corporate Life*, Reading (Mass.).

Dülfer, E. (1980): Zum Problem der Umweltberücksichtigung im "Internationalen Mangement", in: E. Pausenberger (ed.), *Internationales Management*, Stuttgart: 1—44.

Dülfer, E. (1981): Auslandsmanagement in Schwellenländern, in: H. Wacker, H. Haussmann and B. Kumar (eds.), *Internationale Unternehmensführung — Managementprobleme international tätiger Unternehmungen* (Festschrift für H. Sieber), Berlin: 437—458.

Dülfer, E. (1983): Die spezifischen Personal- und Kommunikationsprobleme international tätiger Unternehmungen — Eine Einführung, in: E. Dülfer (ed.), *Personelle Aspekte im Internationalen Management*, Berlin.

Dülfer, E. (1985): Die Auswirkungen der Internationalisierung auf Führung und Organisationsstruktur mittelständischer Unternehmen, *BFuP*, Nov., no. 6.

Dülfer, E. (1988): Organisationskultur: Phänomen — Philosophie — Technologie, Eine Einführung in die Diskussion, in: E. Dülfer (ed.), *Organisationskultur*, Stuttgart: 1—20.

Dürkheim, E. (1933): *On the Division of Labor in society*, Glencoe IU.

v. Eckardstein, D. and F. Schnellinger (1987): *Betriebliche Personalpolitik*, 3. ed., München.

Fayerweather, J. (1969): *International Business Management: A Conceptual Framework*, New York.

French Jr., J. R. P. and B. Raven (1959): The Basis of Social Power, in: D. Cartwright (ed.), *Studies in Social Power*, Ann Arbor (Mich.): 150 – 167.

Gutenberg, E. (1971): *Grundlagen der Betriebswirtschaftslehre*, vol. 1, 18. ed., Berlin – Heidelberg – New York: 285 – 292.

Heinen, E. et al. (1987): *Unternehmenskultur, Perspektiven für Wissenschaft und Praxis*, München – Wien.

Jacques, J. H. (1951): *The Changing Culture of a Factory*, London.

Kulhavy, E. (1975): Multinationale Unternehmungen, in: E. Grochla and W. Wittmann (eds.), *HWB*, Stuttgart: 2723 – 2738.

Kumar, B. and H. Steinmann (1982): Zum Problem des Auslandeinsatzes von Stammhaus-Mitarbeitern im Rahmen des Internationalen Projekt-Managements, in: E. Dülfer (ed.), *Projektmanagement – International*, Stuttgart: S. 189 – 223.

Kupsch, P.-U. and R. Marr (1985): Personalwirtschaft, in: E. Heinen (ed.), *Industriebetriebslehre, Entscheidungen im Industriebetrieb*, 8. ed., Wiesbaden: 627 – 762.

Macharzina, K. (1981): Entwicklungsperspektiven einer Theorie internationaler Unternehmenstätigkeit, in: W. H. Wacker, H. Haussmann and B. Kumar (eds.), *Internationale Unternehmensführung*, Berlin: 33 – 56.

Marr, R. and M. Stitzel (1979): *Personalwirtschaft*, München.

Meissner, H. G. and St. Gerber (1980): Die Auslandsinvestition als Entscheidungsproblem, *BFuP*: 217 – 228.

Ouchi, W. G. (1981): *Theory Z. How American Business Can Meet the Japanese Challenge*, Reading (Mass.).

Pascale, R. T. and A. G. Athos (1981): *The Art of Japanese Management. Applications for American Executives*, New York.

Perlmutter, H. (1965): L'Entreprise Internationale. Trois Conceptions, *Revue Economique et Sociale*, no. 2: 151 – 165.

Peters, T. J. and R. H. Waterman (1982): *In Search of Excellence. Lessons from America's Best-Run Companies*, New York.

Reichhart, L. (1989): *Personalmanagement – reichen unsere Konzepte?*, Speech at the Congress for Organization 1989, "Chancen flexibler Organisation", 19./20. January, Bad Homburg v. d. H.

Schein, E. (1985): *Organizational Culture and Leadership*, San Francisco – Washington – London.

Staehle, W. H. (1987): *Management*, 3. ed., München.

Steinmann, H., B. Kumar and A. Wasner (1979): Der Internationalisierungsprozeß von Mittelbetrieben, in: E. Pausenberger (ed.), *Internationales Management, Diskussionsbeiträge*, no. 5, Nürnberg: 107 – 127.

Tannenbaum, R. and W. H. Schmidt (1958): How to Choose a Leadership Pattern, *Harvard Business Review*, March – April 1958.

Welge, M. K. and M. E. Kenter (1983): Die Reintegration von Stammhausdelegierten. Ergebnisse einer explorativen empirischen Untersuchung, in: E. Dülfer (ed.), *Personelle Aspekte im Internationalen Management*, Berlin: 173 – 200.

Wistinghausen, J. (1975): Personalwesen als wissenschaftliche Disziplin, in: E. Gaugler (ed.), *HWB des Personalwesens*, Stuttgart: 1720 – 1732.

Wunderer, R. and W. Grunewald (1980): *Führungslehre*, Vol. 1: Grundlagen der Führung, Berlin.

About the Authors

Nancy J. Adler: Professor for Organizational Behavior and Cross-cultural Management, Faculty of Management, McGill University, Montreal, Canada

Peter Conrad: Internal consultant at Schering AG, Berlin, West Germany

Eberhard Dülfer: Professor and Head of the Institut für Allgemeine Betriebswirtschaftslehre und Industriebetriebslehre, Philipps Universität Marburg, West Germany

Fariborz Ghadar: Professor at the School of Government and Business Administration, The George Washington University, Washington, D.C., United States of America

Hans H. Hinterhuber: Professor and Head of the Department of Management, Universität Innsbruck, Austria, and Associate Professor for Industrial Management of the Catholic University of Milan, Italy

Ondrej Landa: Professor at the Czechoslovak Academy of Sciences, Institute for Philosophy and Sociology, Prague, Czechoslovakia

Hansgünter Meyer: Professor at the Institute for Theory, History, and Organization of Science at the Academy of Sciences of the GDR, Berlin, German Democratic Republic

Jacques Rojot: Professor of Management and Industrial Relations at INSEAD/CEDEP and Université du Maine, Faculté de Droit et des Sciences Economiques, Le Mans, France

Rüdiger Pieper: President of the Paul-Löbe-Institut Berlin, West Germany

Danica Purg: Director of the Executive Training Center, Brdo pri Kranj, Slovenia, Yugoslavia

Beverly Springer: Professor of International Studies at the American Graduate School of International Management, Glendale, Arizona, United States of America

Stephen Springer: M.A., Industrial psychologist, private consultant, Silver Spring, Maryland, United States of America

Wolfgang H. Staehle: Professor of Organization Theory and Human Resource Management, head of the Institut für Management, Freie Universität Berlin, West Germany

Monika Stumpf: Assistant Professor of the Department of Management, Universität Innsbruck, Austria

Yoshiaki Takahashi: Professor at Chuo University, Department of Commerce, Tokyo, Japan

Wang Zhong-Ming: Professor for Social and Organizational Psychology at Hangzhou University, Department of Psychology, Hangzhou, People's Republic of China

de Gruyter Studies in Organization

An international series by internationally known
authors presenting current research in organization

WALTER DE GRUYTER · BERLIN · NEW YORK
Genthiner Strasse 13, D-1000 Berlin 30, Tel.: (30) 2 60 05-0, Fax 2 60-05-2 51
200 Saw Mill River Road, Hawthorne, N.Y., 10532 Tel.: (914) 747-0110, Fax 747-1326